LOVE IN THE POST: FROM PLATO TO DERRIDA

The Screenplay and Commentary

JOANNA CALLAGHAN AND
MARTIN MCQUILLAN

With additional material by Jonathan Lahey Dronsfield

Heraclitus
PICTURES

ROWMAN & LITTLEFIELD
INTERNATIONAL

London • New York

Published by Rowman & Littlefield International Ltd
Unit A, Whitacre Mews, 26–34 Stannery Street, London SE11 4AB, United
Kingdom
www.rowmaninternational.com

Rowman & Littlefield International Ltd.is an affiliate of Rowman & Littlefield
4501 Forbes Boulevard, Suite 200, Lanham, Maryland 20706, USA
With additional offices in Boulder, New York, Toronto (Canada), and
London (UK)
www.rowman.com

British Library Cataloguing in Publication Data

A catalogue record for this book is available from the British Library

ISBN: HB 978-1-7834-8004-3
        PB 978-1-7834-8005-0
        EB 978-1-7834-8006-7

Library of Congress Cataloging-in-Publication Data
McQuillan, Martin.
   Love in the post : from Plato to Derrida : the screenplay and commentary /
Joanna Callaghan and Martin McQuillan.
        pages cm
   Original screenplay, inspired by Derrida's The post card, with critical
commentary.
   Includes bibliographical references and index.
   ISBN 978-1-78348-004-3 (cloth : alk. paper)—ISBN 978-1-78348-005-0
(pbk. : alk. paper)—ISBN 978-1-78348-006-7 (electronic)
   1. Love in the post (Motion picture) I. Callaghan, Joanna. II. Love in the
post (motion picture) III. Title.
   PN1997.2.L75 2014
   791.43'72—dc23

                                                        2014023927

∞™ The paper used in this publication meets the minimum requirements of
American National Standard for Information Sciences—Permanence of Paper
for Printed Library Materials, ANSI/NISO Z39.48-1992.

Printed in the United States of America

Feature film distributed by Heraclitus Pictures

One of the least deconstructive things you can do in a movie is to point a camera at someone and ask them to say something about deconstruction.

Geoffrey Bennington

To make cinema . . . is to send twenty-five postcards per second to millions of people.

Jean-Luc Godard

CONTENTS

LIST OF ILLUSTRATIONS

ACKNOWLEDGEMENTS

*L*ove in the Post was made possible by awards from the Arts and Humanities Research Council and by funding from Heraclitus Pictures, Kingston University and the University of Bedfordshire, and with support from The Culture Capital Exchange, London and the University of Sussex.

It was also funded through donations by Jorge and Anne Blumenfeld, Terry and Deirdre Callaghan, Julie Callaghan and Paul Hawker, Flo Davy, Vivian Harris, Angela Hunter, Cathy and Neil Ingham, Bridie Ingham, Toby Juliff, Wan-Chuan Kao, Melissa and Patrick Liddy, Lesley Lodge, Rebecca Mason, Angelica Michelis, Nicholas Austin, Michael O'Rourke, Melissa Riggall, Craig Rook, Paula Roush, David Sorfa, Paula Vaccaro, Michele Walliker, Alexis Weedon and Danielle White. We would like to thank all of our sponsors and supporters.

La Carte Postale: De Socrate à Freud et au-delà, by Jacques Derrida, is published by Flammarion (1980) and in English language translation as *The Post Card: From Socrates to Freud and Beyond*, translated by Alan Bass, by University of Chicago Press (1980). We are grateful to the presses for permission to reproduce selected quotations.

An extended version of 'Autobiobibliographies' first appeared in *Libraries, Literatures and Archives*, edited by Sas Mays and published by Routledge (2013). Martin McQuillan is grateful to the press and editor for permission to reprint this section.

Theo Marks's 'Eros in the Age of Technical Reproductability' first appeared in *New London Critique* 20, no. 4 (2014): 1–15. This extract is reproduced courtesy of the editors.

We wish to thank Ken McMullen for the use of an extract from his 1980 interview with Jacques Derrida.

We would like to thank the staff of Rowman & Littlefield International in London, Oliver Gadsby, Martina O'Sullivan, Anna Reeve and our editor, Sarah Campbell. Thanks also to script consultant Lesley Lodge, graphic designer Txabi Jones and Erin Stapleton for interview transcription.

We would also like to thank our colleagues at the London Graduate School, Kingston University, University of Bedfordshire and University of Sussex, as well as our families and friends for all their help in the making of the film and this book: in particular Joachim Bergamin, the true guru. This volume is dedicated to Dante, Oscar and Felix.

TRAILER

Joanna Callaghan and Martin McQuillan

*L*ove in the Post is inspired by the book *The Post Card* by Jacques Derrida. Like the book, the film plays with fact and fiction, weaving together the stories of a scholar of literature and a film director, alongside insights from critics and philosophers.

Theo Marks works in a university department that is soon to be closed. His wife, Sophie, enigmatic and distant, is in analysis. Filmmaker Joanna struggles to complete a film about *The Post Card*. These people are set on a collision course prompted by a series of letters that will change their lives.

The film features a never-before-seen interview with Derrida, alongside contributions from Geoff Bennington, J. Hillis Miller, Sam Weber, Catherine Malabou, Ellen Burt and David Wilson.

Love in the Post is a film that speaks to Jacques Derrida's text *The Post Card: From Socrates to Freud and Beyond* (1980). The first section of the book, 'Envois' [Fr: Sending] is a collection of letters that recounts a love affair between a narrator and his 'sweet darling girl'. It combines the story of the two lovers with philosophical reflection on writing, technology, politics, psychoanalysis, Western philosophy and post cards. Unique amongst Derrida's writing, it gives rise in this film to the story of Theo Marks (an academic working on Derrida's text) and Joanna (a filmmaker who is making a documentary about it).

Love in the Post is as much a film about our contemporary scene as it is a response to Derrida's text. It addresses the importance of the Humanities today within the context of the creeping privatization of higher education. But above all it is a film about love, literature and infidelity. In the words of Theo Marks, *The Post Card* is about 'how people love one another and how people betray each other, and like all literature it's on the side of life'.

Love in the Post is the second collaboration between filmmaker Joanna Callaghan, her production company Heraclitus Pictures and the philosopher and cultural critic Martin McQuillan. Their first film *'I Melt the Glass with My Forehead': A Film about £9,000 Tuition Fees, How We Got Them and What to Do about Them*, was nominated for a British Universities Film and Video Council Award in 2013. Since 2003, Callaghan has been producing films based on philosophical concepts under the research project Ontological Narratives. Her 35mm short film *Thrownness* (2003) is based upon a visual translation of writing by the German philosopher Martin Heidegger. In 2008, she received a research grant from the Arts and Humanities Research Council and produced *A Mind's Eye* (2009) which treats Plato's concept of *eidos* and stars James and Oliver Phelps (best known as the Weasley twins in the Harry Potter films). In 2012, she made *DO NOT READ THIS*, a film about the difficulties of writing which drew from Derrida's work. It features the film debut of Robert Rowland Smith, who also appears in *Love in the Post*. Robert is the author of several works of philosophy and literary theory including *Derrida and Autobiography* (1996) and *Death-Drive: Freudian Hauntings in Literature and Art* (2010). Martin McQuillan has recently completed a film, *Oxi: An Act of Resistance*, with the British director Ken McMullen (also a Professor at Kingston University) based on the *Antigone* of Sophocles told through the financial crisis in Greece. It will be released in Europe through Les films d'en face.

This book features the full screenplay of *Love in the Post* along with a reflection on her film practice by Joanna Callaghan. It also contains theoretical texts by Martin McQuillan on creative practice and Derrida's *The Post Card*, as well as the full transcripts of the interviews with Bennington, Burt, Malabou, Miller, Weber and postal historian David Wilson undertaken as part of the making of the film. It concludes with an essay by Jonathan Lahey Dronsfield on deconstruction and film.

ILLUSTRATION

Martin McQuillan

In part 1 of his 1992 work *Illustration*, J. Hillis Miller offers a reading of Walter Benjamin's 'The Work of Art in the Age of Mechanical Reproduction'.[1] In it Miller outlines the various ways in which the binary logic of Benjamin's text only encourages the reversal and collapse of the categories he establishes in the essay and the propositions he sets up around them. One such instance is the case of the revolutionary potential of cinema. On the one hand, Benjamin would like to suggest that cinema and cinematic technique change forever the way that we understand a work of art, stripping art of its aura through mechanical inscription and projecting us all as viewers from the tradition of auratic singularity into an epoch of the Mass. On the other hand, cinema as a technology of the present can never do more than reproduce the ideological conditions that give rise to it, namely bourgeois capitalism, but Benjamin is conflicted here. For example, and as Miller notes, 'though Benjamin allows that films can "promote revolutionary criticism of social conditions, even the distribution of property", he also says that "as a rule no other revolutionary merit can be accredited to today's film than the promotion of a revolutionary criticism of the traditional concepts of art"' (30). Benjamin's text then opens up a gap between revolutionary film and film as the reproduction of false consciousness, and Miller inserts himself in this space, suggesting that 'the problem with all of Benjamin's oppositions is that they tend to dissolve through the effort of thinking they facilitate' (30). He proceeds to demonstrate that if we think of cinema as a critique of traditional concepts of art, then a division between an age of aura and an epoch of ideology cannot be rigorously maintained, the former being merely an instance of the latter, the latter being an effect of the former. However, Miller goes on to push

1

Benjamin's analogue argument into the digital age, by pursuing more rigorously the notion that a change in the means of artistic production produces a change in the conditions of art criticism. Moving on to discuss our own present of global, digital telecommunications, mass media and so-called cultural studies, Miller notes 'these changes in the media of art have also conspicuously changed the scholarship and criticism that account for art'. From here, Miller's text takes off in the direction of an account of cultural studies as something like the ideological criticism that pertains to digital phenomenality. However, I would like to pause Hillis' fast-forward here and pose a question: what if the distinguishing characteristic of criticism in the age of digital reproducibility was not the heterogeneity of cultural studies, but the very possibility of collapsing the distinction between reproductive technologies and criticism itself? In other words, what if criticism today were defined by the ability to use 'film', for example, as an idiom of criticism. Technological advances in the miniaturisation of apparatus and the compression of data memory have placed the camera within the reach of the graduate school critic. Today, a new generation of critics, philosophers and thinkers are no longer destined to be distanced from the screen as Benjamin was in a cinema seat while a projector gives off its own aura of dust and light behind their backs. Rather, the filmmaker-philosopher of the present is involved in a crafting that is simultaneously both a making and a theorisation of an object. Whether under these technological and theoretical conditions one can continue to talk rigorously of terms such as 'art', 'film', 'the camera' and so on, I very much doubt; the stability of these concepts will undoubtedly begin to dissolve through the effort of making that this technology facilitates. However, if it is true as Miller proposed in 1991 that 'changes in the media of art have also conspicuously changed the scholarship and criticism that account for art', then I want to suggest in 2014 that the greatest potential for such scholarly changes will come in the arena that we for old time's sake continue to call 'theory' and 'philosophy', precisely because it is the task of theory and philosophy to think the limit conditions of such a possibility.

In his essay Miller challenges Benjamin's radical conservatism and finds in the text on mechanical reproduction an unwillingness to accept the possibilities of change that the text itself identifies. No doubt, says

Illustration 3

Miller, the scholar of 1991 will be resistant to the idea that the computer will change the conditions and results of scholarship but we must ask: 'how could a technical device modulate our representations of both past and present cultural forms, make us read Shakespeare, Thoreau or Toni Morrison differently?' (36). I would like to add to that list Derrida and J. Hillis Miller, not because they are objects of the past but because they are part of a vital scene of transformation in which the critic, theorist, maker and their technologies may be increasingly difficult to distinguish. As Miller goes on to state towards the end of part 1 of *Illustration*: 'the work of the artist or of the cultural critic is a response to an infinite demand not only from a heritage to which the artist or critic must be faithful, but from the "other" of that heritage'. In this way cultural criticism is said by Miller to 'transform and reinscribe' the terms of a tradition 'in a founding gesture that is without precedent or ground' (57). This is not to suggest some wide-eyed faith in the revolutionary potential of digital filmmaking, a naivety that would be every bit as conservative and nostalgic as the difficult moments in Benjamin's essay that Miller reads so carefully. Nor is it to suppose that digitisation will finally allow us to slip unbound from false consciousness. Rather, it is to suggest, along with the Miller of the closing pages of the first half of *Illustration* that in a new epoch of scholarly production there can be 'no fixed frontiers . . . drawn between artefact and context' (58). It is not that philosophy on film or *filmosophy* has no genealogy or precedent; on the contrary, it has a substantial history. Rather, what Miller calls elsewhere 'good reading', or plain 'deconstruction' for those of us who want to hang on to that term for political and historical reasons, requires the filmmaker and the philosopher scrupulously to think through, at the frontier of a technological process of crafting, the consequences of a new regime of scholarly technology for an entire tradition of thinking and making. Ultimately, it is to agree with the Miller of *Illustration*: 'the cultural critic must posit anew, as something new, the culture that is studied, while at the same time being faithful to it. This positing also recreates the critic. To some degree it transforms his or her subject-position. . . . [Here Miller invokes the example of the cultural studies professor compelled into a critique of the institution that employs them, I would like to substitute the figure of the cultural critic who picks up the camera that he or she has hitherto chosen to study.]

Such a double contradictory demand is both logically impossible to fulfil and absolutely necessary to fulfil. Responding to it is the first obligation in cultural criticism' (59).

Joanna edits an interview with Jacques Derrida.

NOTE

1. J. Hillis Miller, *Illustration* (London: Reaktion Books, 1992). Miller refers to Walter Benjamin's 'The Work of Art in the Age of Mechanical Reproduction', in *Illuminations*, trans. Harry Zohn (New York: Schocken, 1969).

LOVE IN THE POST

The Screenplay

Joanna Callaghan & Martin McQuillan

INT. GALLERY - DAY

SOPHIE scatters letters.

>   SOPHIE
> 'You have always been "my"
> metaphysics, the metaphysics of
> my life, the "verso" of
> everything I write. My desire,
> speech, presence, proximity,
> law, my heart and soul,
> everything that I love and that
> you know before me'.

JOANNA, a member of the audience watches her.

EXT. STREET - DAY

Joanna walks through a square and onto a deserted street.

EXT. PUB - DAY

A sign outside a pub:

>   'SPEED PITCHING FOR FILMMAKERS'.

A bell rings.

INT. PUB - DAY

Filmmakers pitch their ideas to each other with a ringing
bell signalling the end of each pitch.

>   MARK
>   It's a transgender, cyborg,
>   splatter horror with a Dadaist
>   manifesto.
>
>   THERESA
>   Four friends go to a wedding and
>   one of them falls in love with an
>   American woman who he then only
>   meets at weddings and a funeral!
>
>   DONAL
>   I would have like, room tones
>   from say like a hundred different
>   rooms and they would all run into
>   each other.
>
>   JUSTIN
>   So there is this group of friends
>   and they travel to Texas and
>   there is this crazy guy with a
>   chainsaw and he starts killing
>   them one by one!
>
>   JOANNA
>   I'm interested in films that make
>   you think. I'm currently working
>   on a film inspired by French
>   philosopher Jacques Derrida.
>
>   ANDREA
>   Who?
>
>   THERESA
>   Dar-eeda?
>
>   JOANNA
>   Derrida.
>
>   JUSTIN
>   Is anyone dying in it?

                    MARK
          Is it avant-garde?

                    JOANNA
          Anyways it's just inspired from
          this book. It's actually a love
          story.

EXT. UNIVERSITY OF WESSEX - DAY

A stately building in the countryside.

INT. UNIVERSITY OF WESSEX / THEO'S OFFICE - DAY

Packing boxes lie strewn around in place of furniture.
Sitting on the only chair is MACEY, a mature PHD student.
THEO, her professor, is perched on a stool.

                    THEO
          Have you finished 'The Post
          Card'?

                    MACEY
          Yes, I didn't like it.

                    THEO
          Come on, Macey, you can do better
          than that, why not?

                    MACEY
          It's just heterosexist propaganda
          in which a male academic is
          unfaithful to his wife. It's
          the old clichéd story of male
          philosopher as seducer. It's so
          1970's.

                    THEO
          That's unfair. Don't you think
          the relationship between Plato
          and Socrates is a little more
          complicated than that?

                    MACEY
          So it's a bromance too? Boys,
          boys, boys. Just not interested.
          Why should people continue to
          read 'The Post Card'?

                    THEO
          Well, at its simplest it's about
          people, how they love each other
          and how they betray each other,
          and like all literature, it's on
          the side of life.

                    MACEY
          Theo, you're such a dinosaur.

INT. HERACLITUS PICTURES PRODUCTION OFFICE - DAY

Joanna sits in a chair. Production assistant LUCY taps
away at a computer. A postman enters with a recorded
letter for Joanna to sign.

                    LUCY
          Joanna, on Tuesday 15th you have
          a talk at the Film Academy and
          I'm still trying to sort out that
          cancelled meeting with British
          Screen.

Joanna inspects the recorded letter.

                    LUCY
          Are you going to open that?

                    JOANNA
          'When I am creating
          correspondence, which is not the
          case here, I mean when I write
          several letters consecutively,
          I am terrified at the moment of
          putting the thing under seal...'

INSERT - DOCUMENTARY

                    MARIAN HOBSON
          '...and if I were to make a
          mistake about the addressee,
          invert the addresses, or put
          several letters into the same
          envelope? This happens to me,

and it is rare that I do not
reopen certain letters after
having failed to identify them by
holding them up to the light.'

> MARTIN MCQUILLAN
> Post Card is a very strange
> book. The first part, 'Envois',
> is a series of letters, it's
> fragmented, it has gaps in
> it, some of the letters are
> missing possibly burned. It is
> seemingly autobiographical with
> references to real people such
> as Hillis Miller and Sam Weber
> and a central figure that looks
> something like Derrida.

> J. HILLIS MILLER
> And there are a lot of explicit
> sexual references, some of them
> slightly shocking to me, for
> example, the one in which he says
> 'like when I was an adolescent
> and used to make love against the
> wall'. And you say, 'Really? Why
> are you telling me this, Jacques?
> I don't know that I want to know
> it.'

> SAM WEBER
> Many of the details, as far as I
> know them, were quite accurate,
> but they are given a spin, as it
> were, which takes them out of the
> realm of self-evidence; in other
> words, reality is there but what
> is reality?

EXT. SUBURBAN HOUSE - DAY

Postal historian DAVID and Joanna say goodbye.

> DAVID
> It's been very nice meeting you.

          JOANNA
    I'll be in touch, thank you
    so much for your time, David.
    Goodbye.

David goes back inside. Joanna takes out her phone and makes a call.

INT. UNIVERSITY OF WESSEX / SEMINAR ROOM - DAY

Theo is giving a seminar to students.

          THEO
    It is almost impossible to define
    deconstruction. However you may
    find the following points useful.

Theo's mobile phone vibrates.

          THEO
    Deconstruction is not a method
    of criticism. The idea of a
    method presupposes a set of
    fixed rules to apply to a text.
    Deconstruction has only one
    rule, allow the other, what is
    different, the not me, to speak.

INT. SOUND DUBBING STUDIO - DAY

CHARLES LEAVIS reads an extract from 'The Post Card' from inside a recording booth.

          CHARLES
    'They not only allege that they
    know how to distinguish between
    the authentic and the simulacrum,
    they do not even want to do
    the work; the simulacrum should
    point itself out, and say to
    them: "here I am, look out, I am
    not authentic!" They also want
    the authentic to be thoroughly
    authentic, the apocryphal and the

bastard also. They would like the
counterfeiters to have themselves
preceded by a pancarte: we are
the counterfeiters, this is false
currency. As if there were true
currency, truly true or truly
false currency.'

INT. UNIVERSITY OF WESSEX / CHARLE'S OFFICE - DAY

Charles, Theo's boss, is packing boxes. Theo enters.

          CHARLES
Ah...Theo...
Have you packed your boxes yet?

          THEO
No, I'll do it on Friday.

          CHARLES
Come on Theo, everything has to
go from this building to the
Bazalgette building on Monday.

          THEO
You know I am being passive-
aggressive over this move.

          CHARLES
Your views on the merging of the
literature department with the
communications department are
well known.

          THEO
You are a philistine, Charles.

          CHARLES
The thing you don't understand,
Theo, is that literature cannot
survive the present regime of
telecommunications.

          THEO
Don't quote Derrida at me!

                    CHARLES
          Literature can't survive the
          iPad. Nor can philosophy or
          psychoanalysis.

                    THEO
          Or love letters.

                    CHARLES
          Pack the boxes.

INSERT - DOCUMENTARY

                    GEOFF BENNINGTON
          The 'Envois' has a feel to
          it that is often described
          as literary. It seems to have
          relation with the tradition of
          the epistolary novel.

                    ELLEN BURT
          What an epistolary novel
          in the 18th century does is
          plays with the problem of
          the 'found correspondence', a
          collection of letters found in
          a trunk somewhere, inherited
          and published, that reveals or
          purports to reveal some real-life
          world.

                    J. HILLIS MILLER
          It has to do with the tradition
          in novels that the characters are
          egos; self-identical people who
          remain the same, and when they
          write letters it is a letter from
          Derrida to somebody; there is a
          real recipient, a real singular
          sender. The novel really depends
          on that assumption.

                    MARTIN MCQUILLAN
          'Envois' both plays on that,
          follows in that tradition, but
          also turns it inside out. It's

not clear who's speaking in the
Envois, the French pronouns are
very difficult to follow and are
slippery. It's not clear whether
there are single voices here or
multiple voices.

INT. HERACLITUS PICTURES PRODUCTION OFFICE - DAY

Joanna and Theo are in a meeting.

>   THEO
> Joanna, I've had my fingers
> burned a little bit in the past
> with interviews.

>   JOANNA
> Have you?

>   THEO
> And as you can probably
> appreciate, I am quite precious
> about my book and what it is that
> you are particularly wanting to
> portray in these interviews.

>   JOANNA
> Well I can see your work very
> easily being transferred to a
> very beautiful, very evocative
> film.

>   THEO
> Well thank you, me too, frankly.
> You can point a camera at anyone
> and ask them to speak about their
> thing, but it seems to me that
> I might lose control a bit of my
> project.

EXT. STAMP SHOP - DAY

Theo looks at stamps in the shop window.

INT. STAMP SHOP - DAY

Theo inspects a stamp collection.

INT. THEO & SOPHIE'S APARTMENT / STUDY - DAY

Theo writes in a notebook. The desk wobbles.

INT. GALLERY - DAY

     SOPHIE
    'Again I liked the rendezvous,
    always the same, intact, virgin
    as if nothing had happened. That
    was your choice, and from you I
    accept everything, my destiny.
    Once again we said almost nothing
    to each other (the tea, the lemon
    tart, one thing and another,
    what we said to each other
    then, as so many other times is
    greater than everything, more
    inexhaustible than everything
    that was ever said, even between
    us, greater than the very thing
    that comprehends it and despite
    everything, all the rest, above
    all I admired you; how well you
    know where you are going. How
    well you seem to know where you
    have to go and sacrifice to save
    what you have chosen.'

EXT. UNIVERSITY OF WESSEX - DAY

A camera crew shoots an interview with Theo.

     JOANNA
    Feeling relaxed? OK great.
    Take your time. Ready to roll?
    Everything OK on sound?
    Ready? OK. And...action!
    Why is the book 'The Post Card'
    such an important work by Derrida?

INSERT - DOCUMENTARY

>   THEO MARKS
>   As a work of philosophy the
>   text is engaged with fundamental
>   issue of communication and
>   representation. For example,
>   rather than a letter, that is
>   meaning 'always' arriving 'at
>   its destination', it instead
>   circulates like a post-card
>   arriving in various contexts
>   independent of the intention
>   of its originator, and open to
>   misreading by those who receive
>   it.

>   MARTIN MCQUILLAN
>   A post card puts the idea of
>   destiny under pressure. It's an
>   open letter that can be read
>   by anyone along the way, for
>   example, the postman. So it
>   can have a number of different
>   possible destinations that we
>   can't predict in advance.

>   GEOFF BENNINGTON
>   So for example he coins in
>   this book, the word in French
>   'destinerrance', which is
>   translated as destin-erancy or
>   destinerance, where destining
>   doesn't resolve quite as destiny
>   because of an element of errancy
>   which affects or afflicts it. And
>   this puts some quite difficult
>   questions to philosophies of
>   history, to the idea of a
>   directionality of history,
>   certainly an idea of progress.

INT. EDIT SUITE - DAY

Editor HELEN pauses the Bennington interview and turns to
Joanna.

              JOANNA
          What about cutaways on postal
          stuff? What have you got?

Helen spools through some cutaways.

              HELEN
          (voice off)
          Not much.

              JOANNA
          What about the interview with
          David the postal historian?

INSERT - DOCUMENTARY

              DAVID WILSON
          We use the word 'post' today but
          in fact that refers originally to
          a place where the horses could be
          changed on their journey from one
          town to another and this was a
          changing post.

Helen stops the interview.

              HELEN
          Isn't this going a bit off the
          point?

              JOANNA
          No...No! There is no point; that
          is the point.

EXT. STREET PSYCHOANALYST HOUSE - DAY

Sophie approaches a house and rings the bell.

INT. PSYCHOANALYST HOUSE / CONSULTING ROOM - DAY

Sophie lies on a chaise longue. Her therapist, FRAUKE, heavily pregnant, sits behind her.

                SOPHIE
        I had this dream. It's at the
        seaside and I'm standing on a
        cliff. I'm with Theo. It's quite
        a steep cliff....And then I'm not
        sure who it is anymore, if it's
        Theo...

                FRAUKE
        Or somebody else?

                SOPHIE.
      Yeah.

EXT. ABANDONED CHALK MINE - DAY

Theo runs along a cliff edge. He stops for a rest and looks over the landscape.

INT. THEO & SOPHIE'S APARTMENT / DINING ROOM - MORNING

Theo, Sophie and their five-year-old son BYRON eat breakfast.

                THEO
        Come on. We're going to be late.
        You can eat that in the car.

                BYRON
      Bye Mummy.

                SOPHIE
      Bye.

Theo and Byron leave.

THEO
>   (voice off)
>   Don't forget Benjamin and Esther
>   are coming over tomorrow.

Sophie finishes her breakfast and reads her horoscope.
Her phone beeps with a message. She takes it out of her
handbag and reads it.

INSERT - DOCUMENTARY

>   STEPHEN BARKER
>   'This has separated us, infinitely
>   separated us, but in order "to
>   live", if you can call it living,
>   this separation and in order to
>   love a secret based on it, based
>   on what holds us together without
>   relation, the one addressed to
>   the other, the one backed by the
>   other, yes both.'

INT. HERACLITUS PICTURES PRODUCTION OFFICE - DAY

Lucy works at the computer. The phone rings.

>   LUCY
>   Good morning. Heraclitus
>   Pictures.

INTERCUT - INT. THEO'S OFFICE/UNIVERSITY OF WESSEX - DAY

>   THEO
>   It's Theo Marks. Is Joanna there?

>   LUCY
>   (voice off)
>   *Hi Theo, it's Lucy. She's not in*
>   *at the moment.*

Theo's colleague BENJAMIN enters with mail.

                    THEO
          I wanted to speak to her about
          the contributor release form.

                    LUCY
          Right, what is it that you wanted
          to know?

                    THEO
          (voice off)
          There's something in passage two
          I wanted to clarify.

                    LUCY
          OK, hang on. Let me just get a
          copy. One moment.

Lucy gets up to get the file. She is pregnant. INTERCUT
Lucy's movements with Benjamin's and Theo's in Theo's
office.

Benjamin hands Theo a letter, which he puts in his jacket
pocket.

                    LUCY
          OK go ahead.

Benjamin packs his boxes.

                    THEO
          Quote 'I acknowledge that you
          shall have the sole and entire
          control of the Film and the
          manner and terms upon which the
          Film is produced, distributed,
          marketed, exploited, exhibited
          and otherwise used or disposed
          of in all media and territories
          throughout the world as you in
          your absolute discretion may wish
          in perpetuity'. End of quote.

                    LUCY
          Right, erm...so what was it that
          you wanted to know?

INSERT - DOCUMENTARY

                    GEOFF BENNINGTON
          By presuming somewhere that
          messages have somewhere to go,
          a right destination, a final
          destination and so texts in
          principal if not always in
          practice, would have at least,
          or would open the perspective
          of a true, final, complete
          interpretation in which their
          meaning would be exhaustively
          grasped and successfully
          registered. Derrida thinks this
          is quite impossible.

                    MARTIN MCQUILLAN
          Reading can only ever be
          partial, and reading is about
          understanding the incompleteness
          of reading, and it's a
          sensitivity to that, to what is
          buried, or repressed or remains a
          secret, which makes reading, only
          ever a misreading.

EXT. THEO & SOPHIE'S APARTMENT - EVENING

Lights are on in the top floor flat.

INT. THEO & SOPHIE'S APARTMENT / LOUNGE - EVENING

Theo reads BYRON a bedtime story.

                    THEO
          'A boy had a secret. It was a
          surprise; he wanted to tell his
          grandmother so he sent his secret
          through the mail. The story of
          that letter is the reason for
          this tale. Because there was a
          secret in the letter the boy
          sealed it with red sealing wax.

> If anyone broke the seal, the
> secret would be out. He slipped
> the letter into the mailbox.'

INT. THEO & SOPHIE'S APARTMENT / STUDY - EVENING

THEO works at his desk. He takes the letter Benjamin gave
him from his jacket pocket.

>   THEO
>   (reading) (voice over)
>   Dear Professor Marks, the
>   University of Oxford invites
>   you to give the annual Duke
>   Humphrey lecture. This year is
>   the 40th anniversary of Jacques
>   Derrida's visit to the Bodleian
>   library where he saw the medieval
>   manuscript which became the cover
>   for his book 'The Post Card'.
>   Given your research on Derrida
>   we also invite you to see the
>   manuscript for yourself.

Theo is delighted.
He finds the books 'Love in the Time of Deconstruction'
by Theo Marks and the 'The Post Card' by Jacques Derrida,
and places them on the desk.

INSERT - DOCUMENTARY

Martin shows the cover image of *The Post Card*.

>   MARTIN MCQUILLAN
>   The image shows Plato standing
>   behind Socrates, whose acting
>   as a scribe. Derrida finds this
>   image amazing. We think that
>   Socrates never wrote anything of
>   his own. The work of Plato is the
>   reported dialogues of Socrates,
>   but what we see in this image
>   is Plato dictating to Socrates.
>   So the words of Socrates are

Plato's and not his own. It's
as if Socrates were a character
invented by Plato. So it reverses
the assumed genealogy in which
Plato comes after Socrates. It's
like saying Heidegger comes after
Derrida.

            JACQUES DERRIDA
One morning while I was typing
a passage for these 'Post
cards' the telephone rings and
I hear the operator's voice:
From the United States, do you
accept a collect call from the
United States? I ask who from?
And I hear the voice of my
correspondent in America saying
from Martin Heidegger the German
philosopher who died some years
before. So it was a joke and
I said No, I don't accept this
collect call, and I immediately
wrote down the story in 'The Post
Card', in the book, you could
read it; it's a true story.

INT. THEO & SOPHIE'S APARTMENT / DINING ROOM - AFTERNOON

Theo is making cocktails with Benjamin while Sophie chats
with Benjamin's wife, ESTHER.

            THEO
      (handing Benjamin a cocktail)
Here. Try this, it's my new
invention. I call it a Martini
Heidegger.

            BENJAMIN
Sounds tasteful, what's in it?

            THEO
Equal measures of gin and
vermouth, with a twist of irony.

Benjamin takes a sip.

                    BENJAMIN
          Congratulations by the way.

                    THEO
          On what?

                    BENJAMIN
          On giving the 'Duke Humphrey
          Lecture' in Oxford. It's a great
          honour. I bet our new Head of
          Communication Studies is boasting
          about you to our Vice Chancellor.

                    SOPHIE
          Stop talking shop you two; it's
          boring for the rest of us.

                    BENJAMIN
          It pays the mortgage.

                    SOPHIE
          Can we just have one evening
          without talking about the bloody
          university?

There is an awkward silence.

                    ESTHER
          When will you stop work Sophie?

                    SOPHIE
          In five months and then I'll have
          six months maternity leave.

                    ESTHER
          Will the little one go into
          nursery after that?

                    SOPHIE
          I don't know; when I had Byron
          I went straight back to work. I
          kind of regret that now. So this
          time I might take some unpaid
          leave.

Theo looks uncomfortable. There is an awkward silence
again.

ESTHER
(blurts)
I liked that last book you wrote,
Theo, what was it called?

THEO
'Love in the time of
Deconstruction'.

BENJAMIN
The central thesis was wrong
though.

THEO
Shut up and have another Martini.

ESTHER
No I agree with Theo. There is no
such thing as universal love.

THEO
I didn't quite say that. What I
said was that it is not possible
to derive a universal theory of
love from the particular examples
of individual cases. Because
I love Sophie and cannot help
loving Sophie, it's something
I do involuntarily, that tells
us nothing about the universal
phenomena of love. Sophie and I
have nothing to tell anyone about
love in general.

BENJAMIN
But my point is that it is
possible to love more than one
person at a time--

ESTHER
Oh really?!

BENJAMIN
--and that love is a model that
can be repeated. Think Casanova,
think George Clooney.

              THEO
    Even if that were true, there is
    no reason why George Clooney's
    love for one person should
    resemble that for another. I
    love Sophie and that is what it
    is. If I were to have an affair,
    my love, if it were love, for,
    say, George Clooney, it would be
    quite different from my love for
    Sophie.

              ESTHER
    But would your love for George
    Clooney affect your love for
    Sophie?

              THEO
    It depends if Sophie knew about
    me and George, then...

They all laugh, except for Sophie.

              SOPHIE
    If you were having an affair I
    wouldn't want to know anything
    about it.

              BENJAMIN
    (awkwardly)
    But my point is...

              SOPHIE
    My point is that we should stop
    talking about love as a universal
    phenomenon, as if we were in a
    seminar.

                    MONTAGE
A) Theo works in his study.

B) Sophie on the sofa.

C) Byron on his scooter outside the apartment.

                    SOPHIE
                    (voice over)
                    'You are loved, my beloved,
                    admired by a monster; and yet it
                    is you who are the violent one,
                    my sweet, you who are hacking
                    around in your life and are
                    forcing fate.'

INSERT - DOCUMENTARY

                    GEOFF BENNINGTON
                    One of Derrida's constant
                    interests is to wonder about
                    things happening, about what
                    constitutes an event, more
                    especially what constitutes an
                    event that he would say is worthy
                    of the name event. In other words
                    an event that isn't simply a
                    straightforward causal outcome of
                    earlier events.

                    MARTIN MCQUILLAN
                    This is what deconstructive
                    reasoning is, it is an event.
                    Reading a text as if it were
                    unique, reading it in an
                    inaugural way, as if for the
                    first time in order to articulate
                    the alterity within that text as
                    an experience of the other. . . .

INT. EDIT SUITE - DAY

Joanna and Helen watch the screen.

        HELEN
It doesn't work.

        JOANNA
Why not?

        HELEN
It makes no sense.

        JOANNA
It makes sense to me.

        HELEN
Yes but you've got to make it
make sense to the audience. It's
too hermetic. It's only if you
are in the know that you are
going to get it....I don't know
who your audience is.

INT. HERACLITUS PICTURES PRODUCTION OFFICE - DAY

Lucy is working at the computer. Joanna enters and slams
her bag down.

        JOANNA
What a mess!

        LUCY
I'm really sorry Joanna. What are
you going to do?

        JOANNA
I'll have to edit it myself.

        LUCY
It happens. There's always the
possibility that something better
paid comes along. It's just a
shame it had to happen at this
point in time.

        JOANNA
Well it's not the end of the
world....Her editing was a bit

> clunky anyway. She was always
> trying to make something happen
> with the footage when there
> wasn't anything to happen. It's
> a question of atmosphere not of
> mechanics.

>   LUCY
> By the way Rosalind rang, she
> wants to see you on Tuesday,
> something about copyright
> clearance.

INSERT - DOCUMENTARY

>   NICHOLAS ROYLE
> 'When I call you my love, is
> it you that I am calling or my
> love? You, my love, is it you I
> thereby name, is it to you that
> I address myself? I don't know
> if the question is well put; it
> frightens me. But I am sure that
> the answer, if it gets to me one
> day, will have come to me from
> you. You alone, my love, you
> alone will have known it.'

INT. SOPHIE & THEO'S APRTMENT / STUDY - DAY

Theo writes in a notebook. The desk wobbles. Frustrated
he stops working and throws down his pen.

EXT. PSYCHOANALYST HOUSE - DAY

Sophie rings the bell.

INT. PSYCHOANLAYST HOUSE / CONSULTING ROOM - DAY

Sophie lies on the couch, silent.

INTERCUT - INT. STUDY/CONSULTING ROOM

Theo turns over the desk and finds the wobbly leg. He
takes a screw driver and begins unscrewing the leg.

INT. CONSULTING ROOM
Sophie on the couch, silent.

INT. STUDY
Theo takes the leg off. There are letters wedged into
a hole inside the leg. He pulls one out. INTERCUT with
Sophie's conversation with the therapist.

> SOPHIE
> I realised I was doing the same
> gestures and it felt awkward
> because it's not the same man.

Theo reads the letter.

> SOPHIE
> So I was a bit worried when I saw
> Theo that evening.

Theo very upset, takes another letter from the leg.

> SOPHIE
> I tried to find out if he would
> notice something. Maybe I touched
> him in a certain way that he
> would get suspicious.

Theo is surrounded by letters.

> THERAPIST
> Because you felt changed?

> SOPHIE
> Yes, Yes...I felt changed.

EXT. ABANDONED CHALK MINE - DAY

Theo runs. He stops at the cliff edge. In the distance
Sophie embraces a man. Theo shakes his head in disbelief.
The couple have disappeared. He turns away from the cliff.

INSERT - DOCUMENTARY

          SAM WEBER
          Secrets are really even more
          interesting where they are
          visible, in other words you
          see something but you don't
          know really what is going on or
          what it means. Whether it's a
          language, a face or an activity
          and this remains for me one of
          the important experiences both
          of reading Derrida's work and
          particularly the 'Envois'. The
          point he keeps making about the
          post card being open for everyone
          to read, being public and at
          the same time remaining somewhat
          secret.

          J. HILLIS MILLER
          These letters, though, they
          appear to be addressed to
          somebody particular, 'my sweet
          darling girl' whoever this is. It
          is the theme of 'A destination.'
          That is if you or I as readers of
          these love letters, intercept the
          letters and we are made into the
          recipients of this, so in a way
          they are an attempt to seduce us.

INT. HERACLITUS PICTURES PRODUCTION OFFICE - DAY

Joanna rummages inside her bag, holding aside a stack of
recorded letters.

          LUCY
      Are those all recorded letters?

          JOANNA
      Yes.

          LUCY
      They must be important.

                    JOANNA
          Why do you say that?

                    LUCY
          Because they're recorded, which
          means you have to sign for them,
          so whoever sent them wants to
          make sure you get them.

                    JOANNA
          Well, I've got them.

                    LUCY
          Why don't you open them?

                    JOANNA
          I don't need to.

                    LUCY
          So you know what's inside?

                    JOANNA
          Yes...No.

INT. GALLERY - DAY

                    SOPHIE
          'Your spectre, the other one,
          the bad one, that maternalising
          milliner who dictates sententious
          "determinations" to you, had
          disappeared as if by magic,
          finally alone, the one addressed
          to the other on the floor, very
          hard, huh, the floor, never have
          I so loved the earth.'

EXT. THEO & SOPHIE'S APARTMENT - MORNING

A shower is running forcefully.

EXT. THEO & SOPHIE'S APARTMENT / DINING ROOM - MORNING

Theo searches through Sophie's coat and bag. He finds her
phone and checks it for messages.

INSERT - DOCUMENTARY

                    CATHERINE MALABOU
                    We always have to always think of
                    sending in a determined epoch or
                    period of time so perhaps today
                    we are entering an era in which
                    the technical meaning of sending
                    is disappearing. The goal is to
                    read into the other's minds,
                    into the other's brains. All the
                    technologies that exist today,
                    tend to alleviate, shorten,
                    practically erase the *différance*
                    in order to gain immediacy into
                    reading each others' minds.

INT. METHODIST CHURCH - DAY

Joanna enters the church looking for Sam, a clairvoyant.
On seeing Joanna, Sam touches his forehead and closes his
eyes.

                    SAM
                    It won't make sense yet, but it
                    will. Don't leave home.

                    JOANNA
                    What can you see?

                    SAM
                    Your destiny is tied to something
                    you love...

                    JOANNA
                    What is it?

                    SAM
          You'll have to give up the
          thing you love to reach your
          destination.

                    JOANNA
          And is there life inside of me?

                    SAM
          You already know the answer to
          that.

INT. THEO & SOPHIE'S APARTMENT / LOUNGE - DAY

Byron looks through a stamp book. Sophie watches him.
Byron shows her the stamps. They embrace and Byron touches
Sophie's belly.

INT. UNIVERSITY OF WESSEX / CHARLES'S OFFICE - DAY

Theo is in a performance review meeting with Charles.

                    CHARLES
          Your application for a pay rise
          has not been approved.... Frankly
          I'm surprised you even applied
          for it giving your almost total
          absence of a workload.

                    THEO
          I don't think that's fair,
          Charles. As you know, I am
          working on my three-volume study
          of the history of the post.

                    CHARLES
          Ah, yes. You did mention that.
          You mentioned it last year and
          the year before that.

                    THEO
          I am giving the Duke Humphrey
          lecture in Oxford in two weeks.

                    CHARLES
          That's good news...it's
          prestigious. It's an important
          opportunity for you. What's it
          called?

                    THEO
          (pause)
          'Eros in the Age of Technical
          Reproductability'.

                    CHARLES
          Have you finished it?

                    THEO
          Yes.

                    CHARLES
          Can I read it?

Charles's mobile beeps.

                    THEO
          No.

Charles gets up and checks his phone.

                    CHARLES
          Look Theo, you need to think
          about whether all this post
          card stuff is really the most
          productive use of your time.
          In the new department of
          communications there will be
          plenty of students that need to
          be taught and they will be paying
          £9000 a time. The landscape of
          higher education is changing,
          and writing about post cards
          and 18th-century literature is
          beginning to look like a luxury.

                    THEO
          Charles, whatever happened to
          you? Don't you hate what is
          happening to universities?

Don't you hate all the 'quality
assurance' paper work and the
endless committees and the
research audits, the grade
inflation and now to top it off
we have to call under-qualified
school leavers customers who
are shovelled into universities
because there are no jobs for
them?

        CHARLES
The problem with people like
you, Theo, is that you wallow
in nostalgia for your own lost
undergraduate years.

Theo storms out.

INT. GALLERY - DAY

        SOPHIE
'I would like to be sure that
it is you, uniquely you, alone
and directly, who finally have
accepted the idea of this great
fire, call it "burning". That
there literally will remain
nothing of what we have sent each
other, this entire eternity, that
one day or another we will become
younger than ever and that after
the burning of the letters by
chance I will encounter you.'

INSERT - DOCUMENTARY

        CATHERINE MALABOU
In the 'Envois', Derrida is
in a way, theatricalising this
discussion between the two
principals, that of pleasure and
the death drive. That's why in

the 'Envois' you constantly have
this interplay between pleasure,
love, sex, making love and on
the other hand this tragedy of
destruction, holocaust, dying,
burning.

MARTIN MCQUILLAN
Burning, cinders, ashes...
these are images of a radical
destruction, which is part of
deconstruction. Doing away with
the old order, everything goes up
in flames. But something always
remains, even if it's only ashes.

INT. UNIVERSITY OF WESSEX/ THEO'S OFFICE - DAY

Benjamin & Theo are speaking about the letters.

THEO
Ben, I don't know what to do.

BENJAMIN
I don't know what to say, Theo.
It must be very hard.

THEO
Don't speak like a school
counselor.

BENJAMIN
Ok, it's like this. She had an
affair; it's over, move on.

THEO
What if it isn't over? What if
the pregnancy has got nothing to
do with me?

BENJAMIN
What ifs?!...To be frank, Theo,
for a man who's spent twenty
years teaching western literature
to undergraduates I'm surprised

that you are so bothered by a
little infidelity.

THEO
A little infidelity, is that it?
Like musak in the background of
our lives? All the middle-class
couples are doing it?

BENJAMIN
I don't like to mention Penelope.

THEO
That was different! That isn't
even in the same league as this.
You know what happened there!

BENJAMIN
Professor Pot paging Doctor
Kettle.

THEO
You're on your second marriage!

BENJAMIN
I'm not the one going to pieces
over the fact that some men find
your extremely attractive wife
attractive.

THEO
So you want to fuck her too?

BENJAMIN
Calm down.

THEO
My point is-

BENJAMIN
Go on what is your point?!

THEO
My point is that she clearly
loved this guy and had a long-
term physical relationship with

him and, who knows, might still
be.

                    BENJAMIN
          My point is that it is over.

                    THEO
          How do you know?

                    BENJAMIN
          I don't. You'll have to find out.

                    THEO
          How?

                    BENJAMIN
          I don't know. You're a professor.
          Work it out.

INSERT - DOCUMENTARY

                    JOHN PHILLIPS
          'She used the finest words on
          earth in order to describe what
          she was missing. And that she
          visibly wanted to give me or
          expect from me, that you are "my
          wife" was not obvious at the
          outset and it was necessary to
          multiply marriages and alliances,
          but this is less and less
          doubtful in my eyes, if destiny,
          sort, lot, chance means in the
          end, the end of a life.'

INT. UNIVERSITY OF WESSEX / THEO'S OFFICE - DAY

Theo searches the letters for clues.

EXT. ABANDONED CHALK MINE - DAY

Theo runs.

INT. EDIT SUITE - NIGHT

Joanna is editing an interview with Derrida.

                    JACQUES DERRIDA
          I am actually in communication
          with the ghost of Heidegger
          but not at any time, and not
          according to a script which has
          been set for me. I have my own
          private correspondence with the
          ghost of Heidegger.

There is a knock at the door. A postman enters with a
recorded letter for Joanna to sign. She puts in it her
bag and continues.

                    JACQUES DERRIDA
          I believe that when you read
          someone, that when you inhabit
          or let yourself be inhabited by
          the text of an author -- which
          is a sort of correspondence --
          well the relationship between the
          author and yourself is inevitably
          a phantomatic relationship.
          Heidegger is a ghost for me.

INT. PICTURE LIBRARY - DAY

BETTINA [a forensic expert] is looking at the letters.

                    BETTINA
          Mr Marks, these are unsigned
          letters dated five years ago. It
          will be extremely difficult to
          establish their authorship.

                    THEO
          But can you?

                    BETTINA
          I am an expert in questioned
          document examination, which is

a forensic science. I'm not a
fortune teller.

THEO
Can you tell something about
who this man is from his hand
writing?

BETTINA
Mr Marks! You as a literary
critic are far better placed
than I am to say something
about *who a man is* from what he
writes. You are thinking of the
pseudoscience of Graphology. As
an expert witness in legal trials
my specialism is to establish
authorship in cases of forgery,
counterfeiting, fraud and
identity theft, not to determine
what the author had for breakfast
or whether he loves his wife.

THEO
Please Bettina.

Bettina takes the letters.

BETTINA
Judging by the mannered
handwriting I would say the
author is not a native English
speaker. His calligraphy is
classically European, probably
French. The letters were
written in a state of emotional
intensity, quickly but not
carelessly. An educated script.
He probably has a degree or holds
an executive position.

THEO
An academic?

              BETTINA
That would be impossible to say.
When hand writing is separated
from its origin it is very
difficult to say anything about
the identity of the author....
However, I would say with a
degree of confidence that he is a
Scorpio.

              THEO
How can you tell that?

              BETTINA
(points)
He says on this page.

INSERT - DOCUMENTARY

              MARTIN MCQUILLAN
There is something of the uncanny
about 'The Post Card'.
Themes of doubles, and ghosts
thread themselves through the
book.

              J. HILLIS MILLER
Derrida was a modern, un-
superstitious person -- like
Freud...but he was also
superstitious enough to know that
the quickest way to raise a ghost
was to say I don't believe in
ghosts.

INT. UNIVERSITY OF WESSEX / THEO'S OFFICE - EVENING

Theo opens a special delivery parcel with one hand and
holds the telephone receiver with the other.

              THEO
Yes...Yes...OK. Yes I'd like to
go ahead then. My name is Raphael

                    Schermann. Tuesday at 9.00 am?
                    Yes, thank you. Goodbye

PENELOPE enters.

                         PENELOPE
                    Hello Theo.

Theo gets up, pushing aside the parcel.

                         THEO
                    Penelope!
                    What are you doing here?

                         PENELOPE
                    I had lunch with Charles. He
                    wanted to celebrate my getting a
                    job at Oxford.

                         THEO
                    Congratulations. I love it when a
                    student of mine gets a better job
                    than I've got.

                         PENELOPE
                    Ex-student.

                         THEO
                    I wasn't asked for a reference.

                         PENELOPE
                    After the last time we saw each
                    other, I thought it best to ask
                    Benjamin.

They exchange looks.

                         PENELOPE
                    How is your wife?

                         THEO
                    Pregnant.

                         PENELOPE
                    Again?!

>   THEO
> 'I am the purest of bastards,
> leaving bastards everywhere...'

Penelope laughs. Impulsively, Theo tries to kiss her. She
swerves out of the way.

>   PENELOPE
> Goodbye Theo.

She leaves.

INT. GALLERY - DAY

>   SOPHIE
> 'I couldn't answer you on the
> phone right now, it was too
> painful. The "decision" you asked
> me for is once again impossible;
> you know it. It comes back to you.
> I send it back to you. Whatever
> you do I will approve, and I
> will do so from the day that it
> was clear that between us never
> will any contract, any debt, any
> official custody, any memory even,
> hold us back -- any child even.'

INT. HERACLITUS PICTURES PRODUCTION OFFICE - DAY

Joanna is in a meeting with lawyer ROSALIND.

>   ROSALIND
> I think you'll find that
> reproduction is strictly
> forbidden.

>   JOANNA
> That seems unreasonable.

>   ROSALIND
> And would you want your film
> freely available for anyone to
> download without permission.

                    JOANNA
          It will happen whether we want it
          or not.

                    ROSALIND
          The law takes no account of what
          criminals do.

                    JOANNA
          All we want to do is use a
          10-second clip from a thirty-
          year-old Ken McMullen film. Isn't
          that fair use?

                    ROSALIND
          Fair use is a vexed question:
          Examples include parody and
          pastiche, criticism and
          commentary, news reportage,
          teaching, library archiving,
          research and scholarship. It
          provides for the legal, unlicensed
          citation or incorporation of
          copyrighted material in another
          author's work through a four-
          factor balancing test: purpose and
          character, nature of the copied
          work, amount and substantiality,
          and effect upon the work's value.

Joanna is silent.

                    ROSALIND
          I suggest you run the entire film
          through my office on completion.

She hands the Joanna the paperwork.

EXT. PSYCHOANALYST HOUSE - MORNING

Cars pass.

INT. PSYCHOANALYST HOUSE / CONSULTING ROOM - MORNING

Theo sits with Frauke.

        FRAUKE
So, tell me. . . . why have you
come here?

        THEO
I think my wife is having an
affair.

        FRAUKE
Why do you say that?

        THEO
I found love letters...

        FRAUKE
Found them?

        THEO
Yes I wasn't looking for them. I
had no idea. They were hidden.

        FRAUKE
And what do these letters say?

        THEO
They say that someone is or was
deeply in love with her.

The bell rings. Frauke frowns.

        THEO
They are dated five years ago and--

The bell rings again.

        FRAUKE.
I'm not expecting anyone! I'm so
sorry.

She exits. Theo takes an audio bug from his coat pocket.
He tapes it under the chaise longue.

Offscreen Frauke speaking in a raised voice to a young
man. Door shuts.

Frauke enters.

                    FRAUKE
          I am very sorry. He was so
          insistent.

Theo gets up and rushes out.

                    THEO
          Sorry, I can't do this.

EXT. PSYCHOANALYST HOUSE - MORNING

Theo gets into his car.

INT. CAR - MORNING

Theo takes the audio bug transmitter and tries to tune
it. There is a knock at the window by a hooded teenager.

                    TEENAGER
          Was that alright, mate?

                    THEO
          Yeah fine.

Theo gives the teenager £20 and rolls up the window. He
puts the headphones on and tunes the transmitter. He can
hear some sounds from inside the room. He closes his
eyes.

EXT. CAR - DAY

Theo sleeps.

                    SOPHIE
          (voice off)
          I've taken a step, I've gone
          forward, it's made me stronger,
          bigger; do you understand?

INTERCUT - INT. PSCYHOANALYST HOUSE / CONSULTING ROOM -
DAY

>   SOPHIE
> I went for a walk earlier in the
> park, I looked at the trees, the
> dead leaves, I felt something on
> my face and everything fell into
> place all at once as if everything
> that had happened had made sense.

Theo wakes. He listens to Sophie.

>   SOPHIE
> I didn't know I would still
> be able to feel again all this
> violence after all these years.
> All of a sudden I miss him, I
> really miss him. I love him, I
> love him.

Theo takes off the headphones.

INT. EDIT SUITE - DAY

Joanna edits the interview footage.

>   SAM WEBER
> Can an authority be developed
> by remaining above and beyond
> and outside of the scene it is
> commanding or does an authority
> have to deal with its implication
> in a scene that in some sense it
> is co-creating?

>   CATHERINE MALABOU
> The visual equivalent would be
> the impossibility of really not
> creating what we are saying.
> She has no access. There is
> no telepathy. Cinema is not a
> brain reading. So for me that
> would be the very equivalent
> of what we are talking about
> philosophically. She can't read

our minds, she is listening to
us, but she cannot read into us.
There is no superior ability to
decipher somebody with an image
or a text or with a reading.

EXT. STREET (OXFORD) - DAY

Theo walks through the halls of Oxford.

> THEO
> (voice over)
> 'One day, I will be dead. You
> will come all by yourself into
> the Duke Humphrey room, you will
> look for the answers in this book
> and you will find a sign that I
> am leaving in it now.'

Theo enters the Bodleian library.

THEO
> (voice over)
> The manuscript is a fortune-
> telling book. Follow the
> instructions through the book.

INT. BODLEIAN LIBRARY / DUKE HUMPHREY ROOM - DAY

Theo sits in front of Matthew Paris' medieval manuscript
Prognostica Socratis basilei.

EXTREME CLOSEUP - THE BOOK

The page is MC. Ashmole 304, an image of Socrates and
Plato.

BACK TO SCENE

Theo reads the inscriptions and turns the pages of the
book that lead him through the fortune-telling book.

              THEO
          (voice over)
          Start here. 'An erit bonum ire
          extra domum vel non'. Whether
          it is good to leave the home...
          Follow the trail. A-E-4. 'Ficus
          Fucus' -- The fig. The Sphere
          of Kings the King of Spain. 'Si
          iueris, cum lucro redibis'. 'If
          you shall have gone, you shall
          return with profit'.

Theo looks pensive.

INT. WHAREHOUSE PARTY - EARLY EVENING

Filmmakers, crew and cast mill about. Joanna circulates.
The editor Helen and production assistant Lucy chat.

              LUCY
          Joanna was a bit upset when you
          had to leave.

              HELEN
          Yeah...I don't know how she did
          it. I really don't....In any case
          I haven't been paid.

              LUCY
          If it makes you feel any better,
          neither have I.

              HELEN
          That makes me feel worse.

The party continues. A postman arrives with a recorded
letter for Joanna.

EXT. RIVERSIDE - EARLY EVENING

Joanna opens and reads the letter. She smiles.

INTERCUT - INT. PSYCHOANALAYST HOUSE / CONSULTING ROOM -
FLASHBACK

>   SOPHIE
>   I will go back home, back to my
>   family. I will get back my life
>   with Theo.

INT. LECTURE THEATRE (OXFORD) - DAY

Theo prepares to deliver the Duke Humphrey Annual Lecture
on 'Eros in the Age of Technical Reproductability'.

>   THEO
>   You know I consider 'Envois' to
>   be a truly awful text. So bad
>   I can hardly bear to read it.
>   There is nothing more commonplace
>   than infidelity within marriage,
>   nothing more devastating either.
>   For a long time I've thought
>   about giving this lecture on
>   the topic of infidelity in
>   literature, but where would one
>   begin and end? It would seem
>   that Western literature exists
>   for the collation of infidelity
>   as an experience. When Derrida
>   deconstructs Heidegger or Plato he
>   is betraying the thing he loves.
>   Operating under their law in a
>   transferential way to be sure.
>   Deconstruction is infidelity, it
>   is the betrayal of the loved one,
>   but in the best way possible. I
>   would like to think of the whole
>   of philosophy as the history of
>   a serial betrayal, of pupils who
>   betray their masters. Hegel who
>   betrayed Kant, Marx who betrayed
>   Hegel, Nietzsche who betrayed
>   everyone, Heidegger who betrayed
>   Nietzsche, Derrida who betrayed
>   Heidegger--everyone justifying

> their betrayal as a certain kind
> of faithfulness, the act of least
> violence. And of course Plato who
> betrayed Socrates and who was in
> turn betrayed by Aristotle. Plato
> whose betrayal was never to write
> a word of his own but to use the
> words of Socrates to transcend
> his master. As soon as we have
> writing we enter the domain of
> infidelity. Philosophy relies
> on this structural infidelity,
> without infidelity there could
> be no philosophy, no future for
> philosophy, no literature, no
> thing that we call the university.
> I would go so far as to say that
> there can be no future without
> infidelity, no social bond and
> no politics without it; no
> relationships either.

The audience applauds.

EXT. ROAD - EVENING

By the side of a deserted country road, Theo burns the
love letters.

MONTAGE

A) Theo burns the letters.

B) Joanna throws the letter into the river.

C) Theo and Sophie embrace.

INT. CINEMA - NIGHT

Joanna watches an image of a burning fire on the screen.
Flame light flickers on her face.

                    JACQUES DERRIDA
              (voice off)
              I believe that when you read
              someone, that when you inhabit
              or let yourself be inhabited by
              the text of an author -- which
              is a sort of correspondence --
              well the relationship between the
              author and yourself is inevitably
              a phantomatic relationship.

The fire burns.

                        THE END

CREDITS

Directed and Produced: Joanna Callaghan
Written: Joanna Callaghan, Martin McQuillan
Executive Producer: Martin McQuillan
Director of Photography: Joachim Bergamin
Composer: Peter Coyte
Edited: Ariadna Fatjó-Vilas, Justinian Buckley, Joanna Callaghan,
    Steven Worsley

CAST

Sophie: Birgit Ludwig
Joanna: Lucinda Lloyd
Theo: Leigh Kelly
Macey: Felicity Ferdinando
Lucy: Jessica Boyde
Charles: Robert Rowland Smith
Helen: Amanda Sterkenburg
Therapist: Frauke Requardt
Byron: Dante Bergamin Callaghan
Benjamin: Michael Kingsmith
Esther: Felicity Davidson
Lover: Jason Bennett
Clairvoyant: Edwin Flay
Penelope: Melissa Riggall
Bettina: Amelda Brown
Rosalind: Sarah Woodruff

Filmmakers: Theresa Cole, Mark Harriott, Plamen Kirtchev, Iustin Filip Munec, Andrea O'Donnell, Donal Sweeney.

Extras: Maria Bacro, Lea Bonneuil, Maria Collu, Jodie Crathorne, Sam Darlaston, Joanna Eatwell, Darryl Edwards, Shataksi Ghosh, Jake Godfrey, Gerard Hughes, Lucille Labbe, Jo Murphy, Joe Pognowski, Debbie Spink, Eleanor Webb

DOCUMENTARY CONTRIBUTORS

Geoffrey Bennington
Ellen S. Burt
Catherine Malabou
Martin McQuillan
J. Hillis Miller
Sam Weber
David Wilson

READERS

Stephen Barker
Marian Hobson
John Phillips
Nicholas Royle

Associate Producer: Jonathan Lahey Dronsfield
Assistant Director: Enrico Falzetti
Production Manager: Jo Murphy
Runners: Jake Godfrey, Poppy Corbett
Art Direction: Debbie Spink
Costume: Mark Harriott, Marie-Louise Lowcock
Hair and Makeup: Katrina Flavell , Kaylee Mayles, Didi Vasquez
First Assistant Camera: Rob Storey
Camera Assistant: Iustin Filip Munec
Gaffer: Ray Cook
Sound Recordist: Pete Smith
Boom Operator: Donal Sweeny

Colour grading: Paul Whiting
VFX: Rob Edney
Re-recording Mixer: Dominic Weaver
ADR Mixer: Chips Paul
Foley Mixer: Rob Price,
Foley Artist: Andrea King
Graphic Design: Txabi Jones
Script Consultant: Lesley Lodge

GENEROUS SUPPORT

Jorge and Anne Blumenfeld, Terry and Deirdre Callaghan, Julie Callaghan and Paul Hawker, Flo Davy, Vivian Harris, Angela Hunter, Cathy and Neil Ingham, Bridie Ingham, Toby Juliff, Wan-Chuan Kao, Melissa and Patrick Liddy, Lesley Lodge, Rebecca Mason, Angelica Michelis and Nicholas Austin, Michael O'Rourke, Melissa Riggall, Craig Rook, Paula Roush, David Sorfa, Paula Vaccaro, Michele Walliker, Alexis Weedon, Danielle White

Special thanks for academic research: Jonathan Lahey Dronsfield

THANKS:

Nicole Anderson, Derek Attridge, Bruce Barker-Benfield, Jodie and Graeme Bowman, Charmaine Brady, Michael Brennan, Neil Brown, Justinian Buckley, Sarah Campbell, Jen Clemitson, Mike Chamberlain, Mark Collington, Linda Corocan, Peter Dean, Aggela Despotidou, Flo Davy, Igor Drozdov, Les Ebdon, Christine Edzard, Enrico Falzetti, Deirdre Fox, Jack Garfein, Jaya Garrabost, Alexander Graf, Bill Griffiths, Adele Roberts Hunt, Peggy Kamuf, Michael Kennedy, Mark Layzell, Nick Mansfield, Ken McMullen, Jo Murphy & Jake Godfrey, The Painters Arms, Maksim Popov, Adam Procter, Elissa Marder, Marc Froment Meurice, Frauke Requardt, Daniel Oliver, Szabi Ruczui, Marco Ruffatti, Sands Films, Marsha Sankar, Alexa Seligman, Robert Smith, Claire Birchall, Gavin Stewart, Olivier Stockman, Susan Stone, Angelique Talio, Julie Tetlow, Lyn Thomas, Sue Thornham, Simon Morgan Wortham, Jaime Estrada Torres, Gary Whannel, Maria Wiener, John Paul Zaccarini, Xi Zhao

FUNDED AND SUPPORTED:

Arts and Humanities Research Council, Heraclitus Pictures, University of Bedfordshire, Kingston University London, University of Sussex
Produced: Heraclitus Pictures Ltd, Heraclitus.org.uk

Screenings kindly supported by: The Culture Capital Exchange, theculturecapitalexchange.co.uk

Loveinthepost.co.uk
info@heraclitus.org.uk

REFLECTIONS

Joanna Callaghan

Joanna Callaghan and Martin McQuillan, Bodleian Library Oxford, 2012.

Five years ago I received a phone call from Martin McQuillan that marked the beginning of a significant relationship, creatively and intellectually. To work on 'an enterprise doomed to failure',[1] as Geoffrey Bennington puts it, with a person from a very different background and set of experiences requires a particular set of characteristics: a generous spirit, a quick and curious intelligence, a desire to make things happen and a deep and mutual respect. When it works, such a relationship can yield extraordinary results and *Love in the Post* is proof of that.

When Martin asked me to write something for this book, my response was that everything I have to say is in the film. All that is left to do is to uncover the hidden, the buried, the secret and that which has been left out of the film. I hope this will give you a glimpse of the complexities of the project and of my sincerity in undertaking such a momentous task. But dear reader, I do ask something of you in return: to watch the film with the same dedication with which you read (and I know many of you are very good readers), therefore multiple viewings are advised and a sensitivity to a different kind of language than that to which some of you as text-based scholars may be accustomed.

10 JANUARY 2014—
THE THOROUGHLY AUTHENTIC

In approaching a film based on a source text, the question that arises is one of fidelity—whether to adapt or not. In some ways it is a fairly straightforward decision. That is not to underestimate adaptation theory, which has done much to reveal how complex adaptation processes are, but to point out that fidelity to a text depends largely upon the text itself. Some lend themselves to adaptation; others resist any kind of attempt to bend it into another shape. For a book such as *The Post Card*, part epistolary novel, part essays, part 'end of literature', what kind of approach could be faithful to Derrida's text and, more widely, to his project? In some ways Derrida provides the answer over and over again in *The Post Card*. In the following passage he speaks of the scholars who reported on the authenticity of Plato's letters; it is perhaps a message concerning the impossibility of fidelity:

They not only allege that they know how to distinguish between the authentic and the simulacrum, they do not even want to do the work, the simulacrum should point itself out, and say to them: "here I am, look out, I am not authentic!" They also want the authentic to be thoroughly authentic, the apocryphal and the bastard also. They would like the counterfeiters to have themselves preceded by a pancarte: we are the counterfeiters, this is false currency. As if there were true currency, truly true or truly false currency; what above all throws them off the track in their hunt is that the epistolary simulacrum cannot be stabilised, installed in a certain place, and especially that it is not necessarily, and completely, intentional.[2]

Adaptation from book to film implies that a text can be 'exhaustively grasped and successfully registered.'[3] This resounds with Brian McFarlane's discussion of film adaptation as 'bedeviled by the fidelity issue'.[4] Fidelity criticism depends precisely on there being a single, final, correct meaning to which the filmmaker adheres or otherwise violates or tampers with.[5] Films and filmmakers are judged by how well they adapt the source text, recreating the world of that text through audiovisual media. Complicating this further is the weight of existing interpretations that surround a book. The more that is written about a book, the more burdensome its film adaptation can become.

A few years ago, while writing a paper on director and production designer Christine Edzard, I had the opportunity to consider issues of adaptation. Edzard is best known for her critically acclaimed adaptation of Charles Dickens's novel, *Little Dorrit* (1988), for which she was nominated for an Oscar for best adapted screenplay. All of the French-born director's films have been adaptations, including *As You Like It*, *The Fool*, *A Midsummer's Night Dream*, *The Nutcracker*, *Tales of a Flying Trunk*, *Biddy* and *The Tales of Beatrix Potter*. Her adaptations are startling and innovative, though not as widely known as they should be. In *As You Like It* (1992) staring James Fox and Griff Rhys Jones, Edzard sets the action in a contemporary post-Thatcherite period. The Arden Forest is transported to an urban wasteland by the Thames in London. Shakespeare's play on double meanings is elaborated cinematically through reflections and mirrors and by actors playing multiple parts (a technique also used in *The Fool*). However the text itself is untouched. In this way, Edzard's adaptation works as a form of commentary on the original text as opposed to a reworking of the text into a more palatable language for contemporary audiences. Paradoxically because Edzard does not take liberties with the original text, this is the so-called 'problem' of her adapations according to her critics. In one of very few academic articles on Edzard, José Ramón Díaz Fernández says of *As You Like It*, 'One of the possible problems is that the social parable as well as the setting in a very specific location greatly diminish the poetry and our sense of illusion'.[6] Here we return to the problem of the fixed and final meanings that have grown up around a text.

In 1980 Harold Pinter wrote a screenplay adaptation of John Fowles's *The French Lieutenant's Woman*, directed by Karel Reisz and starring Meryl Streep and Jeremy Irons. It is an intriguing example of an organic, reflexive adaptation from book to film. The movie has two narratives: the original story, presented as a costume drama, and a parallel story of the emotional entanglement of the two main actors playing the roles in the costume drama. There were a number of scenes that Pinter wrote which Reisz left out of the final film. These are characterized by a mix of the two narratives in time and space, for example a scene in which Streep is in her trailer, in period costume and takes off her wig. It's easy to see why Reisz left these out. By keeping the filmed world (the adaptation) and the 'real' world (the actors creating the adaptation) separate, neither is destroyed and both remain inside the overall film world being created. The overlap or convergence of these worlds occurs in the viewer's mind, all the more powerful for its imaginative potential and decidedly less literal.

In the case of *The Post Card*, there were no existing film adaptations. There have been documentary films about Derrida, notably *Derrida d'ailleurs* (Fathy, 1999) and *Derrida* (Kofman and Dick, 2003) alongside drama *Ghost Dance* (McMullen,1983) in which Derrida appears. In 2007 Martin McQuillan wrote a treatment for a film based on the events within the 'Envois'. He presented this at a conference in 2009 and what mostly interested the audience was 'Who will play Derrida?' I was surprised by the assumption that the narrator was Derrida. There was for this audience a real belief in the so-called factual parts of the text. I became intrigued; how could we subvert expectations surrounding the text?

'Envois' has a relatively clear narrative thread, and there are scenes that could be restaged, for example the graveyard walk with J. Hillis

Miller in Zurich (which did happen according to Miller) or the Balliol College lawn incident in Oxford. In working through questions of adaptation and the associated problem of representation (Who *would* play Derrida!) I took a radical approach and considered not producing an 'original' film at all. That is, not to invent a story with actors, sets, locations and so on, but rather, to use existing representations offered by feature films that dealt with narrative episodes of the 'Envois'. I set parameters on the content, as mashups can be time consuming: the films had to be made and set during the period of the lovers' correspondence from 1977 to 1979, must be French, and must take place in France, Switzerland or the United States. Working with four films: *L'Homme qui aimait les femmes* (1977 Truffaut), *Le diable probablement* (1977 Bresson), *L'Amour en fuite* (1979 Truffaut), and *À nous deux* (1979 LeLouche), the clips are cut together to create narrative incidents such as the writing and receiving of letters, clandestine meetings and trips away. The result is *Adaptation*[7] a three-minute film set to Monteverdi.[8]

It was an interesting experiment but not one which could last for ninety minutes, and was one which would pose problems in terms of rights. Like all mashups, it became an essay-like consideration of film ancestry and form. The act was an act of rebellion against expectations about how narrative films 'should be' made and also against those asking, 'Joanna, who are you to make this film?' As another act of rebellion, I didn't read *The Post Card* until after a long time into the project. This might seem outrageous, but it was a genuine attempt to consider the book from a distinct location. To be free to ask any kind of question (including those I was warned against asking) in order to listen to how others spoke about the text. That would be my entry point, the speaking about the text that had 'grown up' around it. In 'To Speculate on "Freud"' Derrida says,

> In other words: the 'author' already is no longer there, no longer responsible. He has absented himself in advance, leaving the document in your hands. At least this is what he states. He does not seek to convince you of a truth. He does not seek to detract anything from the power, the proprietary investments, that is, the associations and projections of anyone. Association is free, which holds also for the contract between the writing and the reading of this text, along with the exchanges, engagements, and gifts, along with everything whose performance is attempted.[9]

I continued to make a number of short films in an attempt to work through problems of adaptation and representation, which included *Deconstructive Film*, produced in 2011. This film was based on interviews I did at the Derrida Today conference in London about film and deconstruction. I spoke with Peggy Kamuf, Geoff Bennington, Stephen Barker, Marian Hobson, Derek Attridge, Marc Froment Meurice, John Philips, Nicholas Royle and Elissa Marder. I asked a range of questions and most of the interviewees answered me patiently, though I understood very little of what they said. One of my favourite interviewees was Geoff Bennington, who, after putting his microphone on, drily began with 'probably one of the least deconstructive things you can do in a movie is point a camera at someone and expect them to say something intelligent about deconstruction.'[10] His example to counter this was the reflexivity that existed in Kofman and Dick's documentary *Derrida*, in which the film crew can be seen filming Derrida. Yet for me as a filmmaker this was one of the least interesting aspects of that film and a very literal illustration of 'deconstructive filmmaking' (whatever that is). During the interviews I became more and more intrigued by what these scholars imagined deconstruction 'looked like'. Peggy Kamuf said Michael Moore's films, Marian Hobson nominated Fellini and Elissa Marder identified Jean Luc Goddard, though for Marc Froment Meurice, Goddard's films were 'not deconstruction, at all, though it looks like it'.[11] He suggested Jonas Mekas's films and later added that 'Deconstruction has to do with a certain overcoming of the ego' and 'reflection and deconstruction don't go together'.[12] His comments stayed with me during this project, particularly in creating the character of the Director in *Love in the Post*. In *Deconstructive Film*[13] these responses are intercut with feature film clips that counter, contest or illustrate what has been said, often not those examples given by the interviewees, but rather my own reactions to what had been suggested and what I saw as a great deal of conflict and disagreement. My conclusion from this research was that perhaps any film could be regarded as deconstructive since it depended upon how it was spoken and not what it 'looked like'.

Joanna receives a recorded delivery letter.

25 JANUARY 2014—THE MATERIAL SUPPORT

Since 2002 I have been producing fiction films that have drawn on philosophical ideas. Early films, *Moments* (2002) and *Mrs De Winter's Dualism Dilemma* (2003), exploited philosophical ideas as content for formal experimentation. In 2004, I produced a 35 mm film, *Thrownness*, shot entirely within studio, which treats Heidegger's concept of *Geworfenheit* through a poem by Matthew Arnold. *A Mind's Eye* (2008) addresses Plato's concept of forms (*eidos*) from the *Timaeus*, using twins to mobilise ideas of essence and copy. In 2012, *DO NOT READ THIS* is a story of a missing manuscript by a recently deceased author. Drawing on Derrida's work, the story explores authorship, haunting and the structure of film narrative.

These films do not attempt modes of adaptation, as there is limited material to 'adapt' as such. A documentary may be perceived as a more appropriate mode to adapt philosophy to screen because of its primarily speech-based approach. Here the text or concepts from the text may be transferred to speech and recorded, whether through interview, on-screen discussion or voice-over. Fictional adaptation is more problematic because of its reliance on narrative. Philosophy does not spring to mind when one is looking for stories, though there are stories, for example, Sartre's *Nausea* (1938) and Nietzsche's *Thus Spoke Zarathustra* (1883).

Vivian Sobchack says film is 'subjectively and existentially becoming before us'.[14] This is true for the director as well as for the audience. I see my films as being created through a series of threads that have different qualities and are contingent. They include the creative source (the story or inspiration, in our case *The Post Card*), the technical and stylistic mobilisation (resources, setting, tone, language of the image), and the director's approach (previous films, personal history, personality). Perhaps the latter is similar to what Andrew Sarris calls the 'interior meaning'[15] of a film. Understanding and articulating this aspect of my films is difficult, as it is often subconscious and can take me by surprise when it surfaces. Sarris also admits that interior meaning is hard to identify because it 'is imbedded in the stuff of cinema and cannot be rendered in non-cinematic terms'.[16] I can recall an experience that might exemplify how my sense or experience of the world became manifest in a film. At the same time it was also entirely on the technical mobilisation available to me.

In 2009 I attended an academic conference where I presented my short film *A Mind's Eye*. During the question and answer I was asked quite aggressively, by the young man who was the panel chair, why I had 'chosen to use a male, blond blue-eyed baby'. (The film features a two-year-old baby in a sequence from Plato's *The Timaeus* which depicts the elemental essences—water, fire, earth, plants—and the somatic essences—horse, baby, man). The implication from the question was that through 'choosing' this representation I was propagating a myth of the perfect man as an Aryan master race.

Before giving my answer, I want to consider this type of question, which is a common one from non-filmmakers. Directors are often asked why they used a particular shot or technique or piece of music, and so on, the assumption being that it was predetermined and can be explained. It sits with the single-author concept of film, that the director has controlled and determined all aspects of the film and, besides being superhuman (as Gaut suggests one would have to be),[17] should be able to articulate and justify the reasons for his or her form of expression. On an extrapolated level my panel chair was talking about my acceptance of responsibility for the representations that I have created. That is one thing, but the concept of 'choice' is another. At the level of filmmaking I am operating, I do not 'choose' my representations. Choice would imply a certain amount of production freedom that you do not have when you are producing a film on a micro-budget. Much of what happens is a process of gathering and hoping, of serendipity and coincidence. It is also dependent upon the enormous amount of collaboration that goes into the production of a film. However, if I want to be known as a successful director, I should not speak too much about collaboration (except with the actors of course!) nor say that much of what happens in a film is chance, coincidence or error. Instead I should declare that I made all the decisions and determined everything and it was all part of My Directorial Vision. I should be able to answer questions such as those asked by my panel chair, coming up with a clever, insightful and hopefully witty answer. My problem is that I do not subscribe to the single-author theory. Behind every director is a team of talented people who together shape the film and the 'representations' created. In the lack of recognition and acknowledgement of the collaborative efforts required to make a film, the single-author director myth is a form of plagiarism, a lifting of others' work and claiming it for one's own. Defenders would say it is impractical to list all contributors and contributions when identifying and marketing a film (think of the already very long credits that exist for films). They may also say that the director made the key decisions in producing an artistic work and therefore has overall ownership and responsibility. Yes and no. Unfortunately, in more and more commercial films made today it is the executive producers and corporations that fund the productions who have become the directors. Decision making has been removed from the director and made in boardrooms and edit suites long after the director is working on another 'job'. One of my collaborators, who has worked in the film industry for many years, finds working on my films satisfying because together *we* make the decisions. His experience reflects an industry where decisions are made and vetoed by committee.

Returning to the question asked by my coincidently blond blue-eyed panel chair, 'Why *had* I chosen to use a blond, blue-eyed baby?' The question was so unexpected that for a moment I couldn't understand it. 'Because it was *my* blond, blue-eyed baby', I answered. On a practical level, using my own baby was the cheapest and most convenient way of putting a baby in the film. On a subconscious level, it was logical I would put *my* baby in a film *I was making* about perfection.

The tension between the practice of filmmaking, the subconscious processes that are at work when producing creative material and the product that arises is a continual source of wonder. I am constantly surprised by what happens in my films and only vaguely understand them upon reflection. I see now when I watch *Love in the Post* that this tension was drawn out through creating a parallel between the story of *The Post Card* and a story of filmmaking. This was shaped by the interviews, which were done before we wrote the script, some of which feature directly in the film, but a great deal remains behind the ideas that are explored in the narratives. Ellen Burt's comments on the material support resonated with me, and in her interview by the Seine I asked her why the book was important, a question Joanna also asks Theo in *Love in the Post*. Her answer was:

> He changes very radically the way that you look at a book or at the medium by requiring a thought on the medium that is like tectonic plates, you suddenly realise again the content is not the matter, it's not just that the medium is the message but the medium effects and finds itself implicated in the developments that the content can take in ways that are very revelatory to us. The fundamental assumptions that we make about our lives and what truth is and what art is, are affected by what it seems is this very tiny little problem of a material support and the systems that grow up around the material support.[18]

How the material support affects the content became Joanna's story. Through her story arc, I could think about and present the problems of filmmaking, of representation, adaptation or interpretation alongside the enormous logistical and practical considerations involved in producing a film. These are not separate; they are intertwined, and this has been misunderstood by many outside of the filmmaking experience, particularly film theorists who focus on reception with relatively little interest in processes of production.

There are ways the material support surrounding filmmaking influences the content. Some of these appear in the film, such as the editor quitting and moving onto another project. Many are behind the scenes; countless actors fired, locations falling through, broken-down kit, parking tickets, unwanted attention, forgotten port-a-loos, and so on. Then there is managing crew from very different backgrounds and perspectives, in particular the technicians: the grips, gaffers, sparks, best boys. Because their roles are highly technical (gaffers are qualified electricians) they are often well paid and accustomed to lucrative expenses, stipends and working conditions. In my experience these technicians often have no interest in the content that is being produced and are unable to distinguish between types of productions, making the same demands of a £1 million pound production as a £100,000 production. I recall a story of a gaffer who exemplifies the industry that has grown up around these roles. His 'trick' was to go around the set carrying a light stand at all times. That way he always looked as though he was doing something while at the same time it ensured he was never asked to do anything.

Film production processes are also plagued by countless documents: actors contracts, crew contracts, location permissions, archive access, copyright waivers, public release forms, and so on. Like all official forms these require the signature as evidence of agreement. It has always struck me that a medium that has above all others the ability to capture presence relies entirely on the written word. The interview footage itself counts for nothing unless the contributor signs the document. (Filmmakers like documentary maker Fredrick Wiseman do not bother with release forms, taking a verbal agreement as binding). In other words, the visual evidence of a contributor willingly answering questions is not proof of their agreement. They must sign a release form and waive all rights to their presence on camera. It is often an aspect of production that makes people nervous, like Theo when he receives the release form from Joanna; he realizes the magnitude of what he is being asked to promise;

> I acknowledge that you shall have the sole and entire control of the Film and the manner and terms upon which the Film is produced, distributed, marketed, exploited, exhibited and otherwise used or disposed of in all media and territories throughout the world as you in your absolute discretion may wish in perpetuity.[19]

In his interview, Sam Weber asks, 'Can an authority be developed by remaining, above and beyond and outside of the scene it is

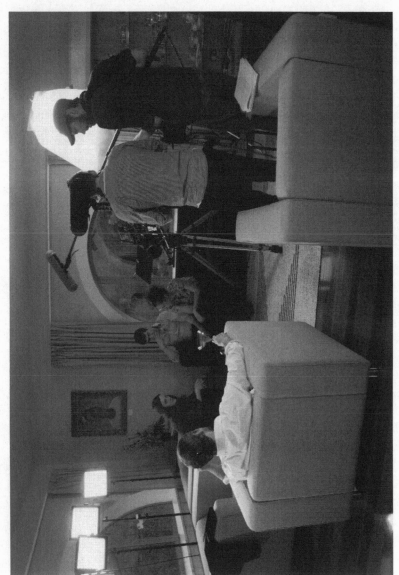

Cast and crew at Dorich House, Kingston.

commanding or does an authority have to deal with the implication in the scene that in some sense it is co-creating?'[20] I used these thoughts to embody the director's struggle for understanding the limits of what she could do in a film about *The Post Card* or indeed 'about' anything. Having struggled for the last ten years to wield industrial filmmaking processes to produce films independently, I am well aware of the huge costs, personal, intellectual and financial, of such an undertaking. I have been an outsider in the filmmaking scene in the UK because of the kind of work I produce and perhaps because of my genealogy. My work sits between camps. It is not experimental enough to be avant-garde, but it also does not obey clearly the rules of narrative fiction as accepted within mainstream filmmaking. It is also not very fashionable work. Intellectual films that are conscious of themselves as films are more akin to European filmmaking, where my work has had more success. So the position of the outsider, who nevertheless wants to be inside, somewhere, is the basis for the character named Joanna.

When I started writing the script, I had not intended to call the director Joanna, but it just happened, and it seemed churlish not to call her by my own name. It also creates a sort of double-take in which for a moment, even if only a few seconds, there is a question: 'Who is Joanna, a character or a real person?' As in the preface of *The Post Card*, Derrida signs 'in my proper name', the question becomes an open one which requires an active reading and an investment which may or may not be betrayed.

18 FEBRUARY 2014—'WHEN HANDWRITING IS SEPARATED FROM ITS ORIGIN'

The importance of accepting responsibility for one's writing is something I have known of since childhood. My father employed a graphologist to find out the identity of an employee who had written expletives about him on the back of a toilet door at the coal washery he managed. He had the door removed and delivered to the graphologist alongside a sample of every man's signature in the plant. Through careful analysis of the handwriting on the back of the toilet door alongside the 170 samples, the graphologist was able to identify the man responsible. The man was called to a meeting along with the union representative and presented with evidence of the offence. He was given two options: admit that it was his handwriting, in which case he could resign, taking with him all of his benefits and entitlements, or deny it and the matter would go to the industrial tribunal. Knowing that the graphologist's specialty was in forensic handwriting analysis, the man admitted it and resigned.

As a twelve-year-old I knew nothing of these adult matters and had no understanding of the environment in which my father worked. I came to know of this story a few weeks later when one evening I answered the door of our home to a strange man. From my bedroom window, I watched the man and my father talk on the veranda. The guilty man, who had been sent by his wife, broke down in tears and apologized to my father, asking for his job back. My father acquiesced and gave him back his job. He had the toilet door painted over and no graffiti was ever seen again.

Theo visits Bettina, an expert in document examination.

1 MARCH 2014—REPRODUCTION PROHIBITED

Just outside of Milton Keynes is one of two dedicated telephone museums in the UK. It is a quaint collection dating from the 1900s to the present, and includes a working telephone exchange, switchboards and a range of telephone memorabilia. Cast and crew had a lot of fun there, telephoning each other, playing switchboard operator, listening in to conversations and witnessing the mechanics of calls through the open exchange. We shot a scene at the museum in which Theo reflects on his conversation with his boss Charles about the 'new regime of telecommunications'.[21] In a dream sequence, that pre-empts developments in the film, Theo is haunted by anonymous calls from the display phones. He runs from phone to phone, picking one up after the other receiving no answer to his questions, this was to be intercut with Sophie speaking on one of the phones:

> I couldn't answer you on the phone right now, it was too painful. The 'decision' you asked me for is once again impossible, you know it. It comes back to you, I send it back to you. Whatever you do I will approve, and I will do so from the day that it was clear that between us never will any contract, any debt, any official custody, any memory even, hold us back—any child even.[22]

The telephone museum scene was dropped though the above extract was used and instead performed in the gallery by Sophie. I spent time experimenting with the editing of the deleted scene and while doing so made a discovery that is an example of the unexpected that happens when working with images and sound.

I have never been one to use storyboards and my director of photography agrees, as the pre-visualisation that the storyboard process encourages is actually very limiting. Instead, when shooting on location, we respond to what we find before us and what happens in the moment. Consequently we shot a number of cutaways in the museum in response to the actor movements that were not planned or envisaged. One of these was a pan across a series of old photographs of switchboard operators. It is a lovely little in-camera moment of time travel as the pan reveals the epochs passing through the change in the women's hair and dress and the technology they operated. When experimenting with this cutaway, I used the above extract from Sophie as voice over and placed it over this shot.

Telephone switchboard operators through the ages. Courtesy of Milton Keynes Museum.

When the voice-over and the picture of these unknown women are put together, the effect is a history that tells of women who have fallen pregnant with unwanted children. The women in the above shot may have listened in (as switchboard operators undoubtedly did) to conversations about unwanted pregnancies but may also have been victims of such circumstances. It has been noted by histories of labour, that in the early twentieth century, telecommunications provided a new respectable source of employment for women and was one of the few technically oriented jobs available to them. Though women were paid up to a third less than men and were immediately dismissed upon marriage, this new industry provided financial and social independence for women that would gradually, along with other developments of the period, lead to significant changes in women's attitudes, lifestyles and sexual habits. It would not be far-fetched to say that the 'new regime of telecommunications'[23] of the early twentieth century led to a number of unwanted pregnancies.

In the 'Envois', pregnancy and 'the child' keep coming back. As early as page 5 there is an allusion to a child of sorts. This child lurks the passages, scooting in like Plato on his skateboard, and quickly disappearing; 'To the devil with the child, the only thing we ever will have discussed, the child, the child, the child.'[24] This child later becomes children: 'As for the children, the last ones I might touch, the holocaust has already begun',[25] and in one of the best known lines from the book, 'I who am the purest of the bastards leaving bastards of every kind almost everywhere'.[26] For me, this child is core to the emotional drama of the 'Envois' as both cause and consequence of all this correspondence. It was essential that a child be present in the film, in this case five-year-old Byron, whose genealogy remains open, but also in the multiple unborn children, visible but not yet real by the surprisingly large number of pregnant women that inhabit the film. It is my play on Derrida's erotic musing; 'Imagine the day, as I have already, that we will be able to send sperm by post card'.[27] Imagine the day that I can make a film which is 'stuffed' full of pregnancies; three women who are pregnant and one who wants to be.

Joanna's production assistant, Lucy, was not written as pregnant. However when five-months-pregnant Jessica Boyde auditioned for Sophie, she was not right for the lead role, but she was very good and

Sophie and Byron at home.

I wanted to work with her. It was easy just to make another character pregnant. This kind of flexibility in casting is rare and usually only possible when the director is also the writer. In mainstream film, creating a secondary character who is pregnant is problematic, as it may raise unhelpful or distracting questions from the central storyline, particularly if it has nothing to do with pregnancy or motherhood. Generally only main characters can be pregnant, yet in 'real life' pregnant women are everywhere—why are they not part of the landscape of films?

In Kelly Oliver's excellent book *Knock Me Up, Knock Me Down*, the use of pregnancy as a central plot device is examined. Unlike motherhood, pregnancy as a theme is a relatively recent phenomenon and has resulted in a new genre of film, the 'momcom'. These films are 'big screen representations of pregnant bellies that promise women romance, love and sex all through the transformative power of pregnancy'.[28] Oliver examines films from the 1930s to the present, and the representation and non-representation of pregnancy on screen including the Hays Production Code which banned the word *pregnant*.

Another character who is pregnant is Frauke, the therapist, who was, in real life, both pregnant and training to be a therapist. I had been inspired to feature a pregnant psychoanalyst from accounts of a friend of mine whose therapist had become pregnant during his treatment with her. He was not one to lie down during the sessions, so instead he watched that belly grow bigger every week from his chair opposite. He was disturbed by the pregnancy and felt 'abandoned' by her. He was relieved when their sessions ended due to the imminent arrival of 'the thing', as he called it. In the film a pregnant therapist could complicate and elaborate themes of pregnancy and psychoanalysis. I wrote a solo scene for Frauke based on an aspect of the therapy process that I have always been curious about: what the therapist did between sessions. According to my sources, a major priority of those ten minutes is to make the couch cold. In the dropped scene, Frauke opens the window very wide, plumps up the chaise longue and brushes off the debris of the previous patient. She takes a notebook from her pocket and quickly scribbles some notes. The scene was left out mainly because it felt too

Frauke prepares the room for the next patient.

laboured. Frauke was not a character that we need care about, and indeed it was better she remain distant for the purposes of the story. This is one of the painful aspects of filmmaking. You bring something to life from the imagination, watch it take shape and marvel at it, and then you have to abandon it, leaving it to be an orphan forever.

11 MARCH 2014—VISIBLE SECRETS

Many sections of the 'Envois' feel like a therapy session, saying things aloud, recounting, reflecting upon them. The gaps in the text are pauses, a loss of train of thought, how one starts a new topic before finishing the previous one. Sam Weber said that Derrida told him he writes in order not to be psychoanalysed, and yet, 'at the same time he was drawn to psychoanalysis as one of the institutionally marginal questioning interrogations of a mainstream systematic body of thinking'.[29]

The ritual of the psychoanalyst between sessions resonated with Weber's further comments on the 'institutionalisation of psychoanalysis',[30] of what in some sense is the conveyor belt of patients who pass through the therapist's room. In 2005 I did a series of photographs in a consulting room. Looking back on it, it was a generous act on behalf of my therapist. I had come to the end of my time with him, and I wanted to mark it creatively.

The process was liberating. I was free to move in that room, to sit in the therapist's chair, to walk about, to capture with my lens my point of view while horizontal. What is missing from the results is the experience of sound. I remember the noises of that North London clinic, doors opening and closing, patients arriving and leaving, muted voices heard through walls and my struggle to catch a few words, to know what was going on in those other lives, those other stories. In another dropped scene, Theo, after planting the audio bug in the consulting room, listens in to a number of therapy sessions from his car. These were to be improvised and combined with extracts from the 'Envois' such as the (very funny) following:

> over dessert, almost without transition, she told me that she could
> only come with someone else. I didn't understand the syntax of her

Image 6: North London clinic, 35mm slide series, 2005: Courtesy of Joanna Callaghan.

sentence right away.—But of course it has to be someone else! And she burst out laughing, understanding that I did not understand. Then she explained to me that she experienced as a kind of delicious pathology of which she was not sure she could be, or in truth wanted to be, cured: everything was staged, from the beginning, so that at the last moment she thinks, imagines, invokes, how to put it?, makes present for herself another than the other who was to be found at that instant coming in her.[31]

I have found that working with actors can be like therapy, though they may not always be willing patients. This resistance can be fertile grounds for development but can also prove unproductive. In an effort to reconsider my approach to working with actors, I attended a month-long course in method acting led by one of the great teachers, Jack Garfein. A self-declared exile living in Paris, the eighty-four-year-old Ukrainian-born director started in the Actors Studio and has worked with Lee Strasberg, Harold Clurman, Dustin Hoffman, Caroll Baker, Rod Steiger, Steve McQueen, Ben Gazzara and many others.

Jack's method is neither Stanislavski's nor Strasberg's; he has his own approach, undoubtedly drawn from these teachers but also unique to him. His experience of directing for stage and screen; his observations of the craft; and a deep and insatiable love of literature, film and theatre inform his approach. He draws from a range of sources including Molière, Miller, Fassbinder, Tolstoy, Brecht, Chekhov, Mamet, Beckett, Williams, Shakespeare, Dostoyevsky and Cervantes. He is a brilliant teacher with a wicked sense of humour. For four weeks in a hot July in the nineteenth arrondissement in Paris, I sat alongside eight French actors, working intensively on texts, word by word, line by line, starting first with improvisations and exercises and developing towards a public performance at the end of the month.

There are very specific exercises and processes one has to undertake in entering into the method that Jack teaches. As with therapy, one has to acquiesce to the process. The first step is a set of strict guidelines for the first reading of the text that has been chosen by Garfein for you to perform. In my case it was Petra in Fassbinder's *The Bitter Tears of Petra von Kant*. For the first reading I was to be alone, undisturbed, reading it through in one sitting. Immediately afterwards I was to note any images that stayed with me and the words related to these images. The words could be any kind, for example a line of dialogue, a prop, a description or a location. Importantly they should not be an analysis of narrative and plot, but specific words from the text that activate images. After this reading, I had then to put the text aside and wait for Jack to phone from Paris (this was pre-course homework). When he did, I was asked for these words, not for the images themselves. I recounted these and he then gave me another set of instructions for the second reading.

Jack's method builds on the actor's personal connection with the words on the page. You are almost discouraged to relate to or consider the story as a whole. Otherwise, only clichés are created or copies of existing interpretations. Once you have identified the images associated with the words (through up to five readings of the text and further exercises) you 'dig in' to discover why these words trigger reactions. These are known as the actor's secrets. They are the stuff they draw upon during their performances. It is their work alone to tap into these to find the situations, memories, experiences that have created them. The role of the director is one of guidance through exercises and not through direct questions. Each line in the text must have an associated image for the actor that is specific and personal to him or her. This is their creative material and what provides unique reactions and actions in their performance. For Jack, the director's role is to provide an environment in which subconscious processes can begin to work; from this place spontaneous and truthful actions surface. In this sense the director works with the actor to build the story from the text up, rather than from a grand narrative down. Authenticity, then, is not about what the actor or the director 'thinks' looks real but what is real to the actor's personal experience. In this way the actor's reactions and images have no literal relation with the story. It is the director who creates these relations through her wielding of the text, and the audience from their understanding of its delivery.

Sophie in therapy.

20 MARCH—THE EPISTOLARY SIMULACRUM

On a rainy day in April 2012 I visited the Royal Mail Postal Archive located a ten-minute walk from Farringdon in London. It has a corporate-looking entrance and a small, rather dreary reading room. The staff were bemused to see a woman of my age and were helpful within their carefully defined rules (no photographs, no pens, no noise). The archivist had 'heard of' Derrida and proved it by saying 'Deconstruction' with a question mark. I asked him what sort of research people do in the archive and he replied, 'Usually obscure'.

I had come to the archive to research stamps, early post cards and the dead letter office. I browsed the shelves where there were many books on the history of the Royal Mail, alongside catalogues from Stanley Gibbons, the London Philatelists and British Philatelic Bulletins. One of my favourite finds was *Dear Cats* by Russell Ash, a history of the role of cats in protecting the mail from rats and mice.[32]

I eventually found a very thin file on the Dead Letter Office. It appears from the lack of material on the DLO and my questions to the archivist that it may not be considered a serious subject for postal historian research. Inside it were no more than ten pages: a collection of newspaper articles, a few old and fragile typed papers and some handwritten notes. On one of these was a short genealogy, written I suspect by one of the archives' obscurists:

1784—Dead Letter Office established—return only important letters
1811—All letters to be returned.
1813—So popular—"Returned Letter Office"(RLO) established
1832—Dead Letter Office and RLO amalgamated
1932—Provincial offices took up the responsibility of returning letters

There were significant gaps in this brief history that the rest of the file did not elaborate. A cutting from the *Belfast Telegraph* reported on the official opening of the National Returned Letter Centre (NRLC) on 6 November 1992. The NRLC is the only place in the UK with the authority to open dead letters. According to the article, a bank of letter-opening machines tackles the large amount of letters that come in. This was 1992, now the NRLC mainly deals with lost parcels, which they auction if they are not able to return—in 2010/11 this raised £1 million for the Royal Mail. One of the most unusual things found in a dead letter was a live snake. I presume it must have been hibernating while travelling around the Royal Mail network before reaching Belfast. Others items include handguns, jewellery and cash including one letter with £30,000. Apparently the NRLC receive a lot of hate mail (not addressed to them) because according to the manager they are 'some of the most poorly addressed letters as senders often don't know much about the objects of their hatred'[33]. How things have changed. Today we have Twitter and Facebook to send hate mail. At least with the kind of hate mail that reached the NRLC, one could suppose it was a cathartic experience for the sender. He or she must sit down, compose the letter (perhaps), seal the envelope, buy the stamp and post it. The ritual may expel some of the hatred, since surely the sender who addresses his letter with 'Neil, Basingstoke', does not expect the letter to arrive at its destination. Twitter on the other hand does reach the person. Like a post card everyone can read it, there is no 'on the way' but it is read by all, on its instant arrival. As Catherine Malabou says, 'I don't think we are still sending things to each other'.[34]

27 MARCH 2014—DEEP THOUGHT AND THE SOUND BYTE

In May 2012 an article was published on the *Guardian* website entitled, "So You Want to Be the New Brian Cox? . . . How to Become a Celebrity Academic".[35] In it there is a mix of advice and accounts of academics' experiences in broadcasting. Ian Peacock, who makes radio programmes on culture and science, was asked, What is the mark of a successful TV or radio don? His answer: 'The best will focus 100% on the audience and not fret about what their peers think'. Historian Dr Bettany Hughes goes on, 'broadcasting and academia are not necessarily comfortable bedfellows—in academia you'll have maybe 15,000 words to make one point, whereas in a one-hour-long programme you might get 4,000 words to put across a huge sweep of history. The mental gymnastics needed to condense your thinking are really testing'.[36]

The presence of the celebrity academic in broadcasting has sky-rocketed. A generation of usually youngish, attractive scholars has enthusiastically grabbed opportunities created by the tough competition between channels and production companies in producing new content for television. Programmes such as *Wonders of the Universe* with Professor Brian Cox are highly scripted, rehearsed, polished, often with dazzling effects, graphics and animations; packaged and sold, becoming very successful television programmes worldwide.

Are these celebrity academics public intellectuals? Mark Jordan from Emory University says they are 'publicized intellectuals' and that there is a choice to be made between scholarship and media success; between the kinds of thinking or writing possible in a university and the kinds permitted by the media.[37] Paul Gilroy talks about the popular intellectual as opposed to the public intellectual saying that in the televisual arena it is difficult to say anything at all, as the pressures of the instant are too great, 'only the sound byte academic can function'.[38]

In cutting together the interviews for *Love in the Post* I often wished I had interviewed more sound byte academics. There were numerous problems caused by length, tone and pitch, the latter being a result of having one Derrida scholar (Martin McQuillan) interview another. There was a lot of hard thinking going on which used a shared vocabulary that at times is inaccessible to a non-expert. If I had been doing my job 'properly' I would have asked them to repeat, go over and simplify their questions and answers as well as shot lots of cutaways and endless amounts of noddies (shots of nodding heads which offer a cutting point). Early on I decided not to take this approach, mainly because it is boring for everyone involved, but more seriously because it would result in the broadcast didacticism we see on our screens all the time.

I am aware that as a result, the content of the interviews will lose some viewers. But I was willing to take that risk in order to emphasize two things. The first is the importance of allowing on-screen thinking to happen. In this case, the interviewee thinks through the question in real time and we watch that process happening. Normally the editor would cut away in order to cut out the hesitations and digressions and to shorten the answer, since apparently, according to broadcast experts, the average viewer has a short attention span. Using a cutaway forces the interview

Joanna interviews Theo.

into a didactic shape, what drives the content is the evidentiary logic, the argument being presented. The sound-byte academic is just another form of presenter (a cheaper one), with their answers scripted possibly by themselves but heavily shaped by the direction to be concise, accessible and to the point. It is a form of in-camera editing, which means less time in post-production, where much of the cost of production has been shifted. For our film, which was concerned with the material support of filmmaking, it would be cheating to use the cutaway to make neat, didactic edits that polished the material, making it comprehensible to the non-expert audience. In other words to un-hermeticise it, just as Joanna's editor suggests doing with her comment that the film 'It doesn't work. It's too hermetic. It's only if you are in the know that you are going to get it'.[39]

The second emphasis concerns expression. When understanding is limited because of language, meaning is shifted to other aspects of the exchange. I compare it to when I first lived in Paris. I was in the early period of learning French, when you cannot follow everything that someone is saying (particularly in a group) but you do not wish to interrupt. Comprehension shifts to expression, vocabulary, body language, subtext—you hear and observe, from a distance, in a different way. This is the way I listened to the interviews. I became interested in the nuance of expression, of how people struggled with their answers, how they chose their words so carefully and thoughtfully and many times qualifying the choices of those words, so that one forgets what they were answering in the first place. I remember mentioning to Martin how I was simultaneously fascinated and frustrated by how these academics expressed themselves. His response was that it was scholarship; that is what academics do or should do. They read, they think, they write and when they make claims they attempt to make them as valid and trustworthy as possible. It sounds obvious but it is something we don't 'see' in broadcast products. The sound-byte academic must conform to the requirements of the media and not the other way around. In my film, I wanted to bend the media to the academic, to do justice to that scholarship, even if it meant losing viewers. My belief is, however, that if viewers are lost, they quickly re-engage through the drama, and that was and has always been my 'trick'. I did learn a great deal from the interviews, but this learning I made present inside the story of Theo, Sophie and Joanna. Perhaps ironically, if there is a didactic quality to the film, it can be found in the drama, not the documentary.

20 AUGUST 2012—INVENTED SCENES

At one moment in the project I wanted to create a series of tableaus of events from the 'Envois' and to shoot these on 35mm film in studio. I imagined these as visually very striking, with elaborate sets, costumes and lighting. Because of time and resources we were unable to produce them.

Tableau: Eating Ashes (Dance Sequence)

In a theatre-style black box, there is a kitchen table, a chair and picture of mountains and a lake, suspended from the ceiling, functioning as an invisible wall. A woman sits at the table with a teapot, a teacup and a pastry. On the table is a funeral urn. She pours her tea and spoons ashes from the urn into the cup, stirring it while dreamily looking out the window. After drinking the tea she begins to dance.

> I'd like to die. In the mountains, a lake, long before you. This is what I dream of, and this postal sorting nauseates me. Before my death I would give orders. If you aren't there, my body is to be pulled out of the lake and burned, my ashes are to be sent to you, the urn well protected ("fragile") but not registered in order to tempt fate. This would be an envoi of/from me un envoi de moi which would no longer come from me (or an envoi come from me, who would have ordered it, but no longer an envoi of/from me as you like). And then you would enjoy mixing my ashes with what you eat (morning coffee, brioche, tea at 5'oclock, etc). After a certain dose, you would start to go numb, to fall in love with yourself, I would watch you slowly advance towards your death, you would approach me within you with a serenity that we have no idea of, absolute reconciliation. And you would give orders. . . . While waiting for you I'm going to sleep, you're always there, my sweet love.[40]

Tableau: Paris's Drawing

A close up of a hand drawing. A wider shot reveals the drawing as that of Matthew Paris's illustration of Plato and Socrates. The hand belongs to Socrates who sits at a desk drawing while Plato stands behind watching him. A further reveal shows Paris sketching the couple in their pose.

The accusation of "plagiarism" was often thrown around. A multiplicity of authors was suspected, more precisely that each letter or all the letters had several authors at once, several masked signers under a single name. Or rather—so as not to confuse signer and sender, receiver or correspondent and addressee—more than one destination. For they know, all of them, what to destine means! This is the unity of the epoch, from Socrates to Freud and a bit beyond, the great metaphorical pancarte.[41]

Tableau: The Drama between Us

In an empty ballroom Freud and Derrida dance a tango. During the performance an audience of scholars take their seats and watch them. At the end they silently clap.

> the discord, the drama between us: not to know whether we are to continue living together (think of the innumerable times of our separation, of each auto-da-fe), whether we can live *with* or *without* the other, which has always passed outside our decision, but at what distance, according to what mode of distancing.[42]

4 APRIL 2014—
LITERATURE CANNOT
SURVIVE THE IPAD

I went to a convent school in rural New South Wales, Australia, run by the Sisters of Mercy. The only relief among all those stern nuns was the English teacher, Miss Badior. She was the most exotic woman we had met in our short lives, she wore scarves, and jewellery and red lipstick. She was in love with the Romantic poets and we were in love with her. We learnt Shelley, Byron, Arnold, Keats, Browning and others. Miss Badior would examine each line and explain how the poet used language and metaphor to create meaning. It developed my imagination and an ability to create images from words. Poetry was also part of my home life, experienced during any long drive (of which in Australia there are many), where my father would recite by heart the poems of Coleridge, Wordsworth and the great Australian poets Banjo Patterson and Henry Lawson, alongside many schoolboy ditties.

I studied Edgar Allan Poe's poem 'The Sleeper' along with Andrew Marvell's 'To His Coy Mistress' and Robert Browning's 'Porphyria's Lover', which gave me an early taste for dark, gothic romanticism and a warning against growing one's hair too long. I do not know why Miss Badior did not delve into short stories, in which case I would have had the opportunity to read Poe's 'The Purloined Letter' much earlier in my life. In later years I read many short stories, which were useful for creating short films, with Jorge Luis Borges and Alberto Moravia particular favourites.

When I read 'The Purloined Letter' I was struck by the elaborateness of the tale. There were so many details that were fascinating, two of which became creative material for the film. The first was the prefect's description of the many places secret letters could be hidden; 'Sometimes the top of a table, or other similarly arranged piece of furniture, is removed by the person wishing to conceal an article; then the leg is excavated, the article deposited within the cavity, and the top replaced'.[43] This is both a brilliant and a desperate hiding place, and I figured it must bear some relation with the significance of the hidden letters. In our film, the letters hidden in a leg of Theo's desk are a further homage to Poe's story by that fact that the very place that Theo writes and works is the least likely place he would expect to look for love letters to his wife.

In 2011 Scotland Yard raided former editor of *News of the World* Rebekah Brooks' flat in relation to the phone-hacking scandal. There on a computer hidden in a cupboard they found a love letter to Andy Coulson, David Cameron's former director of communications. It was unclear when, if ever, the letter was sent. The date, however, indicates that the affair was on going for six years, during which time both Coulson and Brooks were married to other people. In CCTV video available online, Brooks' husband and their security adviser clear the flat of incriminating evidence before the police raid, depositing it in black bin bags near the back of their Chelsea flat. These bags were later salvaged by the police and the contents presented in court. In one of them were nineteen unopened letters. The affair has been documented extensively in court through text messages and e-mail evidence. It is an example of how love letters have been transported into another altogether different medium and the potential for these messages to become public has increased a thousand times over. According to J. Hillis Miller, Derrida never used a computer, as he feared the invasion of privacy that such technology would bring. The possibility of a completely private message has disappeared if it ever existed. Just as Charles says, 'Literature cannot survive the iPad, nor can philosophy or psychoanalysis' and Theo replies 'Or love letters'.[44]

The second detail from Poe's story concerned the episode of Dupin's return to the Minister's flat to take the incriminating letter.

> The next morning I called for the snuffbox, when we resumed, quite eagerly, the conversation of the preceding day. While thus engaged, however, a loud report, as if of a pistol, was heard immediately beneath the windows of the hotel, and was succeeded by a series of fearful screams, and the shoutings of a mob. D—rushed to a casement, threw it open, and looked out. In the meantime, I stepped to the cardrack, took the letter, put it in my pocket, and replaced it by a facsimile, (so far as regards externals,) which I had carefully prepared at my lodgings; imitating the D—cipher, very readily, by means of a seal formed of bread.
>
> The disturbance in the street had been occasioned by the frantic behavior of a man with a musket. He had fired it among a crowd of women and children. It proved, however, to have been without ball, and the fellow was suffered to go his way as a lunatic or a drunkard. When he had gone, D—came from the window, whither I had followed him immediately upon securing the object in view. Soon afterwards I bade him farewell. The pretended lunatic was a man in my own pay.[45]

Here Poe elegantly reveals Dupin's plot. What appears as a fortuitous moment in Dupin's retelling of the story (the gunshot in the street) has, rather, been cleverly orchestrated by the detective. In Theo's case, the plot unfolds in media res, when under the pseudonym of Raphael Schermann (an Austrian clairvoyant and graphologist known to Freud) he makes an appointment with someone over the phone while unpacking a mysterious parcel. The lie about his identity is not elaborated in the scene, as we cannot hear the respondent's voice on the telephone and it might quickly be forgotten with the arrival of Penelope, Theo's former student and lover. It is only in later scenes that these moments may be comprehended, when Theo's actions at the therapist's house are revealed to be part of a Dupin-style plot. Here the scene commences with Theo saying, 'I think my wife is having an affair.' For a beat it appears he may be there to get information directly from the therapist about Sophie. Before he can go on he is interrupted by the doorbell, which startles the therapist and causes her to leave the room momentarily. While she is gone, Theo plants an audio bug under the chaise longue. On her return, he runs out saying, 'I can't do this!' Back in his car, he pays a hooded teenager for creating the distraction and settles in to listen to his wife's session. The writing of this scene was very quick. In some ways the action is all very clunky. Theo is not technical and his equipment is more analogue then digital. But his belief in it and desperation is what drives the plot forward. In this moment we see Theo has the resources to deceive, and he may not entirely be the victim that he first appears to be.

Theo finds love letters to Sophie.

20 APRIL 2014—KEN'S CAN

In the early 1980s British director Ken McMullen filmed an interview with Derrida for his feature film *Ghost Dance* starring Pascale Ogier. This very well-known clip lasts two to three minutes in the movie though the entire interview was around fifteen minutes and shot on 16mm film. When Ken learned of our project, he very kindly offered for us to take a look at the whole interview. He remembered that Derrida had told the story of the Heidegger phone call and thought we might be interested in it, which obviously we were. The location of the negative and its condition was, however, somewhat unknown. Whether the original negative still existed or whether there were copies, whether it was only on U-matic, whether the sound was separate or together—it was like looking for the lost grail; it appeared and disappeared on numerous occasions. Eventually the can was tracked down and after some months I visited Ken's studio to take it for processing. Even then, we were not entirely sure it was the Derrida interview, as Ken had been reluctant, and rightly so, to open the can to check. It was marked 'Jacques Derrida', but it had been in storage for thirty years. I drove to the lab in Soho, as I did not trust the underground with this precious cargo. The technician was amused by my fuss and without ceremony swiftly opened the can. A fine red rust dropped out as he held the film up to the light. I caught a glimpse of that white hair and hoped that Jacques' beauty would be preserved a bit longer. Upon transfer to digital, the film was completely intact and the magnetic sound track also unscathed. The can itself had decomposed and rusted, but not this mysterious and magical material called film. One day later I was watching the handsome, charismatic Jacques Derrida recount the Heidegger phone call. It was one of the best moments I've had in all of this hard work.

1 MAY 2014—NAÏVE FILMMAKING

An academic once commented to me that one of my short films about philosophy was 'a bit naïve'. *Mais si, mais si.* One *has* to be naïve to make films about philosophy. There is not any other state from which to start. If I thought about it too much, I would become paralysed, like many others who dream of making films but are too afraid to do it. A naïve view or let's call it one free of prejudice, perhaps even innocent, is an essential prerequisite of making a 'philosophical film'. I would even say that perhaps all filmmakers are in some sense naïve. For me, this has been a strength. It allowed me to enter what is a very small and closed world of Derridean thought and attempt to open it out (or prise it open).

Love in the Post has been an exhilarating, violent, magical journey that has consumed me for the last three years. It is time to let it go. I send it into the world, to circulate and to reach whoever finds it.

Theo on the edge.

FILMOGRAPHY

Adaptation. Produced by Joanna Callaghan. 2010. London, UK: Heraclitus Pictures, 2011. DVD.

Deconstructive Film. Produced by Joanna Callaghan. 2010. London, UK: Heraclitus Pictures, 2011. DVD.

A Mind's Eye. Directed by Joanna Callaghan. 2008. London, UK: Heraclitus Pictures, 2010. DVD.

As You Like It. Directed by Christine Edzard. 1992. London, UK: Squirrel Film Distribution, 2005. DVD.

DO NOT READ THIS. Directed by Joanna Callaghan. 2012. London, UK: Heraclitus Pictures, 2012. DVD.

Moments, Directed by Joanna Callaghan. 2002. London, UK: Heraclitus Pictures, 2004. DVD

Mrs De Winter's Dualism Dilemma. Directed by Joanna Callaghan. 2003/6. London, UK: Heraclitus Pictures, 2007. DVD

The French Lieutenant's Woman. Directed by Karel Reiz. 1981. London, UK: Juniper Films, 2001. DVD.

Thrownness. Directed by Joanna Callaghan. 2003. London, UK: Heraclitus Pictures, 2004. DVD

NOTES

1. See the Geoff Bennington interview by Martin McQuillan in this book.

2. Jacques Derrida, *The Post Card: From Socrates to Freud and Beyond* (Chicago: Chicago Press, 1980), 89.

3. Geoff Bennington interview.

4. Brian McFarlane, *Novel to Film* (Oxford: Clarendon Press, 1994), 8.

5. Ibid., 8.

6. José Ramón Díaz Fernández, 'Rosalind in Jeans: Christine Edzard's Film Version of *As You Like It*', *Sederi—Spanish Society for English Renaissance Studies* 8 (March 1997): 178.

7. Joanna Callaghan, *Adaptation*, Short film, 2011, Heraclitus Pictures.

8. Claudio Monteverdi, 'Amor (Lamento della Ninfa, Rappresentativo)', Christina Pluhar and L'Arpeggiata, *Monteverdi: Teatro d'Amore*, CD, Warner Classics, 2009.

9. Derrida, *The Post Card*, 344.

10. Geoff Bennington interview, by Joanna Callaghan, *Deconstructive Film*, Short film, 20 July 2010.

11. Marc Froment Meurice, interview by Joanna Callaghan, *Deconstructive Film*, Short film, 20 July 2010.

12. Ibid.

13. Joanna Callaghan, *Deconstructive Film*, Short film, 2011, Heraclitus Pictures.

14. Vivian Sobchack, *The Address of the Eye: A Phenomenology of Film Experience* (Princeton, NJ: Princeton University Press, 1992), 24.

15. Katherine Thomson-Jones, *Aesthetics and Film* (London: Continuum International Publishing, 2008), 53.

16. Ibid., 53.

17. Ibid., 51.

18. See the Ellen Burt interview by Martin McQuillan in this book.

19. See *Love in the Post* screenplay.

20. See the Sam Weber interview by Martin McQuillan in this book.

21. See *Love in the Post* screenplay.

22. Derrida, *The Post Card*, 25.

23. See the J. Hillis Miller interview by Martin McQuillan in this book.

24. Derrida, *The Post Card*, 25.

25. Ibid., 68.

26. Ibid., 84.

27. Ibid., 24.

28. Kelly Oliver, *Knock Me Up, Knock Me Down* (New York: Colombia University Press, 2012), 3.

29. Sam Weber interview.

30. Ibid.

31. Derrida, *The Post Card*, 60.

32. Russell Ash, *Dear Cats: The Post Office Letters* (London: Pavilion Books, 1986).

33. "The National Returned Letter Centre Opens", *Belfast Telegraph*, 6 November 1992.

34. See the Catherine Malabou interview by Martin McQuillani in this book.

35. Louise Tickle, 'So You Want to Be the New Brian Cox? How to Become a Celebrity Academic', *Guardian*, 14 May 2012, http://www.theguardian.com/education/2012/may/14/celebrity-academic-radio-tv-funding (accessed 12 October 2013).

36. Ibid.

37. Mark Jordan, '"My Desperate Life as a Sound Byte!" And Other Tabloid Headlines for the Publicized Intellectual', *The Academic Exchange*, October–November 2002, http://www.emory.edu/ACAD_EXCHANGE/2002/octnov/jordan.html (accessed 12–13 December 2013).

38. Marquard Smith, 'On the State of Cultural Studies: An Interview with Paul Gilroy", in *Visual Culture Studies, Interviews with Key Thinkers* (London: Sage, 2008), 74.

39. See *Love in the Post* screenplay.

40. Derrida, *The Post Card*, 197.

41. Ibid., 84.

42. Ibid., 47.

43. Edgar Allen Poe, 'The Purloined Letter' (EBSCO Publishing: eBook Collection EBSCOhost) PDF.

44. See *Love in the Post* screenplay.

45. Poe, 'The Purloined Letter'.

THE LEGS OF FREUD

A Note on Autobiography in Derrida's *The Post Card*

Martin McQuillan

Throughout the pages of the 'Envois' the narrator is occupied by the writing of a lecture entitled 'Legs de Freud'. As we know, Derrida publishes a similarly entitled essay under his own name in the second half of *The Post Card* as the second part of the extended text 'To Speculate on "Freud"'.[1] Accordingly, the reader of 'Envois' must have pause to think concerning the place of Freud's legs, or 'Freud's Legacy' as Alan Bass decides to translate it in 'To Speculate' but not in 'Envois' where he leaves the bilingual pun to reverberate. We might ask the question as a way of provisionally directing our thoughts, what is the meaning of '*Legs de Freud*' for the narrator of 'Envois'? We should not confuse the narrator with Derrida himself, and to ask the question, what is the meaning of 'Legs de Freud' for Derrida in 'To Speculate on "Freud"' would produce a necessarily different answer. We might say, to be too brief on the topic, that the legs of Freud are what predicate the side step of the beyond that is not a march into the future but a waltz around the problem of who leads in the tango of Freud after Derrida. In relation to the narrative of the 'Envois', however, I think that another answer is possible if we consider this text as a leitmotif in the 'Envois' narrative. However, to offer that answer will require us to entertain a certain ontological difficulty and to assume simultaneously that the lecture called 'Legs de Freud' in the 'Envois' is both the one reproduced in 'To Speculate' and is a completely distinct, fictional and unwritten text. This should not present us with too much difficulty, since the critical commentary on 'Envois' has correctly already chosen to accept the possibility that the 'I' of the 'Envois' is not reducible to 'Derrida' and that in fact such a suspension of referentiality in which we occupy the self-contradictory simultaneity of truth and falsehood is the basis by which we approach all

97

literature and fiction. The premise by which we read the 'Envois' will be, as Derrida says of Rousseau's *Confessions* in 'Typewriter Ribbon', on the grounds of an 'I' for an 'I' in which the self that constructs himself by excusing himself in the *Confessions* is not the same as the I that writes or that I that acted historically.[2]

Such a situation is completely germane to the text 'Legs de Freud' as it appears in 'To Speculate on "Freud"'. There are many significant details in Derrida's essay, but for the moment I would like to concentrate on one particular strand of the response to Freud's story of little Ernst. As we know, Freud covertly installs himself in the case study that he reports as one who lived under the same roof as the child and his parents to bear witness to a psychoanalytic scene beyond mere child's play. However, it is not until much later that he reveals in a footnote to another text that the child in question is his grandson and the mother of the narrative his daughter, Sophie. Derrida is then concerned in his reading with *Beyond the Pleasure Principle* as an autobiographical text and with autobiography as the basis for the foundation of a worldwide science. 'The autobiography of the writing posits and deposits simultaneously, in the same movement, the psychoanalytic movement', writes Derrida (303). However, as Derrida goes on to suggest, there is something distinctly odd about this autobiography, both in terms of presentation of the little Ernst and the motivated spectator who observes his play. This is autobiography but not as we know it, or at least as we might not expect it to be. Of course, as the text of Rousseau, for example, demonstrates, there is always in autobiography the performance of a self that as a presentation of the self will always to a greater or lesser degree result in the exculpation of the self within the conventions of first-person narration. However, Derrida would like to go beyond this in relation to 'Freud':

> This text is autobiographical, but in a completely different way than has been believed till now. First of all, the autobiographical does not overlap the auto-analytic without limit. Next, it demands a reconsideration of the entire topos of the autos. Finally, far from entrusting us to our familiar knowledge of what autobiography means, it institutes, with its own strange contract, a new theoretical and practical charter for any possible autobiography. (322)

So, the autobiographical scene of the grandchild overlaps the analytic scene but does not map onto it exactly, and the gap that opens up between the two is said to institute a 'strange contract' for future autobiography. We might also say for the possibility of any future 'psychoanalysis', but that is perhaps another question. The terms of this 'strange contract' are left open by Derrida. Who is this contract between: the I and the reader, the I and itself, the I and its grandchild? Is this contract subject to the same deconstruction of prolepsis and the performative that one might find elsewhere in Derrida and perhaps most famously in Paul de Man's reading of Rousseau's *The Social Contract*.[3] Derrida points us towards what might be possible under the regime of this strange contract in the next paragraph of the 'real' 'Legs de Freud':

> *Beyond* . . . therefore is not an example of what is allegedly known under the name of autobiography. It writes autobiography, and one cannot conclude from the fact that in it an 'author' recounts a bit of his life that the document is without value as truth, science, or philosophy. A 'domain' is opened in which the inscription, as it is said, of a subject in his text . . . is also the condition for the pertinence and performance of a text, of what the text 'is worth' beyond what is called an empirical subjectivity, supposing that such a thing exists as soon as it speaks, writes, and substitutes one object for another, substitutes and adds itself as an object to another, in a word, as soon as it supplements. The notion of truth is quite incapable of accounting for this performance. (322)

So, the truth of *Beyond the Pleasure Principle* as either science or psychoanalysis does not depend upon the autobiographical scene, and certainly the text of *Beyond* is no less scientifically or psychoanalytically true for the inclusion of (indeed we might say reliance upon) autobiography. In fact, it is the insertion of the autobiography that seems to give the text its value beyond the truth or otherwise of the reportage of the autobiographical scene. There can be no reduction of *Beyond* to the empirical family scene of the Freuds at play and the observation of play. The text performs its own opening as autobiography and the truth or worth of that autobiography is made by the performance of the text itself and is not revealed to us as the truth of empirical facts. As Derrida will say much later on in 'Typewriter Ribbon' concerning de Man's reading of the Marion incident in *Allegories of Reading*, performativity is not reducible to cognition.

Now, to return to the 'Legs de Freud' that appears in 'Envois' and that so preoccupies its narrator, might we say that it is this very theoretical point that Derrida makes clear in the real 'Legs of Freud' that is on the mind of the lover-narrator and perhaps the mind of that other 'I' who writes in the place of the narrator who seems to speak in this text? The pressing theoretical question that imposes itself on the reader of 'Envois' is how are we to understand this text without resorting to what Derrida calls in 'Legs de Freud' an 'empirico-biographical reduction' (328) that maps the historic person of Derrida exactly onto the narrator of the 'Envois', who seems to share similar friends who have the same names as those of Derrida (like Cynthia Chase, Jonathan Culler, J. Hillis Miller and Samuel Weber) and who seems to share similar life experiences to the real Derrida? Might the 'Envois' be an exemplary case of this new and strange contract of autobiography that Derrida offers in relation to Freud's account of his grandson? Might we say that the philosophical truth or worth of 'Envois' neither depends upon its auto-bio-graph-icity nor is reduced by the inclusion of such detail? Rather, can we say that the inscription of a figure that looks like Derrida in the text of 'Envois' opens up a domain in which the pertinence and performance of the text's worth is made beyond its relation to an empirical scene to which it might or might not refer? Just as we might raise questions along with Derrida concerning the non-precocity of little Ernst and the issue of who taught him to play the game with his bobbin, we might equally ask a whole set of questions about the narrator-lover of 'Envois' and those who accompany him in his narrative. 'Envois' as a performative narrative *makes* its meaning and value as philosophy, and its narrative performance can never be reduced to the question of the cognitive revelation of empirical facts. As Derrida will say of the relation between the life of Paul de Man and the fictional narrative of Henri Thomas' novel, *Le Parjure*, all relations are possible and no relations are possible between the two.[4] Thomas' novel is not autobiography and the axis spins slightly differently in this text, but the issue of the performative suspension of reference is decisive in both cases. If one accepts this hypothesis concerning the significance of the lecture 'Legs de Freud' for the 'I' of 'Envois', then surely this is an example of the sort of generational inversion that Derrida finds so compelling in the Matthew Parris image of Socrates and Plato, in which Derrida would be looking over the shoulder of Freud dictating the terms of his autobiographical contract. Empirically speaking, we might say that Derrida comes after Freud and that it is Derrida who reads the performative autobiography of Freud and who writes in a similar way in 'Envois'.

Sophie with her therapist, Frauke.

However, we might also say that after the inaugural invention of autobiographicity in 'Legs of Freud' by Derrida we can never read 'Freud' in the same way again, and what comes after 'Derrida' is the text of Freud that lies before us afresh and needs to be read again, anew and from the beginning. In this way we might discover that as the inauguration of a worldwide science, Freud will always already throughout his entire corpus have been thematising and performing his own psycho-sexual life and that the worth of psychoanalysis is neither reducible to this nor dependent upon it.

NOTES

1. Jacques Derrida, *The Post Card: From Socrates to Freud and Beyond*, trans. Alan Bass (Chicago: Chicago University Press, 1980).

2. Jacques Derrida, 'Typewriter Ribbon: Limited Ink (2)' in *Without Alibi*, trans. Peggy Kamuf (Stanford, CA: Stanford University Press, 2002).

3. See Paul de Man, 'Excuses (*Confessions*)', in *Allegories of Reading: Figural Language in Rousseau, Nietzsche, Rilke, and Proust* (New Haven, CT: Yale University Press, 1982).

4. Jacques Derrida, '"Le Parjure", *Perhaps*: Storytelling and Lying', in *Without Alibi*, trans. Peggy Kamuf (Stanford, CA: Stanford University Press, 2002).

A POST CARD FOR KITTLER

Martin McQuillan

'Sam came to pick me up at the station, and then we went for a long walk in the forest (a man came up to greet us thinking that he recognized me, and then excused himself at the last moment—he must be suffering, as I am, more and more, from prosopagnosia, a diabolical impulsion to find resemblances in faces, to recognize, no longer to recognize). I said a few words about my post cards, asking him to keep it as secret as possible. This morning, in Freibourg, to which he accompanied me by car, I understood that he had immediately spoken of it to Kittler, my host here, and perhaps to his wife (psychoanalyst). The secret of the post cards burns—the hands and the tongues—it cannot be kept, q.e.d. It remains secret, what it is, but must immediately circulate, like the most hermetic and most fascinating of anonymous—and open—letters. I don't cease to verify this.

'S. was to summarize and translate my lecture (at the *studium generale*). I stopped at the places that he himself had chosen and checked off in my text (still on "*La folie du jour*", the title this time), and he took this as a pretext to speak longer than I did, if not, I couldn't judge, to divert the public's attention, or even the sense or letter of my discourse. We laughed over it together and between us laughter is a mysterious thing, that we share more innocently than the rest (somewhat complicated by the strategies), like a disarming explosion and like a field of study, a corpus of Jewish stories. On the subject of Jewish stories: you can imagine the extent to which I am haunted by Heidegger's ghost in this city. I came for him. I am trying to reconstitute all his paths, the places where he spoke (this *studium generale* for example), to interrogate him, as if he were there, about the history of the posts, to appropriate his city for myself, to sniff out, to imagine, etc. To respond to his objections, to explain to him what he does

103

not yet understand (this morning I walked with him for two hours, and then I went into a bookstore, I bought several cards and reproductions, as you can see (I'm also bringing you back an album, *Freiburg in alten Ansichtskarten*), and I fell upon two books of photographs that cost me a great deal, one on Freud, very rich, the other on Heidegger, at home, with Madame and the journalists from the Spiegel in 1968). So that there it is, back at the Hotel Victoria (that's where I called you from), I lay down to flip through the albums and I burst out laughing when I found that Martin has the face of an old Jew from Algiers. I'll show you.'

This is the entry marked as 9 May 1979 in Jacques Derrida's 'Envois' section of *La Carte Postale*.[1] It describes a trip by the narrator to a conference in Freiburg at which he meets someone called Sam Weber and is hosted by a character with the name of Kittler. I could rehearse all the means by which the text of the 'Envois' offers every opportunity and no possibility to be read as a roman à clef, as if there really was someone called Sam Weber or a real person called Kittler. Let us not be so naïve. Upon inspection, and not very close inspection at that, all of the dates and locales of the 'Envois' are out of synch, it is as much about the production of a convincing and undecideable reality as it is a confession of the autobiographical. The affirmation of the undecideable would be the quality of the pretence. So, let us not imagine that in this passage we are confronted with the real Sam Weber, Friedrich Kittler and Jacques Derrida. The last time I sat at this desk in the Bolivar Hall in the Venezuelan Embassy in London,[2] I was speaking on the issue of debt, sitting next to the real Samuel Weber. At least I think it was the real Samuel Weber; he spoke about the onto-theological origins of the so-called 'credit crunch', although, like the man in the forest who approaches the narrator of the 'Envois', I may have been suffering from prosopagnosia, an inability to recognize faces. I might have been sitting next to the 'S' of the 'Envois', this avatar who acts as confidante to the narrator and who betrays his secret within minutes to Kittler. Perhaps, it was an entirely different Sam, the son of Sam, another theoretical Sam, a Beckettian character, or the ghost of another Weber, a name maxed out by the theoretical family. I can no longer remember. I am unable to recognize the face. Like the solitary walker in the forest at Freiburg I can only come up close to Sam and to Kittler and to Derrida and then excuse myself at the last moment. As much as I would like to find or have a 'diabolical impulse to find resemblances' in these faces, I am forced to turn away rather than risk an introduction. A simple greeting would be too much to venture. Perhaps, for fear of rejection; perhaps to avoid a social awkwardness, perhaps out of genuine uncertainty. The introduction is impossible. How to begin a conversation with figures such as these? It would be the madness of the day, the madness of the everyday, an everyday madness. I cannot introduce myself or introduce them. Instead bashfully I will turn away and carry on my lonely walk through this passage. The narrator says that he is also increasingly suffering from prosopagnosia. The turn away is mutual. We might approach each other, convinced that we see a resemblance in one another only to withdraw at the last moment, performing a swerve or a U-turn, our steps creating the loop of the invaginated fold that Derrida describes in his reading of '*La folie du jour*' as the structure of narrative, a story with a single permeable skin, with no inside and no outside and only inside and only outside.[3] This madness, this neurotic compulsion to narrativise results in misrecognition or a failure to connect, a meeting in a clearing (*holzweg*) that does not go anywhere.

So, instead let me say a few words about my post cards. Not the same words which the narrator of the 'Envois' asks Sam to keep secret and which he so quickly passes on to Kittler. Here we might ask the question, what would it mean to betray a confidence to Kittler, to tell Kittler our secrets, to speak to Kittler today and to make a revelation or to pass on some gossip? As soon as we are among the post cards we are once more in the question of media, one more method of inscription and circulation, another mediation, in media res, in-betweeness, the human condition from Socrates to Freud and beyond. The secret of the narrator gets passed around the academics of Freiburg like a post card, from one facteur to another, each reading it in turn before its next posting. At the same time, it remains 'as secret as possible', as if secrecy were possible, and not the impossible condition of all media. 'As secret as possible', which is to say that the narrator has a doubt concerning the absolute secrecy of the secret. This might have more to do with the garrulous nature of his chosen confidante than it does with the possibility of absolute secrecy: 'I understood that he had immediately spoken of it to Kittler, my host here, and perhaps to his wife (psychoanalyst)'. Derrida's

wife was also a psychoanalyst. The psychoanalytic partner, the silent observer of an everyday madness, a keeper of secrets, as well as a reader of
symptoms, of messages and envois. The one who always receives, even
if not the intended or final destination. The producer of the domestic-
analytic scene, or the one who turns the domestic scene inside out into
an analytic moment: a site of transference and countertransference, of
media and mediation. 'The secret of the post cards burns—the hands and
the tongues—it cannot be kept'. There can be no possibility of keeping
the secret of the post card; it must by definition be passed on to the next
facteur, who in turn will read it and move it along. And yet it remains
secret, unreadable, undecideable, like the relation between Kittler and
Derrida, Kittler and philosophy, Kittler and Media. This media that we
say comes after Kittler, or that Kittler is in some way after, a mediation
that is in the manner of Kittler, after Kittler as we say a painting is in
the style of an old master, media after Kittler.[4] This relationship burns
the hands and the tongue; it cannot be held and yet it must be spoken.
'Media after Kittler' must circulate amongst us like a post card that we
must pass on from one to another but do not hold on to for too long,
pass the parcel and do not be caught out when the music stops. Never
cease to verify this impossibility.

Media will always accompany Kittler like Sam Weber accompa-
nies the narrator the 'Envois', chauffeur and acolyte, driver and driven,
automobile and autobiographer, translator and transformer: 'S was to
summarize and translate my lecture', a trans that contains within itself
the sense of beyond (from Socrates to Freud and beyond) a movement
from one side to the other but which never arrives at its destination,
the in-betweeness of translation, another form of media, a beyond that
is only ever mediation. No jump from media to Kittler, no beyond or
after, only the in-between of a sustained thinking of media and the object itself. The object that is also the vehicle of its analysis, no outside
to this scene of analysis. No media after Kittler. Here the after or the
beyond is only another mediation. Let us not speak of 'Media after Kittler'; rather, if this after is just another stage or posting of an extended
and interminable in-between, then let us say 'Media media Kittler'. Kittler in media res, Kittler in the middle, Kittler between philosophy and
media studies, Kittler as the third term of an interminable and impossible
analysis, Kittler as the in-between, a post that receives the secrets of the

post card, the secrets of media that burn the hands and the tongue. Kittler, pass it on. Kittler as a mediation between philosophy and media. Let us not then speak of Kittler after media or of 'Kittler media media' but of 'media, media, media'. The three terms of our scene today all turn around the same impossible secret that there is no outside to the scene of analysis, nothing but the endless exchange of the letter, from one burned hand to another, media, like a hot potato, passed on without end.

Here the translation lasts longer than the original address, like Sam's summary of the narrator's text: the critique outweighs the object. The in-between stretches as far as the eye can see. Like the two characters in the 'Envois' we can laugh about this and this laughter between us will be a mysterious thing. The narrator describes it as being 'like a disarming explosion and like a field of study'. One could read this sentence too quickly; the analogy is not 'like a disarming explosion in a field of study'; the field of study is equivalent to the explosion: a 'disarming explosion', one that demilitarises all ordnance. As elsewhere in the 'Envois' we must take this order of metaphoricity seriously. Derrida is at pains to note that the post card is not a mere metaphor for meaning, the relationship is not to be understood in an allegorical way with one half of the metaphor subordinate to the description of the other. Rather, the circulation of meaning is as much an analogy for the passage of the post card as vice versa. Equally, the field of study and the explosion are equivalent. What if we were to understand Media Studies as just such an explosion? A 'disarming explosion' that left us with no more weapons. Media Studies would be the only field of study that identified its own impossible condition as its object. Here I am not referring to a Media Studies that concerns itself with the weak anthropology of the popular, something like television and film studies in which the idea of study is merely the application of established academic protocols to a new object often unable to justify the weight of academic scrutiny. Rather, this would be an understanding of media after Kittler, the most profound engagement with the conditions of mediation, inscription, technology, and the abyssal prosthetic origin of thought, human and non-human life. A field of study that recognized only the field and understood study to be the active and critical practice of being within that field without horizon or boundary. This media after Kittler would be a dis-enclosure, to use a term translated from Nancy[5] [*la déclosion*], of all the borders and categories of academic classification, running the question of media, mediation, and mediatisation through the university as a problem for the university, perhaps the very condition of the university and of academic life. We might say, following the narrator of the 'Envois', that: in the beginning was media and I will never get over it. No university without Media Studies, equally no Media Studies without the university, no approach to the wider field of digital, celluloid, print media without a critical framework for understanding. No Media Studies without Kittler. No Media Studies without the philosophy of media. Not that philosophy can be asked to speak to media or be used to explain media in a utilitarian way, because media itself is a philosophical concept, perhaps the only philosophical concept, the only thing worth thinking since *Khora* and since the cave. If the narrator and Sam share the mysterious laughter of a corpus of Jewish stories, it is because at their best such stories are a philosophy, they are a repository for a knowledge of their object, a mediation of that object in which the object becomes the media itself as an articulation of its own understanding. Equally, with Kittler today we might share the laughter of a mysterious thing called 'media after Kittler', a disarming explosion, a corpus of philosophical stories, a field of study that would not be recognizable as the Media Studies in our universities today. That Media Studies, so often the *bête noir* of ill-informed politicians and media commentators, who in an act of self-loathing cannot recognize their own work as a suitable object for academic study and so decry the corruption of academic purity by the study of their own practice. Perhaps, such denunciations of Media Studies are a warning, an attempt to make the academy back off from its enquiry into the media: a smokescreen of indignant verbiage that says, do not look behind the curtain, do not inquire further into the construction of globalized meaning and how we the media produce it. While such a Media Studies is absolutely necessary if we are to stay alert to our present conditions of artificatuality, media after Kittler is something more. It is more than the toolkit of ideology critique and semiotic analysis that Media Studies so often contents itself with. Certainly, this 'after' is not a 'beyond' that will transport us to the other side of Media Studies, but it is a critical mediatisation that takes us through Media Studies as just another symptom of the mediatic effects that it first diagnoses. Study here is just one more mode of the in-between, a mediatisation that acts as if it stands on one side of a divide when in fact it is the very act of division itself. Let us not speak of 'Media Studies', rather of 'Media Media', media's own mediatised scene.

What would it mean, then, to pass on a secret to Kittler today? To do so too quickly, fresh out of the car from the forest of Freiburg like the loquacious Weber. Media after Kittler, today Kittler is our host just as he was for the narrator of the 'Envois'. As the etymology runs, he is both our host, the one who brings us all together here, and our guest, the one that we invite into our midst and whom we must treat with the utmost hospitality. He is host and guest and ghost today. You can imagine the extent to which I am haunted by Kittler's ghost in this city. Kittler plays host to the narrator of the 'Envois' not just in any city but in Freiburg, the scene of so much of Heidegger's media effect. Here the narrator seeks out the haunting effects of Heidegger and walks with his ghost ('this morning I walked with him for two hours, and then I went into a bookstore'). The set up here is one of classic elegy in which the poet is reunited with the dead in the landscape with which their lives were most keenly lived, and the poet walks with the dead until dawn. The deceased loved one must always return to the underworld before dawn breaks or the narrator turns into a bookstore, one more false exit into a world of media. He buys two books of photographs, one of Freud and one of Heidegger, as well as a book for his lover of Freiburg in old post cards. Between Freud and Heidegger he introduces a slip worthy of comment. He says of the Heidegger book that it shows the philosopher 'at home, with Madame and the journalists from the Spiegel in 1968'. Once again we are in the scene of the domestic and the observant, ana-lytic spouse. However, this living arrangement is shared with journalists. That is to say, with the media. I am reminded here of Derrida's other, short and under-read text of Media Studies, from a book edited by Sam Weber, 'Above All No Journalists!', on the passing of the command-ments to Moses in which he suggests that the condition under which the Law can be handed down on the top of Mount Sinai is that there are no witnesses present: there can be no revelation, no divine authority or onto-theology with the media.[6] As soon as we have mediation, the Law and everything that depends upon it is ruined. However, perhaps more interestingly in this scene of Heidegger amongst the journalists is that Derrida makes a slip on the date of the *Spiegel* interview known in English as 'Only a God Can Save Us Now'. It took place in 1966 not

1968, significant dates for any follower of European culture. Perhaps, this is not a slip at all; perhaps it is in keeping with manipulation and falsification of dates that characterizes the 'Envois' in general. The narrator is not Derrida, the real Jacques Derrida would know the correct date of the *Spiegel* interview. Perhaps, it is another affirmation of the undecideable that sits so seductively and problematically at the top of every page of the 'Envois' as a false mark in this story of dating. The Hotel Victoria to which the narrator returns to look at his books of photographs may be another comic lodging like the Russell Hotel in London, from which Derrida launched a philosophical and historical hoax in the text 'Racism's Last Word'.[7] The Russell Hotel is of course also the scene of another mediatisation that those who work in Media Studies in the UK know well. But for the moment let us imagine that this is some other interview given by Heidegger to the media, one not on the God of a hopeless onto-theology but on media itself: 1968 after 1966, Media after Kittler, from Socrates to Freud and beyond. Such an interview waits to be invented, a discourse to come that will require all the resources of our poetic imagination, just as the thinking of media after Kittler asks us to imagine another way of working and representing thought and media itself. A gesture as bold as the 'Envois' will be required to find a suitable

Example of the world's first pre-stamped post card, 1867, courtesy of David Wilson.

vehicle for this project. A suitable elegy for Kittler, one that was up to the task of thinking media after Kittler, might not require us to walk with his ghost in the early morning but to pick him up from the station in a fast car and to be the first to spill his secrets before we have reached our destination. He has so much to tell us and we cannot help but pass it on, it will burn our hands and tongues otherwise.

NOTES

1. Jacques Derrida, *The Post Card: From Socrates to Freud and Beyond*, trans. Alan Bass (Chicago: University of Chicago Press, 1987), 188.

2. This text was first given as part of a session with Sam Weber at 'Media after Kittler', Bolivar Hall, London 10 September 2013, organized by Eleni Ikoniadou and Scott Wilson for The London Graduate School. I have retained this marker of its original context for obvious reasons.

3. See Jacques Derrida, 'The Law of Genre', trans. Avital Ronell, *Critical Inquiry* 7, no. 1 (1980): 55–81.

4. See Nicholas Royle's comments in his *After Derrida* (Manchester, UK: Manchester University Press, 1995).

5. See Jean-Luc Nancy, *Dis-Enclosure: The Deconstruction of Christianity*, trans. Bettina Bergo, Gabriel Malenfant, and Michael B. Smith (New York: Fordham University Press, 2008).

6. Jacques Derrida, 'Above All, No Journalists!' in *Religion and Media*, ed. Hent de Vries and Samuel Weber (Stanford, CA: Stanford University Press, 2001).

7. Jacques Derrida, 'Racism's Last Word', trans. Peggy Kamuf, *Critical Inquiry* 12 (Autumn 1985): 290–99.

AUTOBIOBIBLIOGRAPHIES

Derrida in the Library

Martin McQuillan

> '*I hereby undertake . . . not to bring into the Library or kindle therein any fire or flame . . . and I promise to obey all rules of the Library*'.

In the early stages of the 'Envois' section of *La Carte Postale* the narrator is lead through the streets of Oxford by his guides 'Jonathan and Cynthia' towards the Bodleian Library, where he will encounter for the first time the postcard of Socrates and Plato from the manuscript by Matthew Paris: 'I suspect them of having had a plan. They themselves knew the *carte*'.[1] The narrator, let us not call him or imagine him to be Derrida, is concerned that he is being set up as the subject of a spectacle, staged in order to witness the effect the image has upon him. It is only one instance of the paranoia he exhibits in this tale of clandestine love and secret letters that is presented in full as a work of both and neither philosophy and literature. 'Do you think there are listening devices? That our letters are opened? I don't know if this hypothesis terrifies me or if I need it' (16) he comments just before describing his first experience of the post card:

> Jonathan and Cynthia were standing near me next to the glass case, the table rather, where laid out, under glass, in a transparent coffin [*cerceuil*], among hundreds of displayed reproductions, this card had to jump out at me [*devait me sauter aux yeux*]. I saw nothing else, but that did not prevent me from feeling that right near me Jonathan and Cynthia were observing me obliquely, watching me look. As if they were spying on me [*s'ils guettaient*] in order to finish the effects of a spectacle they have staged (they have just married more or less). [16]

The translation seems to add a scopophilic layer to the scene, with the newlyweds on the look out for or lying in wait for [*s'ils guettaient*] the *coup de théatre* and the *coup de grace* of their scheme: *un coup d'envois*, to use a football term, when it all kicks off. Here the library, or more accurately the threshold of the library, not at a bookshelf but at a display case, perhaps outside the library proper, is figured as a space for distrust, obsession, deception, and entrapment. The image of Socrates and Plato is merely an invitation to the narrator to enter the library to discover its secrets. The postcard is bait for the philosopher, a McGuffin in this Hitchcockian scene; what lies behind it is the vault of the library and the trap of writing.

On the one hand, the narrator is taken by the image because for him it disproves a certain encyclopaedic logic of the library. The library as depository of all knowledge, an archive that takes its authority from its comprehensive sweep and genealogy of legitimation:

> Be aware that everything in our bildopedic culture, in our politics of the encyclopaedic, in our telecommunications of all genres, in our telematicometaphysical archives, in our library, for example the marvellous Bodleian, everything is constructed on the protocolary character of an axiom, that could be demonstrated, displayed on a large *carte*, a post card of course, since it is so simple, elementary, a brief, fearful stereotyping (above all say or think nothing, that jams telecom). The charter is the contract for the following, which quite stupidly one has to believe: Socrates comes *before* Plato, there is between them—and in general—an order of generations, an irreversible sequence of inheritance. (20)

The encyclopaedic principle and the culture of legitimation it predicates through the value of presence granted by every image depends upon this protocol of inheritance. This is also why the great libraries are attached to the oldest and most prestigious universities. It is through the sedimentation of generations that they derive their authority and confer it upon those who study there. The idea of the university and the authority of the library are inseparable in this respect. One might go so far as to say: no universities without the library, no library without the universal encyclopaedic principle. The Matthew Paris inversion puts all of this at risk. It challenges the received wisdom of the ages, of every library, and every university, of the entire metaphysical tradition. Brazenly on display, rather than buried, in a transparent coffin [*cerceuil*] or casket in the portico before the pillars of the library it bears testimony to something that deconstruction has previously suspected: that the authority of every received tradition (including that of the university and the encyclopaedic principle itself) depends upon a foreclosure of alterity, whereby metaphysics or the encyclopaedic becomes the very principle by which they justify themselves, as wellspring and effect of their own operation. Rather than being the result of an established inheritance of authoritative generations, they are the outcome of their own textual performance. As the narrator puts it: 'all of this is not without . . . political consequences. They are still difficult to calculate' (21).

The narrator is drawn to the image in the fortune-telling book almost as if it were his destiny to discover it. He is not guided there by accident. However, as the 'Envois' well knows, destination is as much a trap as inheritance. The search for Socrates and Plato lures him into the library and slowly infects him with the sort of archive fever that deconstruction ought to be inoculated against. But the *mal d'archive* is an autoimmunity, something that eats away the narrator's resistance from within. The narrative arc of the 'Envois' takes him back to Oxford to read the manuscript and so answer certain questions accrued through the course of his writing. His destination is the Duke Humphries library, the oldest reading room in the Bodleian, where the Paris manuscript was held in the late 1970s. The Duke Humphries library holds, amongst other things, the archive of the Conservative Party of the United Kingdom. The narrator describes arriving in Oxford from the nominative determinative town of Reading, and is impatient for its oak-panelled splendour:

> I went right over, in the morning, one hour after my arrival, to the Bodleian. The librarian seemed to know me (I didn't understand very well, she alluded to the difficulty that my book [the Paris manuscript] seems to have given her), but this did not get me out of the oath [*serment*]. She asked me to *read* it (it is a question of engaging oneself to respect the rules of the library, the treasures to be protected are priceless). Therefore I read it and handed her back the cardboard covered with transparent paper that she had tendered me. At this point she starts to insist, I had not understood: no you have to read

it out loud [*à haute voix!*]. I did so, with the accent you make fun of all the time, you can see the scene. We were alone in her office. I understood better the marriage ceremony and the profound presuppositions of Oxonian performativism. What would an oath that you did not say out loud be worth, an oath that you would only read, or that while writing you would only read? Or that you would telephone? Or whose tape you would send? (208)

The Paris manuscript presents the cataloguing system of the library with problems, but it is not beyond its parameters. The narrator is distracted by his own desire and does not fully understand what he is being asked to do. The rules of the library must be obeyed and one must affirm this by oath, with one hand on the written word and speaking out loud, one must swear in front of an officer of the archive. The library requires the reader to present and correct, no telephoning in of a performance or sending a show reel. Reading in the library requires a public commitment, like matrimony or collegiate life. One reads in silence and swears out loud:

> Did I tell you, the oath that I had to swear out loud (and without which I would never have been permitted to enter) stipulated, among other things, that I introduce neither fire nor flame into the premises: '*I hereby undertake . . . not to bring into the Library or kindle therein any fire or flame . . . and I promise to obey all rules of the Library*'. (216)

The narrator must promise to submit himself to the authority of the encyclopaedic principle and not to burn the metaphysical house of index cards to the ground. However, as de Man tells us, only a God can promise: only the absolute and indivisible can avoid the inaugural perjury of the oath. The narrator, who as a narrator, is already divided and a ruin of himself, has no hope of keeping the promise he does not fully understand that he is making. Equally, the library, jealous to guard its treasures, does not know what it is allowing to cross its threshold: a postmodern Prometheus kindling the flame of deconstruction, a harbinger of a new Enlightenment that risks the seemingly irreversible protocols of the reading room.

However, our narrator is also bound by the promise he makes. He will persist with it just as his reading undoes those bonds. He is looking for answers in the manuscript known in the Bodleian as 'Ashmole 304', bequeathed to the library as part of the collection of Elias Ashmole, dedicated and ruthless antiquarian, founder of the Ashmolean museum who on one occasion failed to visit the constituency where he was standing as a member of parliament because his horoscope predicted he would lose.[2] When presented with the manuscript the narrator is thrilled by its unexpected colour and by the intricacies of the fortune-telling procedure. His fate is sealed and he is drawn further into the book. Giddy as a schoolboy he is overwhelmed and must leave the library for air, but he cannot resist returning to the book. The temptation to add his own encryption is too great:

> One day I will be dead, you will come all by yourself into the Duke Humphrey Room, you will look for the answer in this book. And you will find a sign that I am leaving in it now (after others, for there has been no lack of barbarians, nor of perjurers, before me) [*après d'autres car les barbares n'ont pas manqué, ni avant moi les perjures*]. [217]

The narrator can only repeat the encyclopaedic gesture of burying a secret deep within the archive. He will be true to the archive, obey all the rules of the library, for despite appearances all the readers of the manuscript who have come before him have also been breakers of oaths, perjurers and bigamists, barbarians at the gates ready to overturn the protocols of inheritance. The narrator will be faithful to the library in his own fashion. He will burn the correspondence of the 'Envois' but not the manuscript and not the 'bildopedic culture' or the 'politics of the encyclopaedic'. These will remain intact as the architectonic principle through which the beloved reader will be guided in order to find this hidden message: an answer to be found in a book.

However, this is a postcard and it is open on both sides for all of us to read. He leaves a trail of breadcrumbs for anyone with a research grant and a rudimentary knowledge of Latin to find the message. The fortune-telling book works in the manner of those flow charts to be found in children's magazines or 'pick your own adventure' books today. From a series of choices made, the reader is guided towards a number of possible outcomes, the logarithmic combination of turns creating the possibility of different destinies. However, like the roll of a dice, the 'Prognostics of King Socrates' can never abolish chance, there can only ever be a finite number of outcomes written down, and ultimately a set number

of routes through to them.[3] The narrator goes on to detail a particular
path through the pages of the book, one that can be retraced with a little
care. The route is complicated and involves the introduction of an initial
limited randomness by the spinning of a wheel, subsequently lost from
the manuscript. This takes us from instructions on how to use the book
at fol. 31r, '*Documentum subsequentis consideracionis quae socratica dicitur*',
followed by the famous miniature of Plato and Socrates at fol. 31v, to:

> On the next page [fol. 32v] a double entry chart, a small computer
> if you will (*Tabula inscripta 'Computentur capita epigrammatum'*) gives
> you, in AE 4, *Spera fructuum* [AE 4 actually reads 'Ficus fruct(us).'—
> MMcQ], referring you thereby to one of a series of circles, each
> divided into 12 sections and 12 names. The circles are six, it seems
> to me (Spera, specierum, Sp. Florum, Sp. Bestiarum, Sp. Volatilium,
> Sp. Civitatum, Sp. Fructuum finally, in which you have just fallen,
> in AE 4, then, and in the section 'ficus'). Are you following? You
> take yourself off then to the circle of fruits [fol. 34r], you look for
> the slice 'fig', as on a menu or a pie [*sur une carte ou sur une tarte*], and
> you read, under the heading 'Ficus', our question, An erit [fol. 34r
> reads 'e(ss)et' though it is 'erit' elsewhere] bonum ire extra domum
> vel non [whether it is good to go out of the house?]. This is indeed
> the question, not so? Underneath, you are referred elsewhere. To
> whom? But to the King . . . and the king of Spain, *Ite ad Regem
> Hispanie*. There are, it seems to me, 16 kings [fols. 39r–40r, with the
> King of Spain at fol. 39r col. I], and each one proposes 4 answers,
> 4 sentences, 4 'verses or Judgements'. Since your figure is 4, your
> sentence is the fourth one. Guess, what it says. [217][4]

The destiny is not the result of pure chance but a calculation based upon
a number of set outcomes. In this sense the fortune is programmed, the
result of a computational logic. It is, in other words, an effect of a certain
encyclopaedic principle. There is only the illusion of destinerrance here,
no deconstruction of the possibility of destination, only an arrival at a
place that the author will have guided us to. It will have been our destiny
as readers to obey all the rules of the library; rules of the 'telematico-
metaphysical archive' that we can in principle never escape but only ruin
by our own perjured commitment to it.

Before we reveal the final score (what the fourth sentence says) in
our own gesture of obedience to the encyclopaedic rules of the library,

it might be worth noting that the Paris manuscript (Ashmole 304) is not an original text. It would seem to be a copy of a previous version of the 'Prognostics of King Socrates', which would have been in circulation. Ashmole 304 is in fact a composite volume, which contains other fortune-telling texts and is constructed from what would appear to be scraps and remnants of parchment used for more significant or sacred books. The inscription and the illumination are of a much higher quality than a later edition of the King Socrates text also held in the Bodleian collection, but nevertheless the conclusion that an antiquarian would derive from the manuscript is that it was intended for private use amongst the monks of St Alban's rather than as a work of knowledge to be held in a library. The medieval mind was quite capable of holding the divine, the secular and even the profane together in a single field of vision and it is in no way surprising that Paris and his fellow monks should read for pleasure this pagan almanac. However, it is, one might say, a re-print. 'I confide to you this solemn and sententious aphorism: did not everything between us begin with a reproduction?' (9) the narrator of the 'Envois' writes to his love from Oxford. The Paris manuscript is a copy, the post card is a facsimile, the oath in the library is the repetition of words printed on a laminated card, the promise is the reiteration of a performance ruined at its origin by the possibility of its own perjury. The love affair, like the commitment to the rules of the library, may obey certain laws and follow a certain logic, but it is a form of mimesis. It copies an inherited model. The 'Envois' obeys all of the conventions of the literary loves and epistolary fictions that come before it. No doubt it subverts these conventions and opens them up to new possibilities but it is always obliged to stay in touch with a model that it at once disavows or betrays and whose laws it is obliged to respect. Everything in the library begins with a reproduction even if it is the repetition of an original perjury or betrayal; the reader is always 'after others, for there has been no lack of barbarians, nor of perjurers, before me'. Quite literally the library, any library, is a collection of reproductions: a warehouse of books, reprints and copies. This is true of even those great libraries like the Bodleian rightly famed for their 'original manuscripts', here we will always find the most decisive logic of reproduction. The Encyclopaedic Principle is first and foremost a Platonism. This is the biblio-metaphyisical culture of the Library as such, and there would be no Western tradition without it.

Sitting in his room at Baliol College, the narrator dreams of writing 'and first to reassemble an enormous library on the *courrier*, the postal institutions, the techniques and mores of telecommunication, the networks and epochs of telecommunication throughout history—but the 'library' and the 'history' themselves are precisely but 'posts', sites of passage or of relay among others, stases, moments or effects of *restance*, and also particular representations, narrower and narrower, shorter and shorter sequences, proportionally, of the Great Telematic Network, the *worldwide connection* [in English in original]' (27). This is a curious encyclopaedic fantasy. The Postal Principle, as Derrida outlines it, may be the very thing, *the necessary possibility of the not* (as Geoffrey Bennington would say) that opens up the closed logic of the encyclopaedic protocol. Here the narrator desires to assemble '*une énorme bibliothèque*' (32) of the '*courrier*', both post person and correspondence, an entire archive that would run [*courir*] away with itself, circumnavigating the entire globe. However, such a library or written history could only ever be part of the history of the Post itself, one relay among many, one more reproduction, representation and exchange. The bildopedic culture of representation must necessarily be a Platonism. A Library that would contain the entire history of the Post must be as big as the world itself. Like the only true map in Borges, it must be an exact copy of the thing it describes. Any other library could only ever be an edited collection of selected or representative works. This selection or editing would remain, says Derrida, as an effect of '*restance*', which as Alan Bass notes in footnote 5 to his translation of 'To Speculate—On "Freud"' means 'that which remains because it cannot be judged, the undecidable excess' (261). There can never be a protocol adequate to the laws of the Encyclopaedia; no ultimate justification for selection and inclusion would be possible. Nevertheless selection occurs and the edition remains to be read, undecidable and unreadable. This is the ruin, the perjury, at the heart of the library: the myth of comprehension, of the comprehensive, the definitive and authoritative. The Encyclopaedic Principle will do everything in its considerable power to cover its tracks here. It will obscure this logic and set up powerful, inertial borders to police who or what may enter into the library. It will require ticket checks, letters of introduction and accreditation, the taking of signatures and the swearing of oaths. However, as a room full of paper it is essentially a tinderbox in which any Prometheus might kindle a flame.

It is educative to note how many libraries refuse or limit reproduction. As the narrator notes of the ironic jussic performative on the reverse of each postcard 'reproduction prohibited' (37). Derrida's own bequest of papers to UC Irvine explicitly forbids digital reproduction in order to put the archive 'on-line'. While a limited amount of reprographics is possible with the due permissions, the scholar of Derrida must first make a pilgrimage to the library and bear witness to the aura of the work of philosophy. The Bodleian has made a selection of images from Ashmole 304 available online but jealously guards the 'image-rights' of its treasures. The library is at once selective and enclosed: these after all are 'special collections'. There can be no access to them without prior approval or supervision. The narrator of the 'Envois' writes, '"Reproduction prohibited", which can be translated otherwise: no child, inheritance prohibited, filiation interrupted, sterile midwives [*accouchers*, lit. one who is present at the bedside]' (39, 44–45). For those who know a little of the autobiographical allusions of the 'Envois' the

Matthew Paris, Ashmole 304, Bodleian Library, University of Oxford.

prohibition against reproduction is intriguing. For those who read in libraries the prohibition is the basis of the Encyclopaedic Principle, one that both predicates the possibility of the library as such and is undone by it at every turn, on every shelf, in every corner, by every reader who gives birth to future generations of thought through their own labour. Socrates' mother, Phaenarete, was also a midwife.

The fourth sentence of the King of Spain in Ashmole 304 [fol. 39r, col. I, 'Rex yspanie', line 4] reads '*Si iueris, cum lucro redibis*', which with the tenses literally translated means, 'If you shall have gone, you shall return with profit'. We should perhaps not be surprised by this paranoid narrator's capacity for sentimentality as the love affair draws to its conclusion. Equally, we should be happy to take this as our own destiny. Whether it is good to go out of the house, to visit the library perhaps, if we go we shall return with profit. This is what happens when we agree to invest in or speculate on a love for the Encyclopaedic.

NOTES

1. Jacques Derrida, *The Post Card: From Socrates to Freud and Beyond*, trans. Alan Bass (Chicago: University of Chicago Press, 1987), 16. Hereafter all quotations appear with a page number from this text.

2. C. H. Josten, ed., *Elias Ashmole (1617–1692). His Autobiographical and Historical Notes, His Correspondence, and Other Contemporary Sources Relating to his Life and Work* (Oxford: Clarendon Press, 1966) 1:220–25.

3. On the question of chance and delimitation see my reading of Mallarmé, 'Un Coups de Dés' in the introduction to Paul de Man's *The Post-Romantic Predicament*, ed. M. McQuillan (Edinburgh: Edinburgh University Press, 2012).

4. For the purpose of brevity I have edited out the start of the trail which goes over two pages of the 'Envois'; however, this is a journey the reader might want to make for themselves. I have inserted in square brackets the pages of Ashmole 304 referred to by Derrida and offered the occasional translation from the Latin. I am extremely grateful to Dr Bruce Barker-Benfield, Senior Assistant Librarian in the Department of Special Collections at the Bodleian Library, for guiding me through the manuscript to this destination.

THE SEX LIVES OF
THE PHILOSOPHERS

Prolegomena to a Thesis

Martin McQuillan

In the 2002 biographical documentary on Jacques Derrida the director, Amy Ziering Kofman, asks the philosopher what he would most like to see in a film about Kant, Hegel or Heidegger. Derrida takes his time before answering, then responds 'their sex lives'. Kofman is taken aback and asks 'why?' Derrida explains that these philosophers never speak about their own sex lives in their philosophy. They present themselves in their philosophy as asexual, but what could be more important to them and to their writing than love, those they love, and the making of love. Philosophy has a lot to say about love in general, perhaps philosophy even began with this question: what is love? But, if Derrida is to be believed, individual philosophers have little to say about their own love lives, at least in their philosophical texts. Philosophy concerns the depersonalised construction of logical and universal systems of thought. Traditionally there should be no room in it for biographical introspection about one's own love life. However, the more one looks into the canon of philosophy the more it becomes apparent that in fact philosophers have had a great deal to say about their own sexuality.

The writing of Plato and Aristotle is replete with references to Greek love. The relations between characters in these texts are not always, shall we say, Platonic. Theologian and philosopher St Augustine of Hippo founded the confessional genre in writing. He writes of his pre-celibate days as a lover of many women, asking God: 'give me chastity and continence, but not yet'. The story of the medieval scholar Peter Abelard and his equally philosophical lover Héloise d'Argenteuil is well known. Their love letters are one of the great epistolary exchanges in the Western canon and Abelard's love poems were at least as influential in his lifetime as his extensive philosophical writing. Jean-Jacques Rousseau makes reference to this in his own epistolary novel *Julie, or, the new Hélo-ise*. Like much of Rousseau, the novel is a mix of fiction and philosophical reflection. In his own *Confessions* Rousseau tells us about his loves and losses, including Madame de Warrens, for whom he served as steward to her household and lover. Rousseau, like Kant after him, has a surprising amount to say about masturbation. Kant offers a treatise on conjugal rights and is quite stiff on the vice of self-love.

As part of his dissertation on ethics, *Either/Or*, Soren Kierkegaard wrote *The Seducer's Diary*, a tale of the seduction and manipulation of young women. It does not take a great leap of imagination to read the novella as a reflection on Kierkegaard's own relationship with Regine Olsen. Diderot was another philosopher who produced erotic writing (notably *La Religieuse* [The Nun]) alongside works such as his monumental philosophical *Encyclopaedia*. Schopenhauer wrote a treatise *On Women*, which is hard to read as anything other than a reflection on his own experiences on the loves and let-downs of the male philosopher divided between scholarly independence, a desire for domestic contentment and eighteenth-century misogyny. Hegel has much to say, philosophical and censorial, about the Christian family, marriage and human sexuality, if seemingly not his own. He reserves that speculation for his letters to his sister and others, some of which were destroyed by his sons to prevent 'misunderstandings' concerning his fathering of an illegitimate child with his landlord's wife. Nietzsche by contrast had little time for sexual repression and hypocrisy in his philosophical writing. His later madness was connected to syphilis, but while there has been much writing about his love for the psychoanalyst Lou Andreas-Salomé, for example, including later novels and film adaptations, Nietzsche's own account is not to be found in his philosophical writing.

In the twentieth century we can find Heidegger occupied with the topic 'Care' in his philosophy but reserving reflection on his affair with his student Hannah Arendt for their now published correspondence, another philosophical relationship that has also been subsequently novelised. Ironically, Arendt's thesis that she wrote 'under Heidegger' was on Augustine and love. Jean-Paul Sartre and Simone de Beauvoir have quite a lot to say about their own love lives and not just with each other. Like Camus such references often take the form of fiction. Roland Barthes' most successful publication was *A Lover's Discourse*, which can be read alongside his posthumously published account of his own sexual encounters in *Incidents*. Michel Foucault is the great philosopher of sex, writing a three-volume history of sexuality before he died of AIDS in 1984. However, unlike Derrida, who makes his own biographical desires and sexual experiences central to a philosophical text like *The Post Card*, Foucault does not reflect in his published writing on his own 'philosophy of the bedroom', to borrow a phrase from de Sade.

It is not difficult to find throughout the history of thought references to the sex lives of philosophers. The question is: how can identifying these moments help us to understand the philosophical text? I do not think that it is possible to suggest, as Niall Ferguson recently did of Maynard Keynes, that sexuality explains thought. That would be a reductive and extremely 'un-philosophical' thing to say. Rather, we might note that often the incidences of philosophers like Kierkegaard, de Beauvoir or Derrida making a theme of their own sexuality occur at the borders of philosophy in the displaced form of literature. Literature opens up philosophy and refuses to permit it to settle on what is allowable and what is not allowable as philosophy. This is no accident since the question of the sex lives of the philosophers is really one of what is permissible and what is not in a philosophical text. It is, in other words, the very question of what is philosophy? I do not think the issue of an author's sexuality will provide us with an answer to this question, but it will allow us to ask it again and again, in order to affirm its complexities and contradictions as a condition of continuing to read philosophy today.

Theo checks Sophie's phone for messages from her lover.

EROS IN THE AGE
OF TECHNICAL
REPRODUCTABILITY

Theo Marks

You know that I consider 'Envois' to be a truly awful text. I can
hardly bear to read it. There is nothing more commonplace than
infidelity within marriage, nothing more devastating either. For a long
time I have thought about giving this lecture on the topic of infidelity
in literature, but where would one begin and end? It would seem that
Western literature exists for the collation of infidelity as an experience.
I then thought I might limit the scope of the lecture to epistolary novels, only to discover that all epistolary novels concern themselves with
infidelity of one kind or another: Rousseau's *Julie*, Richardson's *Clarrisa*,
Laclos's *Liaisons Dangereuses*, Goethe's *The Sorrows of Young Werther*, and
of course Derrida's 'Envois'. Perhaps this will be a more manageable
proposition, as long as we understand that the object of the epistolary
novel is the love letter. The only thing worth understanding in the
context of a fictional exchange—inevitably all epistolary novels concern
themselves with infidelity. All novels, all writing that concerns itself with
the letter, from Poe's story of the blackmail of the purloined queen to
L. P. Hartley's *The Go-Between*, whenever we deal with letters we are
always addressing infidelity, with betrayals of one kind or another. The
reason for this is rather obvious, and let us cut to the chase and not claim
it as a major insight: writing is betrayal. To read and to write, to deconstruct if you will, is to betray the object of our affections. When Derrida deconstructs Heidegger or Plato he is betraying the thing he loves.
Operating under their law in a transferential way to be sure, but also
betraying them as we must always betray the investment in the analyst
to enact the transference. Deconstruction is infidelity, it is the betrayal of
the loved one, but in the best way possible; an infidelity without infidelity, faithful to the necessity of infidelity. One might say that deconstruc-

tion has a commitment to infidelity. But perhaps, this is just the leaver's logic, the one who justifies their betrayal, like the Rousseau of de Man's reading of the purloined ribbon. Equally there will be no closure to such a scene; infidelity opens up the scene of infinite excuse, infinite analysis. This is why its effects are endless and ripple beyond the couple in question, to children, to friends, to parents, into new relationships. One might say that far from being an unusual state of affairs, infidelity is the true state of all relationships, which, as relationships, have no real presence and accordingly are always already betrayed by the fact that they never truly exist. We will our relationships into being, but they are not things of substance, merely illusions of our desire for presence—there is no sexual relation, as a certain Lacan may or may not have written. As soon as there is two, infidelity has already begun, because I can never be faithful to myself, the I that I am is always already multiple. I am always betrayed by my other selves. How much more so the couple; how can I ever be faithful to the me that you project and the otherness of me that constitutes you and in turn dominates me as a superego waiting to be betrayed? Such fidelity is always ruined from the beginning. We are all perjurers who are only ever left with the deconstructive option to betray in the least bad way.

* * *

I would like to think of the whole of philosophy as the history of a serial betrayal, of pupils who betray their masters, according to their own leaver's logic in the best way possible: Hegel who betrayed Kant, Marx who betrayed Hegel, Nietzsche who betrayed everyone, Heidegger who betrayed Nietzsche, Derrida who betrayed Heidegger—everyone justifying their betrayal as a certain kind of faithfulness, the act of least violence. And of course Plato, who betrayed Socrates and who was in turn betrayed by Aristotle. Plato, whose betrayal was never to write a word of his own but to use the words of Socrates to transcend his master. But here we are again in the problem of writing; as soon as we have writing we enter the domain of infidelity. Plato reports Socrates and so betrays him in the best way possible. Philosophy relies on this structural infidelity; without infidelity there could be no philosophy, no future for philosophy, no literature, no thing that we call the university, and of course no thing that we call 'film', the history of film, film theory,

Theo delivers the annual Duke Humphrey Lecture in Oxford.

and film studies. I would go so far as to say that there can be no future without infidelity, no social bond and no politics without it; no relationships either.

Extract taken from:
Duke Humphrey Annual Lecture
University of Oxford, 2013

INTERVIEW I

'An enterprise that is doomed to failure'

Geoffrey Bennington
ÎLSE SAINT-LOUIS, PARIS, SEPTEMBER 2012

Martin McQuillan: So we might begin by thinking about what is really happening in the 'Envois' and in the essay 'To Speculate—on "Freud"' around explaining, for want of a better word, a system of postality, or the postal system. What does that mean for Derrida?

Geoffrey Bennington: Well, it means a lot of things and it goes into the basis of his thinking about a number of things, but the easiest way to approach it is (as he does) with a very concrete example of a postal system, or a postal service, where the idea is very straightforward: that a message can be sent, it can find its way by one means or another through a more or less complicated network and by that principle it can arrive at its addressee. So it's a very simple model of a communicational network and the commonsense view is of course that letters are sent, they travel through, and they arrive. Derrida's brilliant, and I think philosophically very challenging, insight on the basis of that rather simple example is that this could not be called a postal system, or this kind of model I've just been describing could not be called a postal system if it were not, as he puts it, necessarily possible that the letter *not* arrive at its destination. This can seem at first like a strange, or trivial, or convoluted point, but I think it's really a very important one that has implications well beyond obviously talking about the French or British or Heaven forbid, the American post office. The thought is simply this: that if a system were such that it were necessary that a letter arrive at its destination, or a message arrives successfully at its destination and there were no possibility that it failed to do so, this isn't something that we would call a postal system. For a postal system to be worth calling that, there must be a time that the message or letter spends in the network, and so there must be, necessarily, a possibility that it could go astray or otherwise fail to arrive. That's the first point of the argument, which, although not quite the earliest mention, I think it is perhaps the earliest explicit development in Derrida and a very telling development of this, a rather deep philosophical thought of 'necessary possibility', and more especially, of 'necessary possibility that not'. So, 'necessarily possibly not' is then a predicate that is in this case applied to the letter moving through the postal system. Even if it does arrive, even if the system is one that's extremely efficient where in the whole history of millions of letters being sent every single letter has in fact arrived, the point would be that even in a case like that, this would not be something one could call a postal system if it hadn't been necessarily possible that letters not arrive or go astray, arrive at the wrong destination, not arrive at all, not arrive completely, not arrive in legible condition, and so on and so forth. That's the first part of the argument.

The second part of the argument, which is something that the commentators have had probably a little more trouble with, says that because of that necessary possibility, or given that necessary possibility, even in a case where a letter does in fact arrive (you pick up the mail, you open the envelope, you read the letter that was sent to you and intended for you to read), even in a case of success, Derrida is going to argue that that success remains haunted by the possibility of failure without which the success could not have taken place. So, the necessarily possibly not that allows for letters to move through the system (and most often, perhaps empirically speaking, allows them to always arrive at their destination), that necessary possibility, as it is part of what makes a letter a letter and what makes a postal system a postal system, must in a sense still be inscribed in the letter that duly does arrive. That haunting of the empirical success with the 'necessarily possibly not' condition is, I think, a very interesting, difficult thought that Derrida then develops in other kinds of contexts and in other sorts of places up to his very late work where, arguably at least, what his late work most often calls "autoimmunity" is a development or a revision of this postal principle, if we want to call it that as he does in *The Post Card*.

MMcQ: Derrida is quite insistent in *The Post Card* or in the 'Envois' that this is not a metaphor. He is not using this as a metaphor to describe communication. What would that mean, to say that this is not metaphorical?

GB: Well, I think there could be a lot of things we could say about that. In part it's because he is literally describing a postal system and, as you know, in *The Post Card* and the 'Envois' there's a lot about post offices and post cards and letters and stamps and collection times and distribution systems and so on. So at a certain level this is a literal description of that very interesting institution called the post office or the postal system, so I think in saying it's not a metaphor, in part, he is insisting on just how interesting and important that institution is. I remember doing some work on the postal principle and looked at some impressive old histories of postal institutions, many of which made huge claims for the importance of the postal system including the thought that civilization as we know it would have been impossible without something like a post office. Politics as we know it would have been impossible without the post system and so on. So in part, it is not a metaphor simply because in and of itself it is intrinsically extremely interesting.

The other reason that he is very suspicious of the concept of metaphor is that metaphor as it is used in philosophical argumentation usually means taking something known and familiar as a way of illustrating or explaining something as yet unfamiliar and unknown. I think he certainly does not want one to feel that the postal system is familiar and, as it were, easy enough simply to form the basis for that kind of metaphorical extension. So there's no reason to think that the postal service is a metaphor for communication more generally, anymore than there would be to say that the kind of conversation we're having now, in which the postal principle is operative, is a metaphor for the United States postal service. There is no particular priority to be found among these different systems.

MMcQ: Given that letters and parcels also circulate in the postal system, why then post cards? What is the significance of the post card for Derrida?

GB: Well, one of the points about the postal principle that we've talked about and the 'necessarily possibly not' in general, is that in the system letters—lets still call them letters—are exposed to a variety of, let's say, "accidents". So, part of what makes a postal service a postal service is that letters might arrive at the wrong destination, and part of what makes it a postal service is that letters are exposed in other ways during the time and along the paths they take through the network. For example, that exposure could be most easily seen in the case where a letter that you sent to me is intercepted along the way before it reaches the destination, and is opened and read by somebody else. That figure of exposure is something that Derrida tries to capture in the specific instance of the post card. The specific point of a post card, as long as it's treated as a post card and not sent in an envelope, is that the message is exposed. It is explicitly exposed, it is not sealed in or covered over and anybody, for example a postal worker, can pick up the post card and without breaking any seal, or violating any obvious secrecy, can read the message. It is usually next to the address. If the post card is going to reach the address, all the postman needs to do is shift his gaze a few degrees to the left or right and be able to read the message. So the post card is in that sense a fairly clear case of this exposure. Exposure of the 'necessarily possibly not', this is part of the definition of the postal system as Derrida sees it, and of course when I receive your post card (if I am lucky enough to have you send me one) I don't know how many other people will have read the message that you have written alongside my address.

Of course the other reason, which is very explicit throughout the book, especially in the 'Envois' and particularly on the cover of the book, is that the impetus for the 'Envois' section is given by Derrida's stumbling upon a very specific picture post card in the tourist shop at the Bodleian Library in Oxford. That particular post card with its image, which also contains various features that he's going to develop at some length in the book, is another good reason to choose the post card, rather than the letter, as the main figure for this logic of the 'necessarily possibly not'.

MMcQ: Could you help us a little bit with the title of this section of *The Post Card*, 'Envois'; why that term in particular, and how does that play out in the different resonances in French?

GB: Well there are different senses of that word. It is a perfectly common French word used of, let's say, a postal action or event. So my sending a letter is an '*envois*', '*mon envois*' is the act of, for example, mailing the letter or the post card, and it can also be used of the object itself that I put in the mailbox. So the letter or the card is itself '*un envois*', is a sending, a thing sent. But it also has some other connotations which relate to the familiar English word *envoy*. An envoy is somebody who is sent somewhere to represent or stand in for or express the views of somebody who stays at home, typically a powerful, or more powerful figure—certainly more powerful than the envoy—who stays at home and sends him or her to deliver a message. So extending the postal figure only a little bit, a system of international diplomacy or international relations which relies on envoys also illustrates, or embodies, more accurately, the postal principle. Even if the envoy on arrival repeats exactly the message, the imperial message (as in a famous little text by Kafka), even if the envoy were to repeat word for word the imperial message and apparently deliver it to its destination, all sorts of possibilities of mistake, of not, of necessarily possibly not, afflict or haunt the reception of that message. '*Envois*' also has that fairly explicit connotation.

And finally *envois* is just the name from the French verb *envoyer*, which means 'to send' in general, '*envoyer lettre*' or '*envoyer carte postale*' is totally idiomatic, the way we would say in English 'to send a letter' or a post card. It also has a final sense, which is perhaps being ironically played on here, which is that an '*envois*' can also be in French a final little farewell paragraph at the end of a book. For example, here in *The Post Card* it is in the beginning of the book, but traditionally the '*envois*' would be a little piece, possibly in verse, that would send the book on its way, because of course books, including the book called *The Post Card*, which is not a post card in the literal sense, are affected or afflicted by the postal principle: a book itself is *envoyer*. When Derrida finishes *La Carte Postale*, it is sent; it goes out through various networks of different kinds and different orders and its arrival at any particular destination, any particular reader, is marked by the 'necessarily possibly not' logic.

MMcQ: Derrida may also be picking up on Heidegger's understanding of *Being* as something that is sent from an original . . .

GB: Certainly one thing he has in mind, even before we get to Heidegger, whom we can talk about in a moment, is that the philosophical tradition not only has accidentally, or by oversight, failed to think through this postal logic, with its 'necessarily possibly not' condition. The fact that this condition affects all empirical events of apparent successful arrival has not been thought through by philosophy; the philosophical tradition, in Derrida's view, has not explicitly or sufficiently thought through the implications of that situation. Even in some cases where the thinker in question, in this case Heidegger, but in other parts of the book Lacan, for example (himself of course very influenced by Heidegger), where they may seem to have said some interesting things about a logic of sending, they still tend, in Derrida's view, to limit the consequences of the postal principle. So, most obviously between Heidegger and Derrida there's a relation which, as always in the case of Heidegger, is very complex and not something I could lay out in its full detail while improvising. In Heidegger we have a relation between this logic of sending, of destining—of sending something towards a destination—which then is picked up in the figure of destiny. And this destiny still seems to imply something of a good arrival point, an arrival point known ahead of time, which has a hint, at least, of a teleological determination, an appropriate way for things to go, and a right direction for things to travel. In Derrida's view, all of these motifs are under pressure if the postal principle is taken seriously. So, for example, he coins in this book, the idiom, the word in French '*destinerrance*', which I guess is translated as 'destinerancy' or 'destinerance', where destining does not resolve quite as destiny because of an element of errancy, which affects or afflicts it. And this puts some quite difficult questions to philosophies of history, to the idea of a directionality of history, certainly to an idea of progress and all sorts of teleological determinations that thinking about history finds it hard to do without. Accordingly, and more explicitly in the case of Heidegger, Derrida thinks that the philosophical tradition has not entirely taken in, or registered this. A very quick example of that, if I can follow on in a slightly different way, is that one of the implications of the postal principle, with its 'necessarily possibly not' affecting the arrival of messages at their destination and the fact that that 'necessarily possibly not' remains inscribed even in apparent successful arrivals, is that we have to think about what that means for reading in the slightly extended sense where the book (for example, the book called *The Post Card*) is described in terms of the postal principle. Receiving it, its arrival before us, the fact that we can pick it up and look at it, needs to be thought of in the terms of the 'necessarily possibly not' that we've been talking about. One implication of that is the entire hermeneutic tradition, which Derrida is very respectful of and which he finds very interesting, up to and including Heidegger at least, is in his view unduly limiting the effects of that postal principle by presuming that messages have somewhere to go and that they have an appropriate destination, a right destination, a final destination. For hermeneutics, texts in principle, although not always in practice, but in principle, would at least be open to the perspective of a true, final, complete interpretation, in which the meaning would be exhaustively grasped and successfully registered. Derrida thinks this is quite impossible because of the logic of destinerrancy, the 'necessarily possibly not' and so on.

MMcQ: One of the things that you did with Derrida himself was a book entitled *Jacques Derrida* of which your part is called 'Derridabase' where you attempt to outline, systematically, Derrida's thought. Can we speak a little about that book, how it originated and what happens in it?

GB: Well how it came about was reasonably straightforward. I was asked to write a book for a new series at Editions du Seuil, who were doing a series of books on writers and thinkers. They asked Derrida who should do the book on him and he suggested I might do it. We talked about it and in the conversation, one way or another, we came to an agreement that we would collaborate on this project in some way. Thinking about how to do that, I came up with the idea (that I was interested to see he found very striking) that he would write some of the book, and because he would be writing some of the book, I would write without quoting him once in a normal academic way. I would write an account of his thinking that did not quote from his works; he talks about this in his part of the book. I doubt I would have ever had that idea or that ambition in any other circumstance. So, I set out one summer, I think 1988, to systematise, as far as possible, my understanding of Derrida and his work up to that point. I wrote, more or less by the end of 1988, a draft of the 'Derridabase'. The computer reference to database is obvious, as an attempt to capture something of that effort at a systematised account of his thinking. Then I handed it over to him and he kept it for what seemed like an unconscionably long time, during which he wrote the fifty-nine sections of his text which runs along the bottom of the page, called 'Circumfession'. The deal between us was that I would give my best effort to producing an accurate and faithful systematised account of his thinking and he would try to find a way of unsettling that understanding, of writing something that my system could not understand, to put it briefly. Something that I could not possibly have predicted and that did not fall within the parametres of the explanation I had given. I knew that I was writing with a view to that happening, that was part of the contract, as we lay it out in the opening page of the book, and true enough, I think a little over a year later he came back with this really very astonishing text called 'Circumfession', which I think successfully does, at least to some extent, exceed or fall outside of the parametres that I had so studiously and systematically tried to lay down. I think we were both interested in that process and how it happened. But the best proof that he succeeded is that it is a text that I had a great deal of difficulty processing, simply my empirical relationship to that text has always been one of difficulty. I find it a more difficult text than many of Derrida's texts. The paradoxical complication for which I am in part responsible (this is a point I tried to make when the book was launched in Paris, but that didn't go down very well with the Parisian public) is that to some extent, even though I wrote my part of the book and did not quote him—so all the words are mine—it is just him, it is just the system of his thinking, there's nothing of me, in principle, in that part of the book. The other part of the book that he wrote to exceed and surprise my part, I argued (unsuccessfully I thought at the time) at least, in a sense, I could take some responsibility for because it would not have happened had he not been spurred to defy and exceed my understanding of his thinking. So, even though it is a text I did not understand and in some ways still do not, it is a text I thought I might have some signature claim on, and I guess that is marked by the fact that both texts co-exist in the same book.

MMcQ: So there is always something that escapes systematicity, or escapes the system and that would be in keeping with a logic that Derrida outlines in relation to Hegel and Bataille. That is what happens with 'Circumfession'; there is an escape and it is surprising—what's there is a surprise—or it gestures towards something you might not have thought he would have written about. In the same vein, it strikes me that *The Post Card* is a very surprising book, relative to what comes before, and even what comes after it in Derrida's writing: again there is a gesture in there that somehow catches the reader by surprise.

GB: Well, I think there is a similarity in both cases, especially the 'Envois' section of *The Post Card*. The rest of it is relatively recognisable, let's say, and indeed part of it, the famous essay on Lacan, had been published a few years earlier. The long section called 'To Speculate—on "Freud"' is largely only very lightly edited seminar sessions from Derrida's teaching, and the last thing is an interview. But the first part, the 'Envois', has a feel to it which is often described as literary. It is a more literary text; it seems to have something to do with, or some relation to, the tradition of the epistolary novel. It's less like a piece of philosophical writing, even though there are many philosophical arguments laid out in it, and similarly in 'Circumfession'. This is a text that includes a large amount, as indeed does the 'Envois', of explicitly autobiographical material marking dates and times and places that Derrida went, and lectures that he gave, and people that he met and in a more, perhaps traditional confessional or autobiographical mode, feelings that he had, reactions that he experienced. So in both cases there is a sense that the genre or the available genres of philosophical writing are being exceeded to some extent. In a way, the quick way of thinking about it—though it's probably much too quick—is to think of it as literary. 'Circumfession' more so than *The Post Card* is an extraordinarily written text, it's beautifully composed, it's written with all the care, with all the linguistic care, that one might associate with literature perhaps more than a work of philosophy. The point that Derrida is trying to make through that, quite apart from the pleasure one might take in this more literary dimension to his writing, is a point about surprise. He wrote something that was supposed to surprise me, but not just me, the available system, or the systematised version of him. He was also trying to surprise himself, because in the best case scenario, at least, all I did in "Derridabase" was say what he said, so if there's a surprise in the 'Circumfession' running along the bottom of the page, it's also a surprise for him. And one of Derrida's constant interests has been to wonder about things happening, about events, about what constitutes an event, and more especially, what constitutes an event that he would say is worthy of the name 'event'. In other words, an event that is not simply a straightforward causal outcome of earlier events. Derrida wants to say that an event worthy of the name is an event that takes one by surprise. It is something one does not see coming, that does not politely advance from a horizon of expectation and announce itself as it comes towards one. It is something that befalls one, perhaps violently, from above or perhaps from below, or behind or laterally from one side. It is something you do not see coming. So, in both cases of the 'Envois' section of *The Post Card* and the 'Circumfession' section of the book that we did together, there is an effort to not just talk about events, not just to conceptualise or produce a philosophy of events, but to, in a rather striking and perhaps somewhat spectacular way, to produce an event, or to make an event, or to be an event. And that eventful character of Derrida's thinking is something that was there from the start but probably becomes more pronounced in the performance of his texts, if I can use that word, which he late in his life somewhat turned against. The performance of his texts presents something eventful or surprising, which is probably why the quick and easy way of thinking about it is to relate it to something literary, to say these texts have a literary dimension. Literary texts are texts that we are used to thinking of in terms of their performance, what they do, the event they make happen, as much as, or more than, in terms of some conceptual or representational content that they are supposed to vehicle.

MMcQ: If you can recall, what was your experience of first reading *The Post Card*?

GB: I was very surprised by *The Post Card*. I had just moved to Paris in 1979, the book came out that autumn. I remember seeing it, and buying it and going to Derrida's seminar, in fact, and while waiting for the seminar to start, I more or less furtively in my place in the room, flicked through this large, heavy, handsome book that I had just bought (more especially the 'Envois' section). My eyes fell on what subsequently became rather a famous line from the 'Envois' section in French, something like, *'Quand je t'appelle mon amour, mon amour, est-ce toi que j'appelle ou mon amour?'* I am not exactly sure how Alan Bass translates it, but 'When I call you my love, my love, is it you I'm calling or my love that I'm calling?' and this seemed a very striking and strange and somewhat discomforting sentence to find in what I had bought assuming was a work of literary theory or philosophy. I then read the book in a very short space of time with a great deal of enthusiasm, excitement and some puzzlement, and again in a slightly different way, but comparably to my reading of 'Circumfession', with some discomfort as well. This is not exactly what I had expected. I could see a lot in it that responded to things I thought I understood about Derrida's work, but I could also see that there was something else happening which I felt less secure about and

I would have to say today, I still feel less secure about. Things, I would venture to say, that any reader would have to feel less secure about than, let's say, the more recognisably philosophical parts of Derrida's work.

MMcQ: One of the tasks of making a film that responds to the 'Envois' is to translate a text from one medium into another and this involves all the complications that go with translation. I think about this in the sense that Derrida asked the question: not what is a correct translation, but what is a relevant translation? So my question to you, as one of the translators of Derrida, is what are the pitfalls of translation?

GB: Well, translation is nothing but pitfalls. It is all pitfalls. Translation is always going to be problematic. At best, it is going to be a little inventive, it is never really going to be faithful; translation betrays a text but its lies are all true. However, there is a specificity, there is a set of things nonetheless one can say about translating in the narrow sense, for example, about the daunting task that Alan Bass undertook in translating *La Carte Postale* into English and perhaps some slightly different things one would say about, as you say, moving into a different medium altogether, as translating. If one can call responding to the 'Envois' section, in the medium of a movie, a translation. There, of course, it is impossible; there is no good or obvious way to do that. This always has been the case with movies made on the basis of literary texts, and more especially movies made on the basis of the epistolary novel tradition that we were saying earlier the 'Envois' bore some relation to. So, look at the movies made on the basis of Laclos's *Dangerous Liaisons* or Diderot's *La Religieuse* (*The Nun*). These are movies that struggle with extreme difficulty because of one big structural problem, which is, in the case of the epistolary novel, the letters. In the case of great epistolary novels, especially Laclos's novel, the letters play a part in development of the story: the fact of the letters is extremely important in Laclos's book. The fact of the post card and the letters is extremely important in the 'Envois' and moving into the medium of the movies, those letters are still letters, even as the medium of the whole document, if I can put it that way, is moved significantly into a different language, into a different realm of language in the broad sense of language, and different set of technical possibilities. So, it is a quite different matter in the movie of Laclos's novel when you see a character opening and reading a letter. That is a quite different situation from the moment in the actual novel when a character in a letter reports on receiving and reading a letter. Similarly, I think in your movie you will have to be extremely inventive and that invention has to go beyond the normal constraints of what we think of as translation in order to capture something in the displaced medium with which you are dealing. Something that is related to but cannot really be the equivalent of (but nonetheless is related to) the events, if I can put it that way, in the 'Envois' themselves. So to some extent it is, as with all translations, an enterprise that is doomed to failure, and that failure can be interesting. The only prospect for it is a measure of invention, but what that invention should be is not prescribed, or prescribable in anyway. You have to invent it. You have to come up with it without simply applying existing rules, or scripts, or expectations, or programmes. So, the film itself has to be an event in that stronger sense that we were talking about earlier, texts like the 'Envois' or 'Circumfession' and that is the filmmaker's challenge. It certainly cannot be a transposition in any straightforward sense from the medium, the linguistic medium, the printed book medium in which the 'Envois' originally takes place and the really remarkably different medium of film.

Joanna Callaghan: How might you explain to a layperson *The Post Card* and its relation to deconstruction?

GB: Well, I might say something that's not so very dissimilar from what I said in some of the opening remarks I made responding to Martin. Laypeople, assuming we know what a layperson is, 'laypersons', I think, have a familiarity with the post office and sending letters, expecting them to arrive and occasionally experiencing the frustration of their non-arrival or other accidents that can happen along the way. I think, and my own pedagogical experience is, that this is a fairly telling example with which to start a thinking that leads one really quite rapidly to those harder thoughts about dissemination, destinarency, non-directionality in meaning and history, non-finality in general, the open-endedness of possibilities, which is what I call reading. *The Post Card* is the book in which Derrida lays that out perhaps most spectacularly in what are very layman's terms, especially in the 'Envois' section. In many ways, surprising though it was to many readers, 'The Envois' was to Derrida that part of the book which is in some ways shockingly accessible, I think, to the famous man on the Clapham omnibus.

MMcQ: One of the questions that keep me awake at night is to think about the future of deconstruction, thinking about what deconstruction will do, or if there is such a thing as deconstruction, after Derrida. Ten years after Derrida's passing, reading this book several decades after Derrida wrote it, what now are the prospects for deconstruction?

GB: Well, deconstruction is of course not just an academic movement, or fashion, or theory. Derrida famously said many times, "deconstruction is what happens"—events arriving happen in deconstruction. Deconstruction is not an intellectual option that one might choose; to some extent it is completely unavoidable, and even if many academic and intellectual positions would not recognise that fact, I think it is demonstrable that they too are in deconstruction, like it or not. Deconstruction in some ways is a very ambitious and maximal claim, or involves an ambitious or maximal claim along the lines of 'everything that *is*, is in deconstruction', and always has been, and always will be. Now having said that, even if that position is not widely accepted and it probably never will be, there are obviously more specific things that people who have been interested in and struck by and largely convinced by Derrida's thinking will be concerned to pursue. That thought is a ramified and complex thought that is still unfolding before our eyes, so to speak. And part of that unfolding and part of one's accompanying that unfolding in its happening (this is something that will take a while to lay out) is intrinsically to do with a process of reading, in a very broad sense of that term. Reading does not happen once and for all; that is a consequence of the postal principle itself. Reading is always rereading and rereading always entails reading again in the future. So, of course, I have no idea what the future holds in general. It is also a consequence of the postal principle. But assuming in the future there is still a recognisable activity of reading I hope and trust that the strength and resources of Derrida's texts will become perhaps increasingly recognised as an invaluable way of trying to understand the almost incomprehensible things that happen every day.

INTERVIEW II

'We have flipped over the candle'

Ellen S. Burt

QUAI DE SAINT-BERNARD, PARIS, SEPTEMBER 2012

Martin McQuillan: Can you talk a little bit about how the 'Envois' might work as an epistolary novel in that tradition of French literature.

Ellen S. Burt: I think the thing that struck me the most on first reading is that this is an epistolary novel (or in that tradition). I have some experience of the epistolary from my work on Rousseau and I am struck by the extent to which Derrida is very judiciously playing with the tradition, in particular with the question that often gets aired, in a kind of blunt and not particularly refined fashion, of fiction in the epistolary form. An epistolary novel in the eighteenth century plays with the problem of the found correspondence, a collection of letters found in a trunk somewhere, inherited, and published, which reveals or purports to reveal some real-life world from the past, but that has in it, because of its detachment, because of a certain uncertainty as to the status of these found letters in the first place, a kind of fictional destination as well. In Rousseau that is turned up to a second power because Rousseau writes a dialogue preface that says, 'A little dialogue between "R" and "N" as to whether this is a real correspondence or not'. It is important to the speaker or to interlocutor to know that, and R's answer is, 'Well, these questions, I don't really know; I can't really tell you for various reasons. We can only make a theorisation this way or that way'. N becomes more and more irritated and finally he says, 'Come on, just tell me'. And at that point the crafty, persuasive figure 'R' comes up with something like a confession; he says: 'Who could say? Who could say whether this whole air of mystery is not there to hide from you my very real ignorance about what you want to know. In short, I would have to be the

145

author, that I am not sure I am, in order to be able to say to you that I, in fact, wrote this, or didn't write this book'.

So, it is precisely this kind of heightening of this moment of uncertainty that characterises the Rousseau, and I think for me *The Post Card* had something of that effect because it sits in that space of fact/ fiction. To what extent is this a fictional correspondence, or at least a partially fictional correspondence, that in some form or another has been elaborated in order to create the introduction, a possible introduction, to a book on psychoanalysis, Socrates and Freud? To what extent is it a real correspondence that just somehow happens to be obsessed by this particular post card? Those kinds of questions come up very sharply and not, I think, in a way that you just say, 'Oh OK, fact and fiction, that doesn't necessarily much matter', but it changes a good deal in one's reading of it when suddenly you see, let's say, a trope, the poet imploring his mistress or his mistress–muse in a certain letter. The muse here is silent and that is precisely one of the things that happens with a muse. That is a very literary convention; it feels very, in some respects, artificial and gives it this fictional dimension, let's say. From the perspective of characters on the other side, there is the dating, the names of real people, all the things, the clutter of existence, the little love stories and stories of betrayal that get worked out in the thing, and those kind of create a little suspense and novelistic mystery that gets you through it. But maybe the thing that Derrida mostly manages to sharpen for us is the extent to which any letter is in that position. That is to say, on the one hand it is addressed, it has a date, it has a place, a postmark to which it is intended to go, and all of that speaks to a referential language. At the same time, the letter could not be written unless there is an implied absence and in that implied absence, you have suddenly got the possibility of a radical fiction. In part, the letter is operating without any certainty as to its final addressee and its original place of emission. It is as though he had seized onto the problem of the letter itself here and exploited it, which he shares with the eighteenth century, in a way, because that is exactly the issue that such authors are working with. That is one of the points of entry for me in terms of the epistolary fiction, this question of fact or fiction, that leads very quickly to destinerrance, and problems of the way in which *The Post Card* folds into itself; the question of the post office, the question of how the institution of the letter, that grows up around the letter, affects the lives of the people who are writing these letters and reflects on the letter itself, what its possibilities and deadlinesses sometimes are.

MMcQ: We might say that Derrida is not just repeating that traditional form; he is doing something different with it. So, what are those different things? For example, the gaps, what is left out, the bits that are burned, what disappears and what has not been selected quite deliberately. What is going on there?

ESB: OK, well, one thing that is involved there is the suppression of the private details. There is a secrecy involved and a constant reminder of withholding, a reserve, of a private place that cannot be told, for whatever reason. Some of those reasons might be? Well, you just don't know; it is the condition for the interlocutor accepting the correspondence be published, it could be that there are some things that are too precious and too intimate, too private, to be expressed. It could also be simply a reminder of the way in which the letter always contains a secret beyond whatever it is that it exposes, and that is the question of its destinerrance, the question of the post office. It is the question of 'on the one hand' and 'on the other hand': a withheld rereading, a new arrival or something. Those are questions that are raised for me that are not absolutely written up and available, or not quickly available, in Rousseau. I think you could argue that there is something like those suppressions available in Rousseau, but it is certainly much more marked in Derrida; it is a deliberate manufacturing of holes and gaps.

MMcQ: Is it even the right question to ask, whether the 'Envois' is literature or is it another kind of writing entirely?

ESB: It is a good question, because for me in thinking a little bit about *The Post Card* in terms of the 'post cardness' of it, one of the questions that came to my mind was whether this was not really closer to the kind of letters philosophers used to write to one another in objection, or in response, let's say, to the publication of some treatise: Descartes' *Meditations*, say, or Rousseau himself wrote a certain number of letters, or was the recipient of a certain number of open letters that were essentially public objections addressed to an author. The letter to D'Alembert, which is one of his big letters of that sort, seems in some respects closer to *The Post Card* than the epistolary novel that I was talking about—perhaps, primarily, because it is a critical text. It is a critical text in a couple of ways. Firstly, with respect to the Plato-Socrates figures and to the artwork of the 'Envois' (reproduced but nonetheless an artwork) that the narrator at one point goes to the archive to find. Also, in part because it is at some point supposed to become the introduction to a set of critical essays on Freud, and Socrates to Freud and beyond, with a couple of nods back to the fellow logocentric universe in which Derrida very quickly situates himself in his writing. So it seems to me in many respects much closer to that kind of critical and metacritical text. Also, again trying to situate it with respect to Rousseau, Rousseau's letter to D'Alembert was a letter that took on the question of closed spectacles or open-air spectacles—which is better for the Republic? Voltaire and various others of the Genevans are trying to press for theatres to be built in Geneva, and Rousseau writes to say republican principles require the open-air spectacle rather than the closed spectacle, which should be ornamental: people are in the position of spectators, they are watching something out there. This may be a tragedy of sovereignty, representative of power and opposed to the open-air spectacle, which is a spectacle of the participatory, where the spectator becomes actor with a sense in which there is a lack of closure to the thing. In thinking about *The Post Card* and Derrida's insistence that these are not letters (that is ridiculous because they're so long they couldn't possibly fit on a post card), and yet, there is some sense of this problematic in his gesture of opening them up, this private correspondence, making it public, or viewable to the public.

The question of the public spectacle is a question of representation in Rousseau that is not, as he termed it, an aristocratic, monarchical spectacle, a closed spectacle that is removed from the people, in which they are frozen into attitudes of spectatorship. Rather what he was looking for was the open spectacle, where they would become participants. I find it intriguing that Derrida's choice was again not of a letter, the closed letter, but of the post card, that could be read, and not only could be read, but also invites reading by anybody who picks it up. Post cards end up, particularly in Paris, and maybe in London too, I don't know, in antique stores. Old post cards are sold for the images, and there is the extra interest in that image that people have that keeps them holding on to those post cards long after letters have been discarded. All of that suggested to me an interesting relation is taking place in Derrida that reminded me of Rousseau in a different mode, both the metacritical relation, that of a philosophical text and so forth, and a kind of explicit intervention in the scene of where we are today with the question of representation, spectacle, dramatisation and so forth. It is the question of the post card, or the overstuffed post card. It is kind of ridiculous.

MMcQ: Like one of those post cards that you open out with ten different pictures?

ESB: Only, it is kind of almost endless. And the question of whether it is a reflection on the post card, or rather reflections written on post cards that open up in the same kind of way. Anyway, let's say, yes, I agree with you, that I think it is, in many respects, more of a metacritical text than it is an epistolary novel, although there is almost a sort of salacious possibility of reading it in the manner of *Julie, ou la nouvelle Héloïse,* as letters of love. It operates with both, it accepts the risks of operating with both, and I think that is part of what makes it still a very interesting and strong entrance into the world of philosophy and into the world of literature at the same time.

MMcQ: The question of risk here is a very interesting one. We might talk a little bit about the experience of reading the book and the sorts of risks involved in that and the sort of risks Derrida is taking in writing that book.

ESB: Well, I want just to say to begin with that I had an interesting summer reading this book the first time. I was staying in Ithaca in New York, and in Ithaca, as you know, there are gorges; Ithaca is a place that is built by and on gorges. I was reading it in the middle of Fall Creek, on a rock, up above a waterfall that's seventy-five feet high, not an inconsiderable drop. It is not nothing, and there is a lot of ozone up there in a very heady kind of atmosphere, and I think somehow this backdrop affected, or came to represent in some way for me, the kind of sense I had about the book, which was a very heady experience. It was a very interesting and daring kind of move to be making at that moment, when there were other things around. It was not the only risky move around, if you like, but it was an extraordinarily risky one. That rock is gone these days, worn away by the erosion process; one day I almost went over the falls myself, it was an unstable position that I was in, and I felt kind of connected, in some way to this.

So what are the risks that he was taking? Well, one would be that with this book, as with *Glas*, as with *Spurs*, with some of the other things that Derrida was writing and publishing around the same time, it is the consideration that the book is not just a box in which you put a certain kind of content. Rather there is always a perspective in which the book itself can become part of the content, and has to become part of the content. Over and over in those texts he is playing with margins, playing with footnotes, playing with titles, with the space between the first title and the second title, which suddenly allows for ambiguities and so forth. This book is in the tradition he was himself creating at that moment, of very strong and striking and risky sort of speculations for writing. Another risk is to take your private correspondence, and even with a few suppressions, to publish it. Everybody was reading Jacques Derrida's *The Post Card* that summer with the idea that somehow it was a roman à clef. There is a little love story here, so let's find out whom Derrida really knows and loves, and a lot of people were looking in those places. That is risky behavior, just to put the post office together with your personal life; to send so many post cards, to make so voluminous a correspondence as to invite certain kinds of disasters, like the disaster of the lost letter, the lost correspondence that somehow creates extraneous moments of distress. All of those things went into this sense that I certainly had that something was happening here, some intervention was being made that was out of the usual, in the sense of something you had not seen before, some style you had not seen before, but also in the sense that a whole set of topics were opening up that had not been available or at least had not been available in this particular way. It is hard to say how, at once how small, and how huge, a shift this was. It is as though having read 'Envois' you had to reread everything because suddenly the consideration of the margins, what had been left in the margin, had now to be accounted for. That was a risk, a big risk.

MMcQ: On the one hand, it is a risky unforeseen gesture; on the other hand, it is also what happens all the time in literature: this is what literature does; it puts on display, in a way that is disavowable, something of the autobiographical.

ESB: Certainly, yes, it is a literary move I guess. It is the literary move here doubled, very quickly doubled by the critical, metacritical stance, but not just doubled and redoubled, because that already suggests that the critical move is always in that afterthought position; here they are equi-primordial: one does not come before the other. It is not that it is impossible to say that the post cards were created with a view to an introduction to the Freud, because they were. So you find yourself in a position where the critical is not in that secondary position, but rather in a primary position, or potentially in a primary position, in a kind of theatricalised, and therefore literary way, but still critical and reflective at every point thought. I am in the process of looking right now at some other Derrida texts, and one of his signature moves is to look for the place where something escapes, where you know something escapes. Freud, for example. Freud says something and yet he does not really think through the implication of what he has just said, and that is the starting point for a Derridean reflection because it provides him at once with the unthought of the system, with the conditions of the system and its assumptions but also with a point of entrance to see whether or why you need that unthought. What is the rationale for that continued, necessary return of a literary gesture? So, yes, I agree with you that it's an autobiographically fictional kind of move, but I would say always alongside the critical, and the thinking through of the critical.

MMcQ: That reminds me of the reading of Freud in 'To Speculate on "Freud"' where Derrida says autobiography becomes the foundation of a science in the story of 'Little Hans', but then actually we find out this is an entirely fictional autobiography. Autobiography is being used to justify the science, but the autobiography itself is not factual, and that is the slippery move that is going on in the 'Envois' as well.

ESB: Right, with the understanding that what happens, the reason it works and it is not just a charlatanism or whatever, is that in the process of that questioning taking place, what happens is that 'what is a fact' becomes the question. Is the fact a given? No, a fact is being given, or has to be given, and that being given is what we call fiction. So, it is not possible then to say 'fact or fiction, make a choice' but at every point you have to ask what autobiographical reflection comes to be. It is something like the turn back onto the self that consists in asking about the verifiability of one's own representations, so that fact, then, is not fact, but its relation to fiction becomes more stated.

MMcQ: One of the things that interests me in *The Post Card* is the way in which the epoch of literature, whatever that might mean, which might arise in modernity, and might have an explicit connection to something like the epistolary novel, is related to what Derrida calls 'the epoch of the post'. When he is talking about postality in the book, he is at pains to say 'this is not a metaphor', so what is the connection between postality, the history of the post and literature?

ESB: Well, I guess, you are asking about the modernity of literature and the modernity of the post because on some level, it seems that you could say modernity has nothing over Socrates and Plato because it is already there in that image, which reflects a certain understanding. It is already there in Plato's letters, Derrida goes back to Plato's apocryphal letters, and so forth, to find a similar kind of structure. So it is the letter itself, or the writing, let's say, that accretes the postal system. The postal system is part of what a letter bears with it, so e-mail is not much more than an accelerated version of what we already find operating in this early image. On the one hand, you could say there is nothing new under the sun; it is all what it always has been, which is to say, the postal system producing itself, by way of its logic—a logic of what a letter can do, what a letter requires; you send a letter, it can get lost. That means you need a place, you need a dead letter office, where the letters can go and then either be reclaimed by the people who sent them, or claimed by the addressees or through various manipulations sent back, or whatever. That system does not always work; you cannot always find a way. Sometimes people forget to put their return address, so those letters get burnt and that requires extra burning, which the book talks about quite a lot. The incendiary reduction to ashes of a certain number of letters, that is a certain kind of logic working itself out, the logic of the post office that the Phoenicians thought concerning the god Hermes; it is already there as the post office system. On the other hand, you could say, and certainly Derrida, I believe, would be saying this, there are certain innovations that take place over the course of time and one of them is the post office as we know it today or as we knew it in 1970s. It has changed a little bit since then, because, as you know, some parts are falling into ruin. The post office of today is not the post office of the seventies. It was a public institution; now it is more and more a commercial one. Letters now go by SMS texting, or they go by e-mail, or scanned and sent, faxed, and they do not necessarily go through the postman. Nonetheless, there is some modernity, let's say, being explored here. For example, the post card, the image on the post card, that is a relatively modern phenomenon. Papyrus did not do that. The reproduction of a work of art on the post card that is sent through the mail was not a necessary thing, or again the *poste restante* issue, all of those are themes of modernity that show up in the book. You ask the question of literature; well, how does literature show up in that? Obviously, literature starts with the move of other letters, a postulating of an imaginary or absent addressee, and takes place by cutting off from a particular spot, with the possibility of a letter cutting off from a particular spot. Literature starts where letters start, and the accretion that takes place (that is the post office) is in effect very quickly a metaphor for—and not just a metaphor for, sort of part and parcel of—the accretion that is literature, with its systems of sending, second thoughts, corrections, poste restante, dead letter offices, and so forth. All of those, it seems to me, you can see working themselves not just through the epistolary novel but through literature itself, and certainly Derrida's attempt to make the borders of the book show up again in the book is one indication of precisely that.

MMcQ: You are quite right to say that this is a book of the 1970s, and one of the things that strikes me about it, trying to make a film about it now, is that it has the feel of an analogue book for a digital moment. You are right that the post office is falling apart. It is about to be privatised in the UK; it is no longer going to be a state-owned entity. My question, then, is: What is the future of the post, and what might that mean for the future of literature?

ESB: Well this is a question that all of us in the university are concerned with right now because we are seeing reductions, new places in the archive collapsing, in that there are not going to be studies of classics, there are not going to be departments of French, or departments of German. Does that mean the study of the languages will not take place? Does that mean the study of the literature that is related to those languages will not take place? So there is some anxiety around this. On the other hand, it seems to me you can say there is still a future. A great deal of writing goes on, on the Internet for example, and some of it is pretty good. It seems to me, as a somewhat early reader of that kind of stuff, that at this point it is a matter of learning how to sift it, how to make the cuts from the wordy, just blathering, just language, to stuff that is worth recycling, returning to, rereading, and so forth. It does not seem to me that we are not going to be able to make those cuts; it just seems, however, that we have not really figured out systems for doing that, which are readily available for people at this point, or how we might do that. I think students are often at a loss here; they go to the Internet and they look wherever, and faculty do not have the ability to direct them. The result is that some of the training that might be taking place, in terms of how to go and write your own literature is not therefore happening in the ways it needs to. We have some failures around; we have some dead spots in some places where some work needs to be done, but there is a future there. I do not think it has shifted in a major way really. I came here, to France, for the year, with an iPad, and I brought the iPad because I can have 150 books on it. It is not quite as much fun to read the iPad because you cannot underline, you cannot flick back, you do not have the same relation to the materiality of the page, and yet there is some other materiality there. There is some pleasure with flicking with my finger, there is some gesture, some relation to it that is material . . .

MMcQ: There is touch.

ESB: Yes, and that, I think will be how something like a 2012 or 2020 version of *The Post Card* becomes possible.

MMcQ: The sentence in the 'Envois' that I think about over and over again is when Derrida says that an entire epoch of so-called literature cannot survive the regime of telecommunications, and neither can philosophy, nor psychoanalysis, nor love letters. Given what we have just been discussing, could you add the university to that list as well?

ESB: The university in ruins, right? Quite possibly, I think the university has been ruining itself, in ruins if you like, or what is the active verb for that?

MMcQ: Ruining oneself? Self-harm?

ESB: Ruining oneself, not exactly suicide, perhaps? It is at once a ruin and an accretion, because it creates new possibilities, and new kinds of institutions grow up around the edges. It does not fall apart all at once and forever, but living in this epoch where we are dealing with a crisis in the economy with some sense of at once urgency and an inability to figure out how to parse that moment, it certainly feels as though something like the end of the university is at hand, and we need to save it in some way. One can look at it in terms of the kind of logic that *The Post Card* is laying out for us, but it would take some time and I do not want to be too speculative about it, because it seems to me often as though we are starting to get apocalyptic when we think about these things, and that is probably not the way to go. Actually, it carries on in its ruining process; it does not just fall apart.

MMcQ: The University is on fire.

ESB: Ha. OK.

Joanna Callaghan: How would you explain to a student who had not read the book why *The Post Card* is important?

ESB: It is a little hard for me to say whether it is this book only, or this book and few others that Derrida was writing at the time, but let's say the significance for me would be that he changes very radically the way you look at a book, or at the medium, by requiring a thought on the medium that is like tectonic plates. You suddenly realize that the content is not the matter, it is not just that the medium is the message, but that the medium affects and finds itself implicated in the developments that the content can take in ways that are very revelatory to us. The kind of fundamental assumptions that we make about our lives and what truth is, and what art is, and so forth, are affected by this very tiny little problem, as it seems, of a material support, and the systems that grow up around the material support. So, I think I would say to that student, this is going to be a revolution for you in the sense that you are suddenly going to have to ask yourself about something you have been taking for granted your whole life. On the other hand, it is going to come to you as no surprise that something you have been taking for granted your whole life (the post system, the letter, the problem of language) is actually far more important than you originally thought. I think that students would end up buying into that because they would see from this book that this was the case. Derrida was talking at one point—this is in a way a response to Martin's earlier question—in just a private conversation about deconstruction. It was after the de Man scandal, when it had been discovered that de Man had in his early twenties written some articles for a collaborationist newspaper in Belgium and that caused a lot of upset in academic circles. Derrida was dealing with that in a lot of different ways, writing about it, with very considered pieces and so forth. One day he said, you know, people keep announcing the end of deconstruction and it is as though what they had done was reversed. They have tipped over a candle and said, 'look, look, it's gone out, it's gone out, it's all over, it's all done with', and then suddenly what they see is that there are thousands and thousands of little lights around because in flipping the candle over, the material that had been burning, is suddenly found around it in all of these different, smaller ways, but nonetheless burning. I think that is maybe my response to your question of the end of the university. Where are we with respect to the end of the university? We have flipped over the candle, the university is over, but look at all those little lights; it is not in fact over, really. It is a more disseminated university, and I think that possibility of dissemination of the light is actually something that one might consider is something to be celebrated rather more than mourned in a way.

INTERVIEW III

'Cinema is not a brain reading'

Catherine Malabou
JARDIN DU LUXEMBOURG, PARIS, SEPTEMBER 2012

Martin McQuillan: Let's begin by talking about your book co-authored with Derrida, *La Contre-Allée*. How did it come about?

Catherine Malabou: Well, initially it was an order from Maurice Nadeau, who was running a series called *Voyager Avec* . . . . It was part of a series; anyway it was pre-programmed. We had to discuss a writer's travels, and Nadeau asked me to do that with Derrida, travelling with Derrida. So we tried to transform it into something else, into something that would be slightly different from the other books in the series. We decided, in order to do so, to write to each other, to write in the mode of the correspondence. Jacques started to send me post cards from his travels all over the world, mainly from India, Israel, Turkey, and I answered. My text of course was hard because I had to obey the imperatives of the series; it was a little bit more formal. I had to explain to the readers through this correspondence what Derrida's philosophy was. It is a bizarre, strange text, because it is a mix of different tones and genres.

MMcQ: What were the complications around writing a correspondence with Derrida in which you were performing some of the issues that appear in the 'Envois', for example, in terms of the surprise that might arrive with a text or post card that came from Jacques?

CM: The problem I always had with Derrida's elaboration of the 'Envois', and in general the sending and the post, and with adestination, is that despite all he says about that, it seems to me that something of a motive remains very much central in his thought, the motive of the derivation, a 'derive' in French. This schema of derivation, in which you have an origin and something which drifts from the origin, or derives from it, is

157

both deconstructed in Derrida, and un-deconstructed. It remains central and untouched, in a way, because even if he says that this schema, derivation, has to be deconstructed is always already constructed, he nevertheless keeps it in order to explain that the adestination does not derive, or is not a derivation from. Even if he talks about that in the negative form, he keeps this schema of derivation. So this is what I try to address throughout the correspondence and in my commentary of his text. How is it possible to, and is it possible to, give up this theme of derivation totally?

MMcQ: Maybe you could explain that a little bit, the way in which adestination might also be motivated. Is that the same thing as what Derrida called 'destinerrance'?

CM: Yes, it is the same thing, and you are right, he is looking for a non-motivated kind of destination, which is destinerrance. Non-motivated meaning that would be different from Being in Heidegger. Being is also something that is sent, as you know, in Heidegger, which would also be different from pleasure in Freud, which is also presented as a first sending, something which, in a way, launches itself, or something like that. Derrida really wants to distinguish destinerrance from these motivated kind of sendings, these sendings which always have a meaning—the meaning of Being, the meaning of pleasure—but I wonder in the end, if some kind of motivation does not go on haunting Derrida's destinerrance.

MMcQ: Where does the sending come from, if it comes, or is it a sending without origin that only ever has an arriving?

CM: We should not ask precisely this question, we should not ask where it comes from, to the extent that precisely it does not derive from any origin, to the extent that there is no originary presence, there is no source from which something could be able to derive in that the source, as Derrida says, is divided at the origin and there is something like a death of presence at the heart of presence, which in a way makes everything be tardy or late. Everything comes too late because there is no origin. So the origin is in itself a repetition, there is no pure source. This is what explains the unmotivation of the sending, but I wonder if even negatively, this schema of 'derivation from' is not maintained in that deconstruction, the very deconstruction of the derivation.

MMcQ: It is something that remains. Is it the case that it remains because the sending is always recaptured into that kind of schema?

CM: Yes, we cannot call that a metaphor, the logic of the sending, perhaps this should disappear, as such, because as long as you remain within this semantic world of the sending, then the logic of derivation and destination remains pregnant in one way or another. As soon as you have the sending you have the letter, you have destination, you have writing, you have the trace and of course Derrida says that the trace is always erasable, but this erasure itself remains. We are trapped in this sending thing.

MMcQ: That strikes me as very much like Derrida's reading of Nancy on touch, in that one can never escape touch. As soon as you begin with the vocabulary of touch, you are going to be contaminated by the whole metaphysical history of touch, and there will be no sense of touch outside of it. Once caught in an understanding of touch there will simply be a contamination of every touch, which will touch on every concept. So similarly in sending, you are also going to be caught in a structure that you cannot, in principle, escape.

CM: Yes, but at the same time, Derrida acknowledges epochs in sending. So perhaps, he says 'perhaps', when he talks about techne, he says we cannot think about sending in general we always have to think of sending in a determined epoch, or period of time. Perhaps today we are entering an era in which the technical meaning of sending is perhaps disappearing. I do not think we are still sending things to each other in quite the same way. I think the development of technologies today is perhaps making all these metaphors of sending, destination, etc., obsolete.

MMcQ: This is a question that interests me very much, where we are now with technologies of sending. And where we were when Derrida wrote *The Post Card*, which strikes me as two very different places. The thing that is striking about reading the 'Envois' now is that it is an analogue book (about post cards and stamps and post offices) and that is not where we are now in a digital moment. This is not really where we were when *Contre-Allée* was written, but still the post card was used in that book, so why post cards, then, in *Contre-Allée*?

CM: Yes, I think this is a very good question, because I think this is *the* question. He says in *The Post Card* that to consider sending in the way he talks about it, as an epoch of a general technology, a general history of technology, might have been an objection for Heidegger. He says, if Heidegger had been able to read my book, he would have perhaps said, 'Derrida what you are talking about is only an epoch of sending, and now it's over, we are entering another epoch'. Then Derrida would answer, this is what he says in the book, 'No, yes and no, because the general structure of sending, is in a way, wider, broader than a history, of the history of technology'. This is precisely my problem. Is it true that the general structure, let's call it a structure for the moment, of sending is in a way wider than the history of technology? Is the history of technology inscribed within the general structure of sending or, on the contrary, is sending itself just an epoch of this technological development? I think Derrida never really answered this. It is a very big question of course, I do not know who is able to answer it; obviously Derrida did not. That is why, as you say, in the *Contre-Allée*, he is hesitating between two modes of expression, one which is not the sending in *The Post Card*, and the other which is still the same structure as in this book. I think this remains as something unsolved.

MMcQ: And where are we now, today, in June 2012, with sending? We still send a text message, we still send an e-mail; we might even say that we send a tweet? Or does one post a tweet? But that is semantics; that is the same idea to say one is posting. Are we in a moment of 'crisis of destination'? Are we actually at such a point, or, are there only ever moments of crisis of destination? Is that part of the issue about where you draw the line on an epoch? You do not just have epochal breaks and suddenly we are all doing something else.

CM: Well, it is of course difficult to tell because who knows? But I think, so, we are in a moment of crisis, where clearly the goal is to read into the other's mind, into the other's brain. All of the technologies that exist today tend to alleviate, shorten, and practically erase *différance* (with an *a*) in order to gain immediacy in reading into each others' minds. I think this brain thing that is developing, this triumph of neurobiology today, is about that. The ideal is to be able to read in the other's brain. So, is it a continuation of what Derrida has been writing about all his life, is it just a prolongation of that, another epoch of the sending, or is it something totally different? I think we are in this moment today, technical imagery, brain imagery, this is what they, scientists, want to explore: the possibility of reading into each other's brain, as fast as possible, as if technology was not differing, but on the contrary, accomplishing, realising this simultaneously. This would even be more efficient than telepathy. It would be a touch, a kind of brain touch.

MMcQ: Downloading straight into the brain? But that is an old onto-theological fantasy.

CM: Yes, but it is becoming real; that is the difference. If fantasy becomes real, it must be something different from a fantasy. What is happening is part of something else, something different from the old fantasy of reading into each other; perhaps it creates a new kind of subjectivity.

MMcQ: Give me some examples of how that might work today, in neuroscience. What sorts of things . . . ?

CM: For example, people who are totally paralysed: neurobiologists have designed new computers which are able to read into the patient's brain, so you do not have to talk, you do not even have to wink, you just have to be wired into the computer. The machine reads in your neurons, and is able to translate your desires, your wills, etcetera; so this is an example. Also, they have invented these glasses in which the computer is in the glasses. The glasses are two screens, and it is as if you were decoding the real, communicating, being in the real and communicating with the other at the same time.

MMcQ: But that situation still requires an interpretive a/destination.

CM: Yes, of course, so the general schema of sending is perhaps still accurate, but the problem is, and I don't know, I have no answer, but I wonder if writing is still the concern here. Which is the right word for that? Trace? Writing? Is it the right schema, because, in the brain there are no traces, as such; this is not the vocabulary which is used. When the computer is deciphering the patient's brain, it is not deciphering traces. It is deciphering configurations, forms, which change all the time. This is plasticity, this is about neural plasticity, which does not function as, you know, as a magical block or text. This is not the way it functions. So, does it change the general structure, or is it another version of it? I personally think it is a real change.

MMcQ: Whether that is true or not, the question this raises for me is what would the reader of tomorrow then make of *The Post Card*? If we imagine the reader of tomorrow, who may be in an entirely different epoch of destination, or non-destination, or something that looks like an epoch of plasticity, let's say, what might she recover from *The Post Card* in that context?

CM: Loss! There is a very strange motif in *The Post Card* of the Holocaust, of burning, of the disappearance of the archive. I would say this, the notion of total erasure; when I say that there are no traces in the brain, it is true that some neural configurations may disappear without leaving any trace. I think it would be this tragic motif of the total disappearance of the 'vestige', of the archive, something like that.

MMcQ: What then are the implications for philosophy of that epoch of plasticity? One of the lovely passages in the 'Envois' is the suggestion that an entire epoch of literature cannot survive the new regime of telecommunication and neither can psychoanalysis, philosophy or love letters. Why is it that philosophy cannot survive? We must be careful about what Derrida means by 'philosophy' in that sense, but why is it that philosophy cannot survive the process of transformation, and the regime of telecommunication? Or what might philosophy look like, would it still be philosophy?

CM: As you know, logos means 'gathering', keeping, preserving, so the idea that something may be lost, meaning may be disseminated, and maybe destroyed forever, with no salvation, no remission, this is anti-philosophical. This is absolutely contradictory with memory, logos, gathering, and preserving. As you know, even when Hegel talks about destroying, he talks about preserving at the same time, so what Derrida is talking about is the possibility of a total disappearance, total destruction, and this would be the end of philosophy as well. So as you said, philosophy has to transform itself, otherwise, in its traditional form it cannot survive its own destruction, because in fact, Derrida has compared deconstruction to philosophy's self-destruction; philosophy is destroying itself. It is not something like, 'Envois', destinerrance, etc. It is not something which would arrive, which would happen to philosophy; it is philosophy deconstructing itself.

MMcQ: So, we might say that deconstruction itself is the end of philosophy, or the end of a certain idea of philosophy. In that sense, the postal principle as it appears in Derrida, is an equivalent term for deconstruction; or is it something else?

CM: I think it is one of the possible approaches to it. I would not say metaphor, because Derrida refuses this term; it is not an image, a possible approach to it. If deconstruction means, first of all, the deconstruction of presence, then the postal principle is the very expression of that; nothing is, but everything is sent, so the authority of being is shaken by this sending structure. So, in that sense, sending, the postal principle, and deconstruction are one and the same. But, as you know, there are other possible expressions in Derrida.

MMcQ: Well, my next question would be, does something remain of philosophy in these ashes, this immolation, this burning, that is deconstruction? Does something remain that is irreducible? Accordingly, what should deconstruction be doing, if we can phrase it like that, in an epoch of plasticity after philosophy?

CM: Of course something remains, I think this is central to *The Post Card*. This is desire, the desire for philosophy, the philosophical desire and desire for philosophy. As you remember, he always says presence is deconstructed, but presence is what I desire. So, the problem in Derrida is not, well, philosophy is deconstructed so to Hell with philosophy and presence, etc. No, no, deconstruction is still very much enhancing the desire for what is deconstructed. We miss it. This kind of nostalgia, this kind of sorrow about the loss, melancholia, this is philosophical, this is the idea that it is impossible to do without philosophy, to do without metaphysics. We are over it, but we are not out of it, and this remains, and we are dealing with desire. That is why I think he is also talking here with Freud and Lacan about what desire is, and for me, he is talking about plasticity. It is just a way of re-launching, reinitiating this desire, and plasticity is the question of what exactly is plasticity desiring? Plasticity has desire for form; it is a way of re-elaborating a question of form, not of presence, but of form, without which philosophy is impossible.

MMcQ: One of the things that vexes me, or keeps me awake at night, is thinking about what the task, if you like, for deconstruction now might be? If we have understood, to a certain extent, the question of metaphysics, if we might even no longer be in an epoch of writing, and we might be somewhere else in fact, ten years after Derrida, what now should deconstruction as an institutional conjuration be doing? Is it something other than the legacy of commentary on the texts of Derrida?

CM: Yes, this is of course, a very urgent problem, I think that if deconstruction is not renewing itself, that is, if its central scheme—which is writing, trace, etcetera, destination, sending—is not, let's say, actualised, that is, made, or adjusted to our time, then we will have this endless commentary, and it will be a slow death. There will not be any other future than repetition, and one day or another it will end. It will stop, just like what happened to Lacan and Freud, outside certain sects where the thought is celebrated, it will cease to be vital. I think this is the real danger: that it would not appear as a weapon anymore. It will not appear as something dangerous anymore; it would belong to the past, just like Lacanianism; this is what has happened today with psychoanalysis. So something which is to be critical, which is to be dangerous, which is to be a threat to a certain amount of dogma, is becoming harmless, and I think this will happen to deconstruction if we are not aware that deconstruction must change without disappearing, and that there is nothing to lose in this re-elaboration. So what remains of it? I think that we now know that presence is deconstructed already, so we should change this motive, and stop trying in a text or in a philosophy to chase out what remains to be deconstructed. This is not what we should do. We should also give up this literary obsession in which literature has been the privileged field of enquiry in deconstruction. We should absolutely change the framework, we should change the vocabulary, we should change the structure, in order to save the critical force of deconstruction, which is never to accept anything as given, to make it vacillate, to make it shake on its basis, to put everything to the test. This is the only method. This is the only efficient method, the one Derrida has invented. We have to re-elaborate its critical—how do you say, '*tranchant*'—its weapon-like form.

MMcQ: If 'question everything' is the basis of deconstruction, or take nothing for granted, that also includes the text of Derrida, or the inheritance of Derrida, let's say. What should one do then in the re-elaboration of deconstruction, if one wanted to re-elaborate the *The Post Card* or the 'Envois' from the 1970s, how should one begin to approach it today?

CM: *The Post Card?* Radicalise it. Find what seems to be the most radical point in it. Which I think is the possibility of total destruction. The possibility of total destruction is always present in the text but at the same time something that . . . well, Derrida is perhaps not radical enough on that point, because the Death Drive in *The Post Card* and in the other text like 'To Speculate—on "Freud"', the Death Drive remains contradicted by the Pleasure Principle; something remains on the verge of total destruction but is not radical enough. Derrida is playing with total destruction all the time, but it is play. He says it is fiction. What is fiction? It is fiction, the fiction of total destruction. It remains a fiction, in a way. So, if I had to approach *The Post Card*, let's say, from today, I would, I think radicalise Derrida's position about the Death Drive.

MMcQ: Let's talk a little bit about that essay, 'To Speculate—on "Freud"', which seems to be a commentary on the 'Envois' as much as an essay on Freud. What does Derrida do in that reading of 'Beyond the Pleasure Principle'?

CM: In fact, 'Beyond the Pleasure Principle' is a question; the title is a question—is there something? Is there anything beyond the principle? Freud is trying to ask himself, was I radical enough? Is it true that the Pleasure Principle is *the* unconscious principle, or is there another one, another principle which would go beyond it, which would be more radical? As you know, this other principle is the Death Drive. Is the Death Drive, the drive to destruction, more originary than the Pleasure Principle? Is it a more originary law of the unconscious? This is what he tries to explore in this text with the spool, with the compulsion to repeat, etc., and in the end, in the last chapter, Freud says, to cut a long story short, no. In the end there is only the Pleasure Principle binding itself, but the pleasure principle remains the undiscussed major principle of the unconscious, and the death drive is, in a way, subordinated to it. In my opinion, in the 'Envois', Derrida is in a way theatricalising this discussion between two principles: that of pleasure and of the Death Drive. That is why in the 'Envois' you constantly have this interplay between pleasure, love, sex, making love, so many allusions to that, pleasure, etc., Eros; and on the other hand, this tragedy I was talking about, destruction, Holocaust, burning, dying, the Holocaust of the children, he talks about at a certain point. You constantly have this double-bind.

So, the question, if I could talk to him now, I would ask him: so in the end, what is your answer, is it the same as in Freud? Would you say at the end that pleasure is winning? In a way you have shown, just like Freud in his text, that there is only pleasure binding itself, and that in one way or another the Death Drive, self-destruction, total erasure, is always subordinated to pleasure? It seems to me that, yes, if we had to radicalise something today, as you asked me, it would be that. I would like to read once in my life a philosophy of total destruction. Derrida is the closest, but still something remains, this confidence in love, pleasure, etc.

MMcQ: That is just about the most difficult thing to imagine, what that might begin to look like, and yet it might be the only question worth asking on that very basis. I think one thing that is interesting to me about what Derrida does with Freud and the story of the *fort/da*, is the question of why psychoanalysis is so hung up on this obsolete technology. Yet Derrida, himself, is hung up on obsolete technologies, as well, and I'm wondering what might a new technology, which would go beyond the Pleasure Principle, look like. How could we think that now?

CM: Perhaps, this brain reading technology. Perhaps, this erasure of any distance between people, because there cannot be pleasure within this, without distance, it is impossible. This constant threat . . .

MMcQ: Would it be fair to say no pleasure without deconstruction? The pleasure must always be undoing itself from within. It might always be autoimmune in some way, to use that later term, borrowed from biological science.

CM: Yes, you are right, no pleasure without deconstruction. Perhaps, if we were able to intercept each other's thoughts, if these technologies were efficient, perhaps we would not have time for deconstruction. Perhaps, the very temporality of deconstruction would be eclipsed. This is the hypothesis elaborated by Thomas Metzinger in his book *Being No One*, which is a very technical, cognitive book, but it is very interesting. It is a total erasure of time and subjectivity, when it comes to brain reading.

MMcQ: And just as we have discussed, philosophy, or a certain idea of philosophy, may come to an end. What happens to psychoanalysis in this situation?

CM: Well, psychoanalysis was already very ill-treated by deconstruction. I think that even more than philosophy, psychoanalysis has to open itself to neurobiology, to be something like neuropsychoanalysis, otherwise it will just disappear. It needs to open itself to the possibility of a neural unconscious, or that is the end. I would not say that the kind of questions Freud and Lacan ask will become obsolete, no, but there is a change of structure and it is about destruction. Freud writes that the unconscious is indestructible, that no psychic region is able to disappear or to be totally destroyed, that something always remains. You see that with brain lesions this is not true. If you accept identification of the brain with the psyche, then the thesis of the indestructibility becomes absolutely arguable. So of course, psychoanalysts would say, 'Oh, but Lacan has talked about destruction and the Real, and the thing that is a total destruction within the unconscious,' but if we had time, we could demonstrate that this kind of elaboration on destruction is not adequate to describe what happens, for example after a lesion, or you have a neurodegenerative disease. Your psyche is really destroyed without the possibility of re-symbolising it, without the possibility of talking, without the possibility of writing, etc., and this radical destruction is what psychoanalysis has to take into account.

MMcQ: Let me ask about the subtitle of *The Post Card: From Socrates to Freud and Beyond*, this question of the 'beyond' is really what we have been talking about. What is involved in that beyond? What's the meaning of the '*au delà*'?

CM: If beyond has the same meaning as it does in 'Beyond the Pleasure Principle', it means, I remain obsessed by this, the death drive. Will philosophy, or deconstruction ever be able to elaborate something on that beyond, beyond pleasure, and even beyond desire? Will we ever be able to go beyond meaning, at all?

MMcQ: The beyond in the title is one of the terms to be discussed; it is not beyond Freud and Socrates, it is 'beyond' as a question.

CM: Yes, beyond as a question, definitely.

MMcQ: The way one might traditionally adapt or translate a book is to find a way in which (if you are translating from French into English, say) the English does the same sort of work that is taking place in French, but it has to perform as an idiomatic English expression and if you are adapting from a book to a film, you try to make the film reproduce the sort of work that the book does. So given that *The Post Card* is about this postal logic, which is at once a remainder and at the same time an absolute destruction, what might that look like in visual terms? How might you begin to translate that in the medium of film, or the visual?

CM: First of all, I would say, there is no translation without plasticity and what is valid in philosophy is also valid in other domains because what we are talking about is plastic and able to express itself in different languages. There is of course a frontier between the visual and the intellectual, or philosophical but at the same time this frontier is not rigid and there are equivalents. So what is it? What might that be in visual arts? Well, I think it is not an accident that cinema, and film in general, has become the centre of the philosophical reflection today. If you think of what Deleuze is doing, if you think of Rancière, and also of a certain Derrida, you know, the films he made, etc. Cinema has become the motif of a certain philosophical interrogation, and if I had to summarise what it is, which is not easy, I would say it is about consciousness. Bergson was the first one to show that cinema, film, was the closest expression of the flux of consciousness. When you are watching a movie you have the impression of watching a consciousness developing itself, you have the feeling of being in another consciousness, and Bergson says it is deceptive; the film is in fact cutting this consciousness, it is deconstructing it, and I think this deconstruction of consciousness is the very equivalent of deconstruction in philosophy; that presence and consciousness are never effective in cinema, they are always dislocated, fragmented. I would say that the visual equivalent of deconstruction would be the impossibility that perhaps we are experiencing at the moment in this filmed interview, of really not recreating what we are seeing. I think she [the director] has no access, direct access, in the way Bergson is talking about consciousness. There is no telepathy, it is not precisely a brain reading. Cinema is not a brain reading. That for me would be the very equivalent of what we are talking about philosophically. She cannot read in our minds. She is listening to us, but she cannot read within us, into us. The image is not, there's no superior ability to decipher somebody with an image, than with a text or a reading.

MMcQ: Can the visual, the cinematic, be a place in which knowledge is produced, in the way that that occurs in philosophy? Can film know things in the way a philosophical text claims to be able to produce?

CM: Well, I would not say it is the same thing, the same production of knowledge, but for sure, and according to Deleuze it is at the level of the production of affects, that the film is able to produce knowledge through affects, more than philosophy. So it is less through concepts than affects. I remember he has this passage, in 'The Movement Image', on the face and the close-up and when he talks about Eisenstein and close-ups on the face he talks about the face as the substrate of affect. In order to make us understand what he means, he compares it with what Descartes says about wonder, and he says Descartes has to speak about wonder, rather than the film, which is expressing wonder itself. It produces knowledge, the knowledge of wonder through what happens to that face. But I would not be able to describe it more because I am not a filmmaker myself. How is the filmmaker able to transform a surface, like a face, into a production, into a site of production of affects? I would say that the difference is there.

MMcQ: The question would be how we express the postal principle, or express deconstruction, in a way that is not merely a representation of a concept that already comes from philosophy. That seems to me one of the key tasks for a film such as this, to try and begin to do that kind of work.

CM: Godard has talked a lot about that. He says, '*ce n'est pas une image juste, c'est juste une image*'. I do not know if that makes sense in English—not an adequate image, just an image. So there is a play with the word '*juste*' in French, which means, at the same time, 'just' and 'only'. We are not trying to produce any authenticity with our images, but on the contrary, to deconstruct authenticity with images. But I don't know how they do that because I am not a filmmaker myself, but I am sure that the people who know how to deal with images are able to see what I mean. Like deconstructing authenticity, you are not trying to capture a presence; there is something else to be done.

INTERVIEW IV

'But I love literature . . . me too (*moi aussi*)'

J. Hillis Miller
UNIVERSITY OF LANCASTER, MAY 2012

Martin McQuillan: I want to begin by talking about passages in *The Post Card* in which you feature and what that might mean.

J. Hillis Miller: Well the first thing to say about them is that they are all absolutely true; they are not inventions, and I'll speak specifically about them in a moment. That is sort of strange because I like to think of *The Post Card* as a work of fiction, as a great work, a postmodern book, a great postmodern novel. That would not preclude accuracy, but it does mean that one has to be suspicious, throughout, of whether the things that Derrida says are happening actually happened. This would put that in question, because these are relatively unlikely episodes. It is the case, however, and I can attest, that when Derrida was at Yale, one time, I took him sailing in my little typhoon called the *The Frippery*. What Derrida did not know was that the small craft warnings were up and it was a little dubious whether we should have been out there. There were not all that many waves, but that really happened. And it really is the case that de Man and I used to go and pick Derrida up at Kennedy airport, and there was a kind of odd ritual that happened every time. Derrida would eventually appear with his large briefcase and a very heavy suitcase, I don't know what he had in there, and he would ask us to keep them for him for a few minutes, and he would say, 'excuse me, excuse me, excuse me, excuse me', and he would disappear and make a phone call. We assumed he was calling Marguerite, his wife, 'I'm safely . . .' but who knows? Because he never said, and then eventually he reappeared and we had great difficulty persuading him to let us carry these heavy objects. He wanted to carry them, struggle out to the car with them. So that really happened. There is a place I noticed just today where he says he was leaving after his stint at Yale for that year, and he said, 'Paul took me to the train station . . .' and it is true we did not drive him to the airport when he left, so that's undoubtedly factual. And the great episode of the visit to Joyce's tomb we made. I was teaching in Zurich one summer, he came to give a lecture there, and we went together to visit the tomb of James Joyce, which is right in the back of the cemetery up by the zoo. While walking, we walked back by a slightly different route and we came upon the tomb of Egon Zoller, '*Erfinder des Telephonographen*', he was the inventor of the ticker tape, and on his tomb is a ticker tape with the tape going across from one side to the other and it says Alpha, Omega. Derrida, who was working on *The Post Card* at the time, and on the general question of communications, stood for ten minutes just looking at that tomb, meditating about it. Neither of us had a camera, but I mailed a good, old friend of mine in Zurich, named Maya Hostettler, and said, 'Maya, could you take a photograph of that, of the tomb of Egon Zoller and send it to Derrida?' So somewhere in Derrida's papers is a photograph of that tomb. I am trying to remember if there are any other places where I appear. There is one memorable Derrida story about Yale that I remember, but I don't think it gets in *The Post Card*. Harold Bloom and I were going to have lunch with Derrida, who was staying in one of the residential colleges, Ezra Stiles, which is a modern-design building, Saarinen or something. There are stone steps going up to this residential suite that he had, and Bloom, who has published a fair number of books, as I had, but not quite like Derrida, we were going up these steps, and the closer we got to the door, the louder we heard the Derrida typewriter, like a machine gun: brrrrrrrrrrrr! I looked at Bloom, and Bloom looked at me, and we said, 'shall we interrupt him?' and we said, 'yes' thus putting a stop to whatever great piece of creativity. But I think the theoretical issue here is it is possible to read *The Post Card* with the idea that these episodes may have borne some relation to things that really happened but were not necessarily, strictly speaking, accurate. I think they probably are. When he says that 'I'm writing this on the train back to London from Oxford', I think that is probably where he was when he wrote it. So the question of where the very strict, pointillist kind of realism, shades off into fiction is a very hard line to find.

MMcQ: Thinking about these episodes in *The Post Card*, which may or may not be true, how then should we read the 'Envois' in terms of the history of literature? If it is literature, the first question might be, Is it related to the history of the epistolary novel? How should we think about it as a piece of writing in terms of what Derrida discusses in 'The Ends of Man', toward the end of that essay, as a new genre of writing, a new idiom of writing that would be something other than philosophy.

JHM: That is an interesting question; as you know, there is a very interesting passage in the 'Envois' which is very important to me in which he says, 'I met the other day the young American woman who is writing a PhD dissertation, and I suggested it to her that she write something on the telephone in modern literature, meaning modern, early twentieth century', and she said, 'but I love literature', and Derrida says, 'me too (*moi aussi*)', and then he says, '*mais si, mais si*'. That is hard to translate, because it means 'but yes', but also 'no', '*mais si, mais si*'. Then he goes on to say that an entire epoch of so-called literature, as well as psychoanalysis, philosophy and love letters (so he is very specific, on so-called, '*soi dite*', literature, philosophy, love letters and psychoanalysis) will come to an end, with the end of the print epoch with what he says is a new regime of telecommunications, and from that point of view, the political regime is not important. It is an interesting claim, a claim that the telecommunications regime beats out the political regime and you could say that the Arab Spring has been that, the cell phone was so important in this, you could say that it brought down those regimes in North Africa. The cell phone was absolutely essential to communication among people in Libya, but that's a pretty strong claim. I suppose it was probably Avital Ronell who went on to write a book about the telephone, a very good book; it was a smart suggestion on Derrida's part, Derrida knew Avital Ronell. So it would be in that context that you could say Derrida, on the one hand, is writing something which is an epistolary novel, there is a long tradition of that. On the other hand, he is writing it in such a way as to attempt to participate in that end of literature in various ways. So it is both continuous with the history of the novel and really a novel that is supposed to make novels impossible, or something. Why and how? He is very specific about that; it has to do with the tradition in novels, that the characters are egos, self-eidetical people who remain the same, who can be identified, and when they write letters, as in the letter from Derrida to somebody, there is a real recipient, a real singular sender. The novel really depends on that assumption, even quirks it, complicated as it is. It quirks it as a personality, an individual person, and *The Post Card* attempts to put that all in question, quite explicitly. At the beginning, in the preface, or whatever it's called, he says, 'you may distrust this signature'. The copy he gave me, by the way, he actually signed, so it says 'Jacques' up there at the top, and then there's a footnote that says, 'doubtless you are dubious about this signature'. He says, 'you are right, we are more than one (*nous sommes plusieurs*)', so there is a quite deliberate attempt, and it is theorized elaborately, to put in question this idea that the characters are selves, single selves, that there is a destined recipient of the post cards. By the way, it always seemed to be quite implausible that such long texts were written even on a stack of these post cards six inches tall. That is a part of it that I find dubious. So, it is both a novel and something to put novels at an end. I would add one more thing to that, which strikes me as important now. In reading *The Post Card* the range of telecommunications would strike one today as being very old fashioned. There is nothing in there but text written on post cards and telephone calls. There are typewriters and so on, but these are very antiquated technologies. Derrida never used e-mail, for example; he feared the invasion of privacy that would come, and it was quite a long time before he used a computer, not at the time of writing the 'Envois'. I think the texts, whatever form they had, were typed out. In the famous 'Martini Heidegger' episode, where the phone rings and it is an American graduate student probably, who says it is a collect-call, the operator says, 'We have a collect call for Jacques Derrida from Martini Heidegger', and Derrida says quick as a flash, 'I refuse'. He was not going to pay for this, it is a hoax, not a call from Martini Heidegger. I do not know quite what you make of that. Derrida was like my wife, who doesn't use e-mail but does use the telephone, and writes letters by hand. Derrida was, for reasons that he is quite explicit about, fearful, really fearful, of the new telecommunications, even the ones that were available to him. Later on you could not e-mail Derrida, you could send him a fax, but the fax machine broke down, and he never got it fixed. From that point of view, the technology of *The Post Card* is quite old fashioned, it belongs to a moment. On the other hand, all the stuff about the fifty-two characters, spaces, stuff left out, and other hijinks, the scrupulous dating, June 10, an often implausible number of things he claims to have written always on the same day (but he was a fast writer), all of that would correspond to certain features in what's called postmodern fiction. Postmodern fiction also uses extravagant typographical devices and so on. So, I would place Derrida halfway between the maintaining of a tradition of fiction that is dubious about its realistic referent and, at the same time, trying to write something which would put an end to novels, which would cooperate in the new regime of telecommunications. Do you know, by the way, can you tell me, are there any manuscripts of *The Post Card*, of the 'Envois' left?

MMcQ: They are in the Irvine archive; there are versions of it, and also the Egon Zoller photograph, along with a whole lot of things that he assembled, like photocopies of encyclopaedia entries about the post, and things he had taken from the British Library, and that—

JHM: Right, but not any of the texts with the missing passages; one would like to know what he left out.

MMcQ: Well I suspect he did not leave anything out, this is just a ruse. I suspect he never wrote them.

JHM: That is what I suspect too.

MMcQ: There is the essay 'Telepathy', which emerges as something that had been cut out of the 'Envois', but I suspect that is another deliberate ruse on his part.

JHM: I have taught this essay of Derrida's that I immensely admire and quite recently, actually, written about it, so that I know the textual stuff where he says, 'this was accidentally left out of the text, and I found the manuscript too late to incorporate it because the proofs had been made.' It sounds very implausible, but Derrida is always ahead of you, 'so as I know you will say this is a Freudian slip, that I forgot without forgetting', so you say, 'why, would he leave this out? This is great.' It is dated, pieces of it are dated, it is just like the rest of the text, and the only explanation I can give (although there might be various explanations) as to why he deliberately left it out, is that it makes or explains the technique of the 'Envois' a little too explicitly. It gives you a theoretical armature that is based on the telepathy, the ideas in 'Telepathy' so you can take the essay 'Telepathy' and use it as a way of reading the whole of *The Post Card* and say, 'ah, now I understand what he was doing because I read "Telepathy"', but I think he wanted it to remain inscrutable, and he says that over and over again. It is a cryptic, indecipherable text, out in the open, completely out in the open, but nobody is going to be able to figure it out. Also, 'Telepathy' is quite remarkable because it was written, apparently, over just a few days, in the dates that he refers to, and it's a very learned, wonderful, wonderfully funny account of Freud's ideas about telepathy with the typical Derrida ploy, which is also there in Freud, which he nails Freud on more than once. It is Freud saying, 'I do not believe in telepathy, my only access to telepathic experience is through my patients', like the male patient who calls him on the telephone in one of his telepathy essays, while at the same time Derrida is right that Freud really did believe in telepathy. He just knew that people would think he was not very scientific in believing that. It is the same ploy in Freud in the great essay on the uncanny, where Freud says, 'I've had no experiences of the uncanny, so I have to base my account of the uncanny entirely on texts', like Godivar or the Hoffmann story and so on, but before you get to the end of that Freud thing, a great essay on the '*unheimlich*', Freud is giving you two wonderful examples of his own experiences of the uncanny. One of which is being in the little Italian town and finding himself in the red-light district, and feeling this was not the right place for the great Doctor Sigmund Freud to be, so he tries to leave, and every time he tries to leave, he finds himself back again in the red-light district. He says it was uncanny. The other example that Freud gives is even better. He is in a train compartment and suddenly the door swings open and reveals to him, sitting across from him, an unkempt old man in a beard. Freud says, 'to whom I took an instant dislike'. Well it is his own reflection in the mirror of the door. So, it is a double and as you know doubles appear frequently in the uncanny. That theme of the uncanny and of doubles and of ghosts, no doubt with the Freudian provisos, threads its way through *The Post Card*, which keeps coming back to the question of ghosts. The general rule I think would be, for Derrida was, like Freud, a modern suspicious person, but he was also superstitious enough to know the best, quickest way to raise a ghost is to say, 'I don't believe in ghosts'. That is a dangerous thing to claim.

MMcQ: Could we think about literature itself, in the relation to this book, in relation to that passage in *The Post Card* about the epoch of telecommunications? As a Professor of literature who has had a distinguished career in the academy, I would like to ask you the question, have we reached that moment in which we are moving into a different epoch, one in which literature is now becoming less important?

JHM: That is a very good question. In fact I have given seminars here, and will give the second half of it tomorrow, that are, in a way, about that question: does literature still matter, in the old fashioned sense of printed books and novels and so on? I think too, one has to say two or three things at once, that Derrida probably also foresaw in *The Post Card*, ironically and contradictorily, there is no doubt, I think, no doubt that less literature is being read these days, than it used to be. Or the social world of printed literature is not quite the same. Why? It is obvious, because so many people now spend so much time on Facebook, sending e-mails, playing video games, computer games, and doing all sorts of other things than reading Shakespeare. So there is a gradual replacement of printed book technology with these new technologies that Derrida anticipated and feared enough not to enter into. On the other hand, huge numbers of Harlequin romances are sold every year still, and they're as printed books. One out of every four Americans in the year 2005, or something, admitted to having read a romance during that year. So the print epoch is not entirely over. I think one thing that has happened to it is a fairly rapid shift to reading in Kindle or some other eBook reader. I was on the airplane the other day, coming back from my annual Irvine seminars, in this case flying to Washington, so it was a long flight, and I walked down the aisle and a very large percentage of the passengers were reading. Eight out of ten of them were reading an eBook. I would say only 20 percent of them were reading actual printed books. As far as I could tell (it was a little difficult, awkward to bend over and say, 'by the way is that a novel you're reading?' but I did as best I could to look) it looked to me that they were not playing computer games, and they were not reading the history of the West, but they were reading novels, they were reading fiction. So, that would be a way of saying that literature has not died, it has simply been transported into this new medium. That would then lead you to ask, 'Well, what's the difference between reading *Great Expectations* in a book that I hold in my hand, and reading it on Kindle?' and that is a very hard question to answer. I have thought a lot about that. I started off assuming there must be a difference. I guess there are various specific things you can point to: the Kindle version is searchable, which the printed version is not, unless it happens to have an index. If you're reading a book of *Great Expectations* you cannot do that, it is an added value, it is a value for me doing literary criticism. My example of that is reading James' *The Wings of the Dove*. I was writing about that and it was online like almost everything else. I would not read it online, yet I am not hostile to it, or afraid of it, the way Derrida apparently was, but it is very difficult to make that transition. But, I got very interested in the word 'Oh!' or the expletive 'Oh!' There is a passage early where Densher is meeting Lord Mark and is introduced to him by Kate. The nobleman does not say, 'Oh, I'm pleased to meet you', he just says, 'Oh', and then there is a whole paragraph in which James says, 'it was not the "oh" of an idiot, a lot of expensive education went into that "oh"'; he explicates the 'oh'. So then I began to be interested in 'oh' to see if there were other cases where the 'oh' was used, and there are four or five of them. The climatic one is at the very end, where Kate says to Densher, 'I'll marry you in a minute if you can tell me that you're not in love with her memory', (Lily) and Densher says, 'oh, her memory'. I was interested in that 'oh' and how Densher caught the habit of saying 'oh', it begins to appear a couple of times earlier for Densher. So I was interested, had I missed any? They are very hard to find in a big book like this, I would have had to turn all the pages looking for 'oh'. But in a minute online I could look for 'oh'. By the way, I had not missed any, there did not seem to be any 'oh's that I had overlooked . . . and that is valuable as a use of the online version. But that is different. The other difference, and I am not sure that I understand this, would have to do with context. If I have a printed book in my hand, the context of it is other books, whether in my own library, or like Derrida's library in that film, or the Library of Congress or something. The context is the assemblages of printed books, usually alphabetised so you can find *The Wings of the Dove*, etc. An online book that I download from cyberspace has as its context the whole unimaginable complexity of the things that are in cyberspace, which is not a 'space', it is rather a way of taming cyberspace. I think it is not a space because everything is there at all times. All you have to do is put the URL in and you can get anything from anywhere. So you say, 'where is the online version of *The Wings of the Dove* located?' There is no answer to that because it is in servers all over the place, it is flying around from one part of cyberspace to another, and I think that makes a difference in the way you feel about its existence.

It makes a different community of readers, so I do not think literature is coming to an end. The other, final thing to say would be that you could argue that whatever you mean by literary or by literature, there is a huge amount of transposition of language, of uses that we normally think of as literary, into things like television ads. What do I mean by that? Well, we watch television news at night, and the news on NBC from 6:30 to 7 about half of that is advertising. So we see these over and over again, and I have started to get interested in how literary they are. They are very literary, if you mean what most people mean by that. For example, there is one that shows a little dog, rushing around with a bone, trying to find a safe place to put this bone, in the dog house, in a safe, he can't find his way into a bank, so he's very anxious about what to do with this bone. It turns out it is an ad for an investment company— very clever, and very funny. Then there is an ad, which is not so funny, for the American oil companies, coal and gas companies, in which this charming young woman comes forward and says, 'it is wonderful news, we have enough oil and gas and coal to last for a hundred years, there is no problem at all with sources of energy, etc.' What she does not say is that by using this stuff we are going to raise the level of the water at my shore-side property on Deer Isle, so I won't have two acres of beautiful shore property but two acres of plain flats and other disastrous things will happen. The actors for these things are either very charming young women or bearded scientists, intellectuals and so on; it is not the actual, I would say, somewhat sinister white men who own these companies and are receiving billions and billions of dollars from them, like Dick Cheney (Cheney was an oil man like George W. Bush). So, the one conclusion I make is teaching people to read literature in the old fashioned sense of printed books is a help in protecting yourself from television ads, which millions and millions of people watch, and other forms of lies that politicians are wont to emit.

Joanna Callaghan: I am trying to read *The Post Card*, I find it a sensual book, quite sexual, and I'd like to know what you have to say about that.

JHM: Oh yes; after all, it is a book of love letters. They are love letters in the literal sense in that they are an attempt at seduction, and they are often fairly explicit in their reference to that. It is not a dirty book. On the other hand, you are right, it is sensual and there are a lot of explicit sexual references, some of them slightly shocking to me. For example, the one in which he says, 'when I was an adolescent and used to make love against the wall', and you say, 'Really? Why are you telling me this, Jacques? I don't know that I want to know this.' So, whoever these love letters are written to, yes they are quite a sensual form of seduction. You might say one reason why he might have left 'Telepathy' out is because it does not seem to fit the love letter aspect of the thing. He keeps speaking in English, actually in the French edition, of 'my sweet darling girl'. There is a lot of caressing and all this compulsive telephoning, 'I just talked to you on the telephone, it was wonderful to hear your voice', etc. I would say he picks this up from the tradition of the epistolary novel, such as Richardson in English literature, more eighteenth century than nineteenth century, and indeed it did have a certain period that was earlier with Marivaux and Laclos. Those tend to be love stories and sometimes quite explicitly erotic ones, as in the *Liaisons Dangereuses*, so there is a tradition of doing this in the epistolary form. What is the point of the epistolary novel if it is not a love story? What is the point of a love story if it is not fairly explicitly sensual? So Derrida certainly picked that up and follows that convention, but I have no doubt and it certainly seems fairly straightforward to me, that on the other hand, as you remember, these letters, though they seem to be addressed to somebody in particular, 'my sweet darling girl', whoever this is, that is they are part of the theme of adestination. As he says, if you or I, as readers of the love letters, intercept the love letters, we are made into recipients of them, so that in a way they are an attempt to seduce us. And though there might be a difference between male and female readers, it is not entirely clear that such a distinction can be made.

Joanna Callaghan: and Derrida himself was a very attractive man . . .

JHM: We put ourselves, male or female, in the position of the recipient of these letters, and he theorizes about that. He says I write a post card to somebody, somebody intercepts the post card, and says, 'oh, this is meant for me, I am the person to whom this is directed', and in this book I give you another example of this in action. Yes, he was very attractive and both to men and women, though, so far as I know, he was entirely heterosexual. I watched him, and it is of course customary in France to kiss men as well as women. He kissed my wife when we would meet, on the cheeks, whereas he and I never kissed. However, I witnessed him kissing people like David Wills, and so on, and men in a perfectly innocent kind of way. One of his great seminars is a whole seminar based on the single phrase '*je t'aime*', and how do you get two hours just out of the phrase '*je t'aime*'? Well, he could do it; the difference between 'I love you', which is plural, there is no distinction, as in French, '*je t'aime*' etc. The general theory is parallel to what we are talking about, that '*je t'aime*' is not a statement of fact, but it is what he would have called a performative. It creates both love in the person to whom you are saying 'I love you' ('*je t'aime*') but also creates me as the person who is in love. So it functions as a speech act, according to Derrida. But in the course of these two hours, in a big room full of people at Irvine, a hundred and fifty people listening to him (graduate students, faculty, people who came from all around, other campuses and so on, a lot of people) at some point he said, 'of course, there's a distinction in speech act theory between use and mention'. Mention would be, what I've just being doing, just quoting '*je t'aime*', not using it. Using it would be to actually function as a speech act, and Derrida at some time in the course of these two hours said, 'I'm only mentioning this, but of course, you cannot make that distinction' and I realised that this was two hours of a kind of collective seduction of this whole room full of people because he'd said, '*je t'aime, je t'aime, je t'aime*' over and over again. It was quite remarkable. And Derrida was certainly very aware of his seductive presence. I do not think he sat down and said, 'and now I will write a seminar in which I attempt to seduce an entire room full of people in a big lecture hall'; nevertheless, it functioned that way. But of course, I have just been citing, I have not been using it. Right?

MMcQ: There are three other things that are said to end with the epoch of telecommunication: psychoanalysis, love letters and philosophy. So what happens to love letters, psychoanalysis and philosophy?

JHM: Yes, that is interesting. He does not say, except for psychoanalysis. Psychoanalysis is easier to explain. You do not even have to take for granted that Derrida always knew what he was talking about, but I think he means with love letters, as a means of seduction and maintaining a love relationship through love letters, written by hand on a piece of paper and sent to your beloved, that the medium is absolutely necessary in this case. That would be one I would put in question, because there are lots of love letters that are now written by e-mail, not to speak of Facebook and other things, that sometimes lead to successful sexual and marriage relations. My son met his present wife online, by e-mail. They started corresponding by e-mail and that led to a very happy relationship and to marriage, so they exchanged love letters by e-mail. So I am less worried about that, but I know what Derrida meant. Psychoanalysis is easier to talk about because he mentions it. What he means is that psychoanalysis depended absolutely on a certain stage of postal communication. These fellows, the early Freud and his disciples and so on, had to communicate by letter or by telephone, and Derrida wants to say that psychoanalysis as a science or discipline depends on that technology. Psychoanalysis would have been very different if he, Freud, had been able to communicate to Ferenczi and the rest of them by e-mail. That is the claim and he does spell that out in the text 'Archive Fever'. Philosophy? I do not know. I guess he meant the same thing, for what we normally think of as philosophy is, like literature, dependent on the epoch of print. Hegel and Kant and so on, were only able to philosophise in a way that depended on their work being published in books that people read, and so on. In this way the whole institution of philosophy depended on existing in a print epoch. I do not know what that means for Plato and Aristotle, since they did not have printed books. He does not comment on that.

McQuillan: I am not sure about that, because he would be far too sophisticated about the idea of what philosophy was to think of it just in those terms. I think here he means metaphysics or the tradition of Western metaphysics. What comes to an end would be Western metaphysics, or the idea of metaphysical closure is somehow opened up by a new relay of telecommunications.

JHM: So there would be something else, there will be something, but it will not be philosophy. He does refer to this in other places, of Heidegger's fear even of the typewriter. For Heidegger, philosophy was something you do with pen in your hand, and as soon as you start using other prosthetics—but of course the pen is a prosthetic device too—you were not doing philosophy. Philosophy has to be done by hand. Nietzsche used the typewriter, from quite early, he was not afraid of the new thing. Heidegger was afraid, so Derrida caught from Heidegger a little bit of this anxiety. Why could there not have been any phone call from Heidegger? Probably because in that hut up in the Black Forest there was no telephone, there was nothing but pen and ink and note-books, etc. Derrida moved, as you know, from handwriting (the early manuscripts are in quite illegible handwriting) to the typewriter as in my story of Bloom and I interrupting his typing; then from a little por-table typewriter finally to the computer, a little portable Mac. He used the most primitive word processing programme, 'MacWrite'. Nobody uses MacWrite anymore! When he used to give me disks, which I still have, of his seminars, beginning from about the time he started using the computer, they were in MacWrite and I had to use my translation thing to get them into Word so I could read them. Obviously, I do not have MacWrite. Derrida, as you know, was very generous both with his books and with his manuscripts, I think because he had this fear that the stuff would all vanish, that there would be a fire in the rue d'Anjou. So, he distributed the stuff around and I was one of his depository libraries. I have a pretty complete set of things, including discs that go back to '92, or something like that. There was a long history of that. Whenever I would have to miss one of his seminars I would say, 'Jacques, I will have to be away during the lecture, could you give me the seminar that I am missing' and he would very generously do that. Then when he started using the computer, I didn't ask for this, but he would give me in a disc the whole set of seminars for that year so I would have them. The last time I saw him, when he broke off his seminars at Irvine to go back to Paris where he was diagnosed with the cancer, the last thing he did was to give me the disc with the last two years of *The Beast and the Sovereign* seminars, which was a nice gift because he was only beginning the second year of those seminars at Irvine since he was always a little behind the Paris sequence. He did not have time to do the seminars in Irvine but those last seminars are amazing. They are the ones about *Robinson Crusoe* and Heidegger. Heidegger's basic concepts of meta-physics and *Robinson Crusoe*, what else? It was typical of Derrida. Why *Robinson Crusoe*? Because the seminars were supposed to be about the animal, the sovereign human above and the animal below. A graduate student at Irvine had given a paper about animals and *Robinson Crusoe*, so Derrida who had not read *Robinson Crusoe* since he was a child, reread *Robinson Crusoe* and amazing things happened as always happens with Derrida. But it is not about animals, it is that section in *Robinson Crusoe* about solitude, absolute solitude. It is a most striking solipsistic passage where he picks up Crusoe's isolation on the island and says, 'from my selfhood, to any other selfhood, there's no bridge, isthmus, connection, transport, I am condemned to total solitude, I will never communicate with anybody else my inner self.' He also picks up from *Robinson Crusoe* the fear of death because there is a passage where Crusoe feared to be buried alive; that really worried Derrida and it led to an impasse, as you know, in Derrida: the question of whether he should be cremated or buried? It is a total impasse, because if I am buried, I may not be dead. I may be underground but wake up and find I am not dead, like Mary Baker Eddy, the founder of an American pseudo-religion, who had a telephone in her tomb, in her casket, in case she woke up and could call up to say, 'Hey, I'm not really dead'. So you say, 'Well, you should be cremated', and this was interesting to me because this would not worry me about being cremated, but he said 'if you're cremated' (and he imagined ashes being scattered) 'then there's no place, no locus to mark where you're buried'. So, either way, you've had it. Actually he was buried as far as I know, not cremated, although I have never visited his grave. So that part of that final seminar is not about animals at all. It is typical of Derrida that he would deviate rather than following up with the student. The graduate student was what led him to reread *Robinson Crusoe*, but he did not do the obvious thing, which is to say, 'now I will tell you about animals', he went off on a tangent and did his own thing.

Joanna Callaghan: Would you like to tell us about your own copy of *The Post Card*?

JHM: The copy I have Derrida gave me. As his books came out he gave me copies, and I think my copy of the translation is also a gift, but the French one does have his signature. It has, as with all the books he gave me, an inscription in the front, very politely dedicated to both me and my wife, 'Hillis, Dorothy, your affectionate friend, Jacques' or 'toujours, Jacques' and then a place, Laguna Beach perhaps, and then a date. These are very valuable actually, and I've got a whole wall of them. I used to kid Derrida and I would say, 'Jacques, in my old age, I am going to live on proceeds of selling these books, one by one'.

INTERVIEW V

'The rubric of narcissism that no one escapes'

Samuel Weber
MONTPARNASSE, PARIS, APRIL 2013

Martin McQuillan: Perhaps we could begin by reflecting on the background to the 'Envois' and the context in which you appear as a character in the book.

Samuel Weber: Well, you know the question of background is sometimes hard to delimit. I first met Derrida eleven years before the date of the 'Envois' when Peter Szondi and I invited him to Berlin to give a lecture. I had been reading him for a few years before that, so there was a long prehistory to that, and then part of the closer background was that I had been invited that year by Lacoue-Labarthe and Nancy in Strasbourg as a visiting professor to help them organise a conference there on genre at which Derrida presented on 'La Folie du Jour'. My role was to help them invite people from Germany and the United States to this international conference. So one of the people that was invited was Kittler, who took advantage of the occasion of Derrida coming to this conference to invite him to Freiburg, which is close by, an hour and a half or so from Strasbourg. That was his visit. We drove to where he gave the lecture, and met Kittler, who was to become a leading figure in German media theory, and so on. There is not much of the conference that is shown in the 'Envois', it seems almost like a kind of private visit, but there was the background of a large international conference to which he alludes briefly. Two points, I guess, are interesting to mention. One that strikes me in the second passage that I read is his anxiety about time. Jacques Derrida was always very anxious about time in general and one of the forms that took was that he was always very worried about missing a plane, missing a train, and so on. So in this famous drive to the train station, in Strasbourg, if I remember correctly, we were there in plenty of time, but we got caught in a traffic jam and Jacques was ready to jump out of the car and run the last thousand metres because he was so sure he was going to miss his train, which seemed to me a bit exaggerated at the time. However his characterisation of me was not wrong, and ever since then and the publication of *The Post Card*, I tend also now to come very early to train stations, appointments, and so on. I am the one who is waiting for others now, usually, but at the time, he was absolutely right about that. His relation to time I think is very interesting because it involved an anxiety of finitude and of urgency, and immanence, and really he turned that into an enormous productive power in his writing. Anyone who has not really read his work and only gets it second-hand can easily miss out this sense of urgency that was extremely deeply felt; it was really visceral, with Jacques Derrida. I think that was one of the reasons he also responded so strongly to the earthquake situation in Southern California when he was there. As anyone who has gone through that knows that you have a sense of time as being totally fragile, totally discontinuous; you never know if you're going to be there two seconds later, and so on. He was very moved in all sorts of ways by that, and reflected on this question of fear and trembling, the earth trembling, as well as himself trembling, so that is the first thing that occurs to me there in connection with that. The second was the secret, and again he is absolutely right, one of the fascinating things about the *La Carte Postale* (and I'm not the first to have noticed this) is the mixture of reality and fiction, of veracity and imagination, if you will. Many of the details as far as I know them are quite accurate, but they are given a spin, as it were, which takes them out of the realm of self-evidence. In other words, reality is there, but what is reality? And in a certain sense, I think what troubled and fascinated Jacques Derrida was to be in the situation of being ventriloquised, as it were, at the conference. In other words, at very short notice, I had to give summaries in German, not my native language, to be sure, of his French, which is not the easiest French to interpret or to translate. As I remember it, I really got into it. As he writes, the audience was very much hanging on every word that I could give them, responding to it and I certainly exploited it to the hilt, much to his discomfort, as he found himself sort of an outsider at his own lecture because of the question of translation.

MMcQ: You are one of many characters who appear, Hillis appears, and Paul de Man, Jonathan Culler and Cynthia Chase appear, can you recall the first time you read the 'Envois' and realised that you were in it? When you realised that your personal relationship with Derrida, that secret, had been put on display?

SW: I'm afraid not, perhaps because it was so traumatic to discover myself exhibited in this way, a mixture of being flattered and being shocked such that I actually do not have a direct memory of a first time. But certainly it was not only the first time, once you are in that situation there are many other times that follow and it becomes impossible to distinguish the first time. I can only imagine being both shocked and flattered, playing however small a role in this epic, this epic text. But just to come back to this question of the secret, I guess it is worth mentioning that whereas most people tend to think of the secret as something hidden from view, Derrida was playing here on something Lacan also plays on in his 'Purloined Letter' essay, that secrets are even more interesting when they're visible. In other words, when you see something but you do not really know what is going on, or, what it means and so on: whether it is a language, or whether it is a face, or whether it is an activity. This remains for me one of the important experiences in reading both Derrida's work and, in particular, the 'Envois'. This is the point that he keeps making about the post card being open to read for the public and at the same time remaining somewhat secret. I often think today in the age of the Internet this is what happens when people send e-mails without thinking, that the e-mails can easily be made public to an unlimited audience, it is a little bit like the post card, amplified a million times, almost globalised. Potentially unlimited.

MMcQ: The 'Envois' is a kind of departure in Derrida's writing. There is nothing like it before; previously there have been very rigorous philosophical essays, that become book collections, but are really stand-alone essays. He is really an essayist and so this is a total departure. There is nothing really that much like it again in Derrida's writing. So what is he doing with writing and genre, since that was the nature of the conference, in this text?

SW: It is true that this form is unique in his work, but if you look at his work as a whole, I think you'd feel that he is always extremely aware of his relationship to an audience, what I have called at various times, what I consider to be a kind of 'theatrical dimension'. He is always very aware of performing, even in the earlier work, where he is very cautious in academic writing on Husserl, for example, but there is still this sense of fascination with theatre—the act of writing as an act of exposure, an act of communication that necessarily escapes the intention of the person's communication, and in some way also conveys more than that person is actually aware of. I think there is a constant effort on his part to play with that situation, although it definitely takes different forms. I have always felt his texts after *La Carte Postale* seem to be more theatrical, I have the feeling he is using the situations, colloquiums, conferences, et-cetera, as occasions to stage something. In French we say a '*mise-en-scène*', to stage a scenario, and it involves both an enormous amount of control and in some sense, also the recognition that the greatest control cannot prescribe the way it is going to be received or the effects that it will pro-duce. I think that is where you find this mixture of play and enormous mastery in his work, but you are absolutely right, this is very unique. I can only think of *Circonfession* as a text that is extremely personal and autobiographical, but in a different way that does not remain confined within the private sphere. He was in some ways an extremely private person, but at the same time he was aware of the fact that this privacy was going to be very public as well. He also had what his son, and also some of his students, called a kind of 'exhibitionist' flare to him as well, which was shocking. It was shocking from somebody coming from an academic, not to say philosophical, background indulging not just in confessional forms but in a kind of erotic play, as he did in the 'Envois'. I think the erotic dimension is very important; that is why I find the very end when he talks about pleasure and rhythm, going beyond pleasure and the idea of a certain type of rhythm, quite interesting.

MMcQ: But how far can it strictly be called autobiographical writing?

SW: Certainly as long as one takes the word literally, the '*autós*', the self, this is a function of the writing and is not just a function of the writing expressing itself as it exists above and beyond, before and independently of the act of writing. I would say that throughout his whole career he was fascinated by the '*autós*', by the *auto*, whether it is the auto-affection in his discussion of Husserl or autoimmunity later on and what he called 'ipseity' with the deployment of this self. But what is unique about it is the way in which he connected that fascination with a process of networking, of articulating, of signifying, of communicating, of exposing in ways that very few people had done before, or have done since. Also, in other words, that through the experience of what seems to be a private self, or an 'autós' or certainly a singular self, with its own distinctive history, there are elements offered for people, or others, with their own singular or distinct histories to participate in, to tap into, as it were. So there is a kind of communication that goes on that presupposes separation, but it does not involve identification in a way that would abolish differences. It seems to be, for me at least, what is most impressive and imposing about his writing.

MMcQ: One of the things I'd like to talk to you in particular about, given your own interests, is the place that Freud plays in the 'Envois', in that whole history of relays and the encyclopaedia of the post that he develops throughout the work. Psychoanalysis and Freud seem to have a particularly prominent, even privileged place within that, so why is Freud so significant in that history of the post?

SW: I could answer in part by picking up on this question of singularity. In other words, what Freud develops, in some ways parallel to what Derrida is developing, is an approach, a method of writing and of thinking that is not directly, or simply generalisable. Freud does not start a science of Freudism, as Marx could be conceived to do with Marxism, and Derrida is in a somewhat similar situation because of singularity of his writing and of his thinking. It is not something that can be fully, directly generalisable, taught, or passed on, the way you could in certain sciences or disciplines. What fascinated him, particularly in 'To Speculate—on "Freud"', is the question of a name, the proper name, making a name, making a name for oneself by invoking a different term. In the case of Freud, instead of 'Freudism' you had 'psychoanalysis'; in the case of Derrida, you had 'deconstruction' for a long time. Although I think he had an ambivalent attitude toward that process, but he recognises it as probably strategically necessary in order to continue the reach and development of his thoughts. At the same time, he analyses all the traps that are involved in this process of making a name for oneself. But that is I think in part, perhaps, one of the underlying factors, that drew him to Freud and to psychoanalysis. Freud found himself in a situation that I think Derrida also found himself in, which was that of trying to rethink the relation of the singular, of a singular experience, to commonality. So for example, in the 'Interpretation of Dreams' one of the things Freud starts off by saying, in contrast later to Jung, is that you cannot hope to have a key to dreams. Even though you can analyse symbols and so on, ultimately the analysis of each dream has to be idiomatic, has to be based on an encounter with a specific configuration of the dream. If you see water, you cannot just say that this means libido, or something like that. I think Derrida was in a somewhat similar situation, with the necessity to communicate, teach and interact, and make claims of generality (he certainly was not interested in just developing a private experience). Obviously he had huge ambitions, but at the same time insisted on the singularity, the singular source of those experiences. This is something that I try to conceptualise *post facto* with the idea of the encounter, which you find in so many other terms and uses by Derrida. You have a singular trajectory encountering factors and elements, occasional elements, and out of that comes something that can be shared but in the process of being shared has to be transformed. That is why I think Derrida on a certain level perhaps, in contradistinction to Freud, in part, probably also felt himself attracted to having things in common with Nietzsche, in not simply being the founder of a school. So whenever he talked about deconstruction he tried to avoid it being called an '-ism', deconstructionism. He tried to suggest that it is a process that is going on independently of what any one writer, including himself, could contribute to it and so on. Obviously there are all kinds of inconsistencies and problems of which he was aware of to think about under the rubric of narcissism that no one escapes, and that in a way he tries to dramatise, and theatricalise in this text, in order to allow it to demonstrate elements that can be shared, that do not just go back to an ego. Singularity for Derrida was always an aporetic concept that involved communication with others, and never just a self-identity. It is not the same, therefore, as the individual.

MMcQ: There is a particular question in *The Post Card* about psychoanalysis and technologies of communication, particularly psychoanalysis and the telephone, for example. It seems to be connected to a reading of *Beyond the Pleasure Principle* and the '*fort/da*', do you want to unpack some of that? What is happening in 'Envois' around psychoanalysis, and its development, and both the question of the postal principle and the question of the pleasure principle?

SW: Yes, I think the postal principle at that point was one way that Derrida was trying to think this difficult connection of singularity and generality. In other words, how do you establish communication, commonality, on the basis of an experience that remains to some extent irreducibly singular? So, here is where the unconscious comes in, and the problem of the institutionalisation of psychoanalysis, and institutionalisation in general, which often tends to operate under a logic of subsumption of the individual under the general, and so on. It is precisely this problem that always fascinated Derrida, but I think that he was trying to think alternative models too. So, the postal system was, you know, at that point one such model of a communication that on the one hand, reaffirms distance, reaffirms separation (you do not send a post card usually without having that kind of separation) but on the other hand he was also interested in the fact that post cards, not always but often, are exposed to view. I mean obviously you can send post cards in envelopes, that makes it a bit different, but he was fascinated by the way in which the post card, which was a communication from one singular being to another, had to travel through a network that exposed it to others and exposed it also to not arriving at its destination, to winding up at the dead letters office, and so on. All of these factors introduce a kind of discontinuity into a circulation so that the question of identity, and the relation of the singular to the general, becomes perforated, and becomes a function of circulations. Today we might call it 'networking', but there are problems with that term.

MMcQ: Can we have a look at those essays that come after the 'Envois'? The book as a whole is a collection of different genres of writing and writing from different moments. For example, the section 'Freud's Legacy' is itself a character in the 'Envois'; it is the lecture that he is working on and that he finally delivers. Maybe start with 'To Speculate' and take us through the argument of 'To Speculate'. What is the significance of that text in Derrida?

SW: It is hard to say, it is hard to summarise, because there are so many aspects to it. For me it is one of the most impressive essays he ever wrote.

I am not going to give you an objective summary of everything that is in the text, but rather some of the elements that have impressed me the most. I would point to the very complex relationship, for me at least, in the question of authority, of how Freud, having established a certain system around the pleasure principle, then revokes it. In a certain sense the *'fort/da'* is not just a game of alternative presence and absence, but a game where presence and absence are superimposed on each other. It is not just an experience of a child on its way to mastering its relation to the world, but it is also a structural experience. I think he felt that Freud was always going through this, and Derrida was confronted with it as well, so there was constantly this question of the revocation of authority. I remember how he describes Freud at the end of the essay *Beyond the Pleasure Principle* suddenly saying, 'people ask me do I really believe all this nonsense about a death drive, and drives and so on, all these things that cannot be directly clinically observed and measured and calculated'. Freud then responds in various ways, I remember him saying that 'the question of belief is not really decisive here, whether I believe it or not, or whether it really happened' and Derrida picking up on that saying that this is the point where Freud does not give an answer, a clear answer, after he has unsettled what seemed to be the stable basis of his system. Derrida says that at this point, for the group that had gathered around Freud and the school of psychoanalysis, it is not as if Freud's authority becomes any less, but in fact it becomes even greater, because of Freud being intangible, as a result of him not giving a positive answer to this question of whether he believes it himself, or not. This strikes me as one of the most fundamental gestures that you can also find in Derrida's deconstructive writing, which has often frustrated many readers. At the end you do not come up necessarily with a thesis or a lesson that you can sort of carry away and that you can use to guide you through the uncertainties of the future, but in fact you come up with a challenge, with a tension, what he would call later on an 'aporia', which you have to work out, and which also functions as much at the level of feeling as it does at the level of intellect. I think there is a reassessment of the relation between thinking and feeling that is implied in all of this. I think he is showing us Freud as far from being a dispassionate observer but totally implied in the scenes that he is describing, but then generalises that to say that everyone in writing is implied in some way in what they seem to be describing. That is why for me the notion of staging, of mise-en-scène, replaces the notion of observation or description in the work. Everything that you would describe in an other, you are in some sense projecting and describing in yourself as well, but as Derrida writes this, it is not set up as, or from the basis of, a reductionist de-masking. Rather it is a dynamic, because you can never escape from it; at least, that is the suggestion. So, in that sense the *fort* is the *da*, and the *da* is always *fort*. They coincide rather than opposing each other and that is why at the end of the essay he comes back to Nietzsche, the great questioner of opposition and the structure of metaphysics, and tries to pick up the notion of rhythm instead of the notion of oppositionality in thinking difference.

MMcQ: One of the parts of 'To Speculate' that I particularly like is the reading of *Beyond the Pleasure Principle* in which Derrida is reading the story of the '*fort/da*' and Freud says 'this was told to me by the grandfather', but it turns out Freud *is* the grandfather, and Derrida goes on to talk about using autobiography to found a science, only to then to find out that the autobiography was fake.

SW: This is it, I do not think that Derrida simply stops at the point of saying 'ah ha, we've unmasked Freud as a fraud' because he claims to be describing something objective and in fact he has actually 'created it' or projected it. Derrida feels that this is a fundamental, inevitable characteristic of participation in anything. It is a little bit like, or roughly equivalent to, the Heisenberg uncertainty principle. You cannot measure the position and momentum of a sub-nuclear particle, because the process of measurement itself has forms. You can do the one or the other, the process of measuring is part of that which is being measured and there is something of that in Derrida's work. The challenge that leaves for me is to try to examine what it is that can be shared, what is it that one can have in common and communicate within this process, rather than saying 'Ah ha, we've caught Freud', or Derrida for that matter, in a kind of 'petitio principii'. I do not think Derrida had a notion of objectivity that would be cut off, or separate or ascertainable totally, from the process of its articulation. I think that is the whole point of his emphasis on language and textuality.

MMcQ: There is a lot in that essay, as you describe it, which seems to be suggesting that Derrida's project finds a lot of echoes in Freud, or in Freud's development of psychoanalysis, but the relationship between deconstruction and psychoanalysis is also one of critique. Here and in other essays by Derrida, he is critical and reads perhaps a certain Freud against a certain Freud. So what would be the nature of that critique?

SW: Well I already suggested that at one level of his discourse Derrida never tried to present deconstruction in the way Freud tried to present psychoanalysis, as something that could in any way be seen as something that is an independent discipline or science and so on. In other words, I think he felt that Freud was naïve in that way. To what extent Derrida succeeded, I think is another question but I think he had a critique of the system that was perhaps more radical than Freud there. I think deconstruction owes an enormous amount to a philosophical tradition of which Freud was very suspicious and which Freudian categories did not always acknowledge, in the way that Derrida acknowledged a certain philosophical tradition as an indispensible prerequisite of the work he was doing: Husserl, Heidegger, Kant and so on. Although both Freud and Derrida shared at some level a critique of metaphysics, it was a very different type of critique. I think that Derrida felt that you could go much further criticising, or deconstructing, the axioms of a logic of identity, or the logic of presence, by precisely mobilising the resources of philosophy, rather than in some way or other trying to build this critique on a discourse of observation. Now, Freud's psychoanalysis is not a discourse of observation, either, simply, but it is certainly more dependent on a clinical moment than deconstruction would be. I think you are absolutely right, as a matter of fact Derrida once told me that he writes in order not to be psychoanalysed, and I could really believe that because his writing did have that to some extent. It was a process of, a kind of, continual self-analysis. At the same time, Derrida was both drawn to psychoanalysis as one of the institutionally marginal questionings or interrogations of a mainstream, systematic body of thinking that had been institutionalised, and in some ways wanted to keep his distances from it, for both intellectual and emotional, personal reasons. Nevertheless, one of the things with this book is that he brings those two things together. He brings the 'Envois' which is his self-staging of a certain erotic scenario, together with a discussion of Freud. In so doing you really have the tension there in a discussion of psychoanalysis that would seem to be largely theoretical but which also then brings it back to autobiographical elements and so on in a scenario which is autobiographical, but in the sense we were speaking of before, the 'autós' is really a function of the—and the 'bio' is a function of the—writing, as a condition of it.

MMcQ: Another of the essays included here is the essay 'Le facteur de la vérité', the reading of the Poe short story, which for a long time became a really significant text in the exposition of deconstruction, primarily because it seems to be a critique of Lacanian psychoanalysis. Could you just unpack that a little bit? What is happening in that essay, why it's such a significant essay?

SW: I think for two reasons. On the one hand, and I was very much a part of this myself, many of us at the time felt that despite whatever personal polemical differences there could be between Derrida and Lacan, there was also be a great deal of commonality in their projects, at least for me, based on an attention to language and performance. In both cases it is not just accessory, or instrumental, but a constitutive medium of thinking, so that, in other words, a relation of theory and practice that included linguistic performance, theatrical performance was essential. It was all the more interesting, given the polemical opposition of many of the followers of each of the figures, to see Derrida take a position toward (to actually try to deconstruct in a reading of) Lacan. This in many ways had a lot to do with what he was doing around the question of exposure and the open secret and the erotic background and so on. I always felt, coming from an Anglo-American literary training, that Derrida in his critique of Lacan demonstrated his sensitivity to literary problems precisely by focusing on the narrative framing, the position, again the authority position of the analyst. In playing on the word 'dessein' and 'destin' at the very end of the quote, Lacan's quote from Racine, or he is quoting Poe quoting, we have the difference between, on the one hand, organising interpretation around the notion of destiny, which is also familiar as a Hegelian and a kind of Heideggerian notion, '*schicksale*' or '*geschickt*', which is not the same, and on the other hand, the 'dessein,' which was more textual and involved the actual implication of the narrator in the narrative. That is the critique, at least as I remember it; I have not had a chance to reread it so recently, but Derrida's critique or deconstruction of Lacan has a lot to do with a question of authority. What is an authority? Can an authority be developed by remaining above and beyond and outside the scene it is commanding? Or does authority have to deal with its implication in a scene that in some sense, it is co-creating? This is, as I remember, a key difference, or point, that Derrida focussed on, and for many people, at least those coming from a literary background, this was very familiar. This is partly because of the whole literary motif of the unreliable narrator, which, interestingly enough, in literary criticism had really not been extended to the critic. In other words, there was an established criticism of unreliable narrators, but there was very little on the critic himself or herself being involved as an unreliable narrator. That, for me at least, as somebody who worked with texts of both Derrida and Lacan, was ultimately the difference between the two. Lacan seemed to me to be presenting himself as what he called a 'guide', he often used that term in the *Ecrits*, to help people confront uncertainty. Whereas it seemed to me that the Derrida was very much a question of staging uncertainty in different ways and not presenting himself, not directly at least, as a guide. Whether, indirectly or not, deconstruction functioned that way is another issue, but at least that seemed to me to be the contention of Derrida. That is why this essay can fit into the whole complex of texts in *The Post Card* where it is always a question of how authority is constituted, given its dependence on language.

MMcQ: You have done extensive work on Freud. You wrote a book that is actually cited by Derrida in the footnotes, even though it had not been finished when *La Carte Postale* appeared. Do you want to say a little bit about what you do in your book with Freud?

SW: To some extent, what I have been describing here I tried to retrace in *The Legend of Freud*, how Freud starts out by trying to establish a certain scientific objectivity to observation, but then quickly allows himself to be drawn into a process in which the idea of observation becomes very problematic, and he acknowledges that. It is really much more of an interpretative involvement that he is dealing with rather than an observation as we find the empirical sciences. I tried to retrace that and tried to formalise that, using the German term that Heidegger had also actually used, '*auseinander setzung*', which in French they translated as '*explication*'. In other words, the idea that whatever you postulate is postulated in interaction with the other and the result is a centrifugal movement, '*auseinander*' in German also means 'to scatter' as well as, literally, 'out of another'. It is an ordinary word that exists. I tried to show how Freud likes to work with oppositional categories, but these oppositions tend to break down, and he then he has to find other ways of dealing with matters. One line of thinking that I have continued to follow, even today, many years after, is the status of anxiety in Freud's work. Recently, I have published an article on the Uncanny, an interest in Freud that I shared with Derrida, in which I tried to say that Freud writes the essay on the Uncanny as a last ditch effort to domesticate and integrate the problem of anxiety which he had been concerned with from very early on. He had thought this was a question which would be able to deal with the pleasure principle, and which after (when he moves beyond the pleasure principle) returns to with a vengeance. I am still working on that, but I think it unsettles the Freudian conceptuality, so I tried in my own way, in some ways very influenced by what I had read of Derrida at the time, to try to get at the driving factors in Freud's work that could not simply be contained in a systematisation, the way psychoanalysis is often considered. What I learned from the experience of working on Lacan, and above all the Lacan reception that I later on found in the United States when I returned there from Germany, was that people are really very much in need of guides. They want 'führer' and they want terms they can hold on to. They want terms that can survive the fragility of singularity and that give them a sense of being able to navigate securely in an uncertain world. The more uncertain the world, the stronger the need, and I think that has partially been one of the reasons why so much of these impulses of early post-structuralism and deconstruction have had an increasingly hard time in the academy as the social conditions of life become more and more precarious, as people have more and more need of certainty and less and less tolerance of uncertainty and tensions.

MMcQ: Derrida writes in the 'Envois' of the secret pleasure of you and he sharing Jewish jokes. Tell us a joke, Sam.

SW: Derrida claimed, I think it was in *Mémoires: Pour Paul de Man*, that he was not very good at telling stories. That really surprises me because I found him a very excellent joke teller. I am very bad at telling stories, but I think I can maybe remember one that he told me. It is short, a

Jewish joke. It is about an Orthodox Jewish family, the son is getting ready to be bar mitzvah-ed and they ask the son, 'What would you like as a gift for your bar mitzvah?' The son thinks for a minute and says 'a Yamah'. And the father, mother say, 'What? A Yamah?' The parents did not want to show their son that they did not know what this meant so they went to the Orthodox rabbi and they say, 'We asked our son if he wanted something as a gift for his bar mitzvah, and he said he wanted a Yamah'. And the rabbi said, 'a Yamah? What's that?' So the parents say, 'Well, we don't know either'. The Orthodox rabbi bit the bullet and went to his colleague, a Reform rabbi, who he thought might be closer to what the young people are thinking these days. And he said, 'The son of one of our temple, is being bar mitzvah-ed and he says he wants as a gift a Yamah, do you know what a Yamah is?' and the Reform rabbi says, 'No problem, 'Yamah', it's a Yamaha, it's a motorbike'. The Orthodox rabbi says, 'Oh thank you so much'. And the Reform rabbi says, 'Can I just ask you one thing?' The Orthodox rabbi says, 'Sure'. So, the Reform rabbi asks, 'What's a bar mitzvah?'

This is a very un-politically correct joke by Derrida. *Voilà, ce tout.* That too will wind up on the cutting floor.

INTERVIEW VI

'It is called "deltiology"'

David Wilson
LUTON, UNITED KINGDOM, JUNE 2013

Martin McQuillan: Let's begin by talking about the history of the postal system in the UK, dating back to the earliest organised postal system.

David Wilson: Well, I suppose the first organised postal system was set up by Henry VIII when he appointed his 'Master of Posts'. It was of course largely due to royalty and the landed gentry wanting to communicate with each other; this was certainly not open to the public. Mail was often delayed, and Henry VIII was not pleased about this. His items were not getting through, so he introduced the idea of there being some sort of date put on letters (letters in the general sense, not letters that we recognise today) so that you could tell whether mail was, in fact, being delayed, but it was a difficult task. People did not always put dates on letters. By the late seventeenth century, post became a little more organized. We use the word *post* today, but in fact, that refers originally to a place where the horses could be changed on their journey from one town to another, a changing post. That is where the origin of the term *post* comes from. It was slow to develop, partly because it was expensive. It was expensive because any items that we would think of as letters today had to be paid according to distance travelled. So, for somebody to send a letter thirty miles, it might be the equivalent of half a week's wages. It was very slow to catch on.

MMcQ: What begins to accelerate the growth of the postal system?

DW: I suppose it was the fact that more people needed to communicate that charges came down, and you also have to bear in mind, it was not the person sending the letter that had to pay for it; rather, it was the person receiving the letter who paid. For centuries families had lived in the same town or the same city; when people were spreading to different parts of the country due to industrialization, the only way they could easily communicate with each other was by post. So, it became essential to have a postal system.

MMcQ: When does that change, that it is no longer the person who receives, who pays, and it is charged to the sender?

DW: Well, it was in 1839 that Roland Hill made a proposal that there should be a universal payment for postage. That it should be the same amount, irrespective of distance, irrespective of the number of sheets of paper involved, and with the introduction of what everyone knows today of the 'Penny Black' postage stamp, one penny which would take your mail anywhere in the country. There was a changeover period, whereby people had the option of paying that penny in advance or not paying it. The penny black was your receipt that you had paid, and if it went through the postal system without prepayment, the recipient could still see their letter but only if they paid double the amount. So, it became more the norm that you paid in advance.

MMcQ: Just to go back a stage, when was the first public postal system introduced into the UK?

DW: By that I assume you mean when the postal system was not re-stricted to royalty, or the landed gentry. Well, you have to bear in mind, the ability to write a letter, to become literate was a very slow process as well, and I suppose we can relate this to the education system, when people in general were taught how to write. Previously, in your village there would be a lawyer or somebody of high note who had learned how to write, and they would write the letter for you. If they were writing the letter for you, you were dictating it for them. This meant that you could not really do anything that would be personal. So, as more people became literate, and they were writing about and between themselves, the number of letters needing to go through the post increased tremendously, and in 1840, with the introduction of the penny postage, millions of letters were being sent daily.

MMcQ: So, by the beginning of the nineteenth century, you have a universal postal system in the UK, and it is quite normal for ordinary citizens to be sending things by post.

DW: That's right, and it was one penny, for one sheet of paper, folded, because envelopes had not come in common usage yet. One penny for one sheet of paper, any distance in the country; tuppence for two sheets of paper, providing it did not exceed a particular weight, and for mail going abroad there was a much higher rate, of course.

MMcQ: And by this time, the general post office had been founded?

DW: The term *general post office* had been in existence for a longer length of time, it was based in London, as you might well expect. 'Royal mail' is another phrase that came about, because it was the prerogative originally of royalty. Even today, you will still see the remnants of 'royal mail' on all our pillar boxes; we have the royal crest, it might be 'EIIR', 'GVIR'—if it just has 'GR', then that's George V; it couldn't have been any other George, because George IV was well before the system evolved. So, really from 1840 onwards, we see the postal system, very much, as we still have today. Postal workers had a very distinctive uniform. They had to go on parade in the morning, to be inspected before they could carry out their duties. Imagine that today!

MMcQ: What does the growth of the railways do to the post?

DW: The growth of the railways had a very big influence because it meant that mail could be travelling around the country very quickly indeed, and in some ways, in the late nineteenth century, mail was actually travelling at a faster rate than it does today. The difference being, of course, there was not the volume, and one can find examples of mail, clearly postmarked on a particular date in London, perhaps addressed to, let's say, somewhere in Switzerland, and in those days, the letter would have a receiving mark (in other words, when it arrived in the town, the destination town, it would cancelled once again) and one can see that it had arrived the following day. Now that was largely due to the railways.

MMcQ: What is happening in the rest of the world at this time in terms of postal systems?

DW: Well, in terms of postage and stamps as we think of them today, Great Britain was the first, and that is the reason why Great Britain is the only country in the world that does not have the name of the country on the postage stamps. After all, when they were introduced, it was not anywhere else. However, it was very quickly recognised that this was a very efficient system of giving a receipt of prepayment and it was not long—shall we say the first ten years, up to 1850, certainly by the 1860s—before many countries, worldwide, had their own postage systems, modeled on the British system.

Very often if a letter was going abroad, it would have, apart from the postage stamp, a little hand stamp attached to the letter with the letters 'PD' which stood for 'paid to destination'. So postal authorities in non-English-speaking countries, for example, would recognise that the correct postal rate had been paid for its destination, although the currency might be quite different. To ensure that British stamps, for example, were recognised as being the genuine item, whenever a new design of a stamp came out, copies of that would be sent to all other countries in the universal postal union. They would be cancelled with the word 'specimen', for example, so that the postal authorities abroad would recognise them as being genuine. In this way it was not necessary to have different stamps of different countries.

MMcQ: A question arises from that—the prepayment has been made somewhere in London, and the post card or the letter is sent to Switzerland, say, but the 'invoice' [*envois*] has not been paid to the Swiss postal system. At this stage, what is in it for the Swiss to still deliver the letter, for which they have received no payment? How can there be a universal system of post in which the post has been paid somewhere else, but is delivered by another authority?

DW: It's reciprocal. So in the same way as items originating in Switzerland, to use your example, we accept them in this country; you might argue, what's in it for us? It is a universal, postal union that recognises each other's system. I believe the universal postal union came into place around about the end of the nineteenth century, 1874, founded in Berne, Switzerland. It was essentially set up so that every signatory to the UPU would recognise each other's postal system.

MMcQ: So, that creates the reciprocity across the world. That is a systemic underpinning that changes the way in which the world works entirely, all of a sudden. Rather than delivering items by hand, or having somebody delivering things thirty miles away, you have a worldwide system of reciprocity for the exchange of mail, which underpins modern development.

DW: It does, and you have got to think of what that means if you ask the question, what is it that the postal systems of the world have done for social development? Obviously, it is a tremendous amount. It means that—remember this is before electronic communication—communication is available to the masses. You could communicate with members of your family across the country. In the case of post cards, you could exchange information; for example, this is what this holiday location looks like, so travellers abroad would always send a post card to members of their family. You would have people, say, who were interested in architecture visiting one particular country who could now communicate that because of a picture post card. One could learn a certain amount about fashion of the time, dresses for example, because these were always portrayed on post cards. Photographers of the time had a field day producing post cards. You could go to a studio in a town, have your own photograph taken, put onto a card, and that could then be posted to members of the family. I am just thinking of the British scene, but I am sure it would be true throughout the world; in a similar way the postal system has a lot of positive aspects to be accounted for.

MMcQ: The postal system is a form of mass communication. Email is as well, it is essentially the same thing. At its height, if we have reached its height yet, what was the volume of post flying around the UK at any one time?

DW: I believe the post office will tell you that typically they handle something in excess of seventy million items per week. Obviously, when it comes towards Christmas there will be a peak, but seventy million items a week is the average. Nowadays, it is recognised that because of the Internet, social networking and so on, the volume of personal mail has decreased quite a lot, but on the other hand, commercial mail, or what many people think of as being junk mail, has increased. One of the reasons why it has perhaps increased, and this is not generally known, is that whereas members of the public will pay so much for a First Class or a Second Class stamp, a commercial organization actually pays less per item. So this is why you might receive an item with what appears to be an underpayment—why am I paying 50p, when it says 46p, for example. So, commercial mail has perhaps increased; personal mail has decreased. As a philatelist, I could say it's rather dire because whereas you can go down to a post office today, a main post office, and have your own stamps printed on the spot, some people, some purists say they are not postage stamps. However, it serves the purpose, it is still a receipt for payment. I suspect that probably within twenty to twenty-five years, the postal service as we recognise it today will either be in a completely different form or it will not exist at all, particularly as Royal Mail has lost the monopoly. [The Royal Mail in the United Kingdom lost its postal monopoly on 1 January 2006 and was later privatized by the Coalition government on 15 October 2013].

MMcQ: What is the cultural significance of the Royal Mail losing its monopoly?

DW: I do not know if I can necessarily answer that accurately; mail is still delivered through our letterboxes through Royal Mail, but there are a number of other companies nowadays who have taken on the job of sorting mail itself. But for the last mile, so-called, it is handed on to Royal Mail for delivery. If you look at a lot of mail that we receive today, it will say on the envelope 'delivered by the Royal Mail', but in fact it may have been a European company, such as TNT (three different European companies are actually responsible for all the handling up to the last mile) and that 'last mile' usually means up to that last sorting office.

MMcQ: So, the reason why the postal system may, in fact, die out, is simply because of the lack of personal exchange going on? Because it all happens by telephone or email that volume of messaging is just disappearing?

DW: If you needed to send an urgent message twenty-five years ago, and it was not possible to use the telephone for whatever reason, you could take a letter down to your post office, and pay a supplementary fee for what at one time was called 'express mail', and it would arrive that much sooner. Today, you can pay something in excess of £5 over and above postage for special delivery, and it would be guaranteed to be delivered by 1 PM the following day or, by paying a little more, by 9 AM the next day. On the other hand, you can, through your mobile phone, or the Internet, or Skype, or any of the other social networks, you can contact somebody instantly, and that is where the postal system is losing a lot of its custom. Telegrams, for example, do not exist anymore. Yes, that was a form of sending messages very quickly. You paid by the word, I believe, and that is why you got very stilted messages; unnecessary words were omitted because you paid by the word. I think the last telegrams that existed in this country were the so-called 'greetings' telegrams; somebody was getting married, or a birthday, but I believe that was 1960s or early 1970s when that was phased out. It is really a question of economics.

MMcQ: Let's talk a little bit about post cards because they are a unique form of 'envois' or sending. What are the origins of the post card?

DW: I suppose one could say that the origins of the post cards go back to the eighteenth century, when people attending a dinner would sometimes leave what we might today think of as being a business card, or visitor's card. It would have their name and address on, perhaps they might sign it, and there was nothing more to it than that. It was not sent through a postal system, as such. But the idea caught on, and it was in the 1870s or the late 1860s in the Austro-Hungarian Empire somebody came up with the idea of having a larger card, larger than a visitor's card, to send through the postal system. It would be much cheaper than a letter, because it would be open; anybody could read the content. And the idea caught on so quickly that by 1870 in this country the post card as we understand it today, in its very simple form, came about. On the first of October 1870, in London alone, there were well over a million of these post cards used on the first day. So it must have been publicised in the newspapers of the day, and it just mushroomed very quickly. These were pre-stamped—this was the important thing—so you could send a post card for half the postal rate. They were pre-stamped for a halfpenny. They were blank on the back and on the front was the space for writing the address of the recipient; on the back you wrote your message. These kinds of post cards are known as postal stationery. On the other hand, the picture post card—perhaps the kind of post card we would see if we were visiting Brighton, or the seaside, or a foreign country—on one side it would have a picture and the other side was limited to the address only. Therefore, if you wanted to send a message, you had to write over the picture itself, or around the margin, which of course was not very satisfactory, because there was not very much space to write. It was not until the early twentieth century, I believe it was 1902 or 1907, that the rules were changed, whereby the side that did not contain the picture was divided in two halves. One half was for your address and one half was for your message, but these post cards became very popular, very quickly.

MMcQ: The message on a post card can be read by anyone as it passes through the postal system or through the sorting office. What kind of issues does that throw up?

DW: I would imagine that such issues did not actually come about until the post card was being delivered, because the postmen and women would perhaps not have time to sit down and read what somebody else had written. If we are talking about British post cards the message was probably only about the weather when you were on holiday. However, such issues did arise among more wealthy people, living on Estates, where perhaps they did not handle their own mail immediately after it had been delivered to the correct address. It would be the butler or one of the maids who had access to their master's mail, and of course they could read it before handing it on. This is where a controversy might arise, because it could be personal; it could be the master had a mistress somewhere who was writing to him; there are all sorts of things that could arise from that. But it was cheaper; this was the point. Somebody could now send a post card for a rate that was cheaper than the ordinary rate, and it served, and suited the masses.

MMcQ: What sorts of developments then follow in the history of the post card?

DW: Well, one of the developments was the so-called 'reply paid' post card. If you were writing to somebody, and you wanted a reply back straightaway, there was a thing called a reply-paid card. It was essentially a two-part post card—the two halves attached, either by a strip of linen or one piece of card that was perforated down the centre—and the re-ply part was already prepaid. It was an encouragement to get your reply straightaway. Somebody would not have to go out and purchase stamps, or whatever. The other thing was that post cards became acceptable for sending abroad, again at half the standard letter rate. So, we had this rather strange situation towards the end of the nineteenth century where the postal rate to send a letter to France, for example, was tuppence half-penny, but you could send a post card for a penny farthing and it's the only example of a farthing used in postal circles in Great Britain.

The idea of the pre-stamped message endured for some time. The last examples of pre-stamped stationery are only a matter of years ago, not necessarily on the post card, but you had aerograms (air-letters); they were pre-stamped. You had certainly within Queen Elizabeth's time quite a number of examples of postal stationery where the items are pre-stamped. I cannot think at the moment of there being any existing examples. I think it was the aerograms were the last ones to be pre-stamped, and they are being phased out now. Now you buy a post card and you put a stamp on it, so it is the same price as sending a letter. This is because in the 1960s when we had the introduction of the so-called 'first-class' and 'second-class' rate. The post office will tell you that for first class they will guarantee something like 95 percent of those items will arrive at their destination in Britain the following day. Second class, they say two to three days, although in some cases, it arrives the following day as well. So you have the choice of how quickly your item of mail is sent through the system with first, or second class.

MMcQ: This is interesting because before the 1960s it would seem that innovation within the postal system was geared towards introducing an ever-faster means of delivery. With the consumer choice that comes with first or second class we have a two-speed system with only one route for express delivery. While, as you say, the instantaneous nature of SMS texting, for example, may result in the physical post card disappearing altogether.

DW: If you go down to a holiday resort in the summer, you will see, as you walk along the promenade, large numbers of stalls selling post cards of that particular town. The mere fact that they are on sale does not mean that they are being used. I suspect that this is one area where the number of post cards being sent has decreased, and is not likely to increase again for the reasons that electronic communication is far quicker and the younger generation cannot go anywhere without their iPhone, texting the person walking even twenty yards behind them. But at the same time you can go to the National Gallery, say, and in the shop of the National Gallery, the entire collection is there in the form of post cards. In this sense people might now be collecting the post card rather than sending it. This is another matter altogether. Post cards, after stamps and coins, are probably the third most collectable item universally because you can depict so many different things on them. It may be a copy of the *Mona Lisa*; it may be a copy of a particular item of ceramics; it could be a picture of a particular building. It will not be long I suppose, maybe it has already happened, that some of the newer buildings in the London skyline, I am thinking of the Shard, for example, will appear on post cards. People will collect these if they have a particular theme: it may just be insects; it may be birds; it could be anything. They are collectable items, and a very small percentage of these, I would suggest, ever actually go through the post. The term for post card collecting, it is called 'deltiology'.

Joanna Callaghan: If you came across a letter but did not know about its origins, what sort of information could you garner from the postmark and stamp?

DW: A postmark is going to determine where and when, by date, and often by time, a particular item entered the postal system. Now some postmarks are extremely scarce—they may only have been used for one or two days—perhaps at an exhibition somewhere. I can think of an example in my hometown here of a postmark that was only used for two days and that is extremely rare. The reason why it was only used for two days is that the regular one broke down and so an emergency one was used. I can think of mobile post offices that used to visit agricultural exhibitions. There used to be, up in Scotland, on the Clyde, steam paddle-ships, which had a post office onboard. In the early twentieth century it was fashionable to go for a trip on one of these paddle-ships; if something was posted on board and received that postmark, then that is a very collectable item in itself. We also have examples of where British stamps have been used in British post offices abroad. One example is where stamps of one country can be used in another country, and perhaps the only way you will know that it has been used abroad is because of the postmark. There was a British post office in Constantinople, for example, as well as post offices in Malta before Malta had its own stamps: the list is quite long. So, postmarks, themselves, can tell you a lot of information.

On the other hand, stamps would give it away, because every country has to have its name on its stamps. It may be in its own language, but it will be there as the name of the country, with the exception being Great Britain. As to the letter itself, the envelope may not give you any clues, unless there is something printed on that envelope in another language. But there again if it was something in French all that would tell you is that it came from a French-speaking country, not necessarily from France. So the stamp will tell you and the postmark, if it is clear.

MMcQ: Tell me a little bit about how the dead letter office works.

DW: As far as Britain is concerned, the so-called 'dead letter office' is actually a large warehouse in Belfast. An item of mail might be undeliverable for any one of a number of reasons; it may be the building no longer exists, but the person sending the letter did not know that; it may be that it has been incorrectly addressed; it may be to a number in a street, and the street exists but the number does not exist. Any item that cannot be delivered and does not have a return-to-sender address on the outside, will then be sent to the dead letter office in Belfast, where a large team of postal workers have the task of trying to find out where it can be sent back to (if there is an address inside and they have the authority to open it). If there is not any means of identifying where it originated from, it is dealt with, according to the post office, 'by the appropriate means'. Now, the appropriate means may be that after three months, it will be shredded. If, however, it contains an inclosure, it might go to auction if it is something that is valuable. It might also be confiscated, and I can think of examples in the past where (not so much in a letter) but in a small parcel or packet that contained a firearm, such items would not then be posted onwards. If the items are not claimed or traced within three months, they are usually destroyed, but the operatives in the dead letter office in Belfast would claim that a very high percentage of what they receive and have to deal with, are successfully returned to the sender without an additional amount levied. Additional amounts are levied if an item is underpaid or not paid for originally at all. It used to be the case that whatever the deficiency was, double that deficiency would be called for. For example, if the postal rate was 10 pence, and no stamp had been put on at all, you as the receiver would have to pay 20 pence to accept, to receive that letter. Nowadays it is a set fee, plus the missing postage.

MMcQ: I am interested in postcodes.

DW: The first postcodes were actually a long time ago, when it was decided that London should be divided up into regions. When I say a long time ago, I am talking about the Victorian era, when, geographically, London was divided up into North, South, East and West and then the individual areas, so you would have North-West, North-East, South-East and South-West. The North-East region was done away with quite some while ago, as indeed was South. So the city was divided up into regions and it was found that mail could be sorted far more efficiently by people using those London postcodes. So much so that this spread to Glasgow, Birmingham and Liverpool and other main cities. Nowadays, of course, we see a development of the British idea of postal codes that have been used in Germany, in the United States, where they refer to them as 'zip codes'. It was back in 1959, I think, when the postmaster general of the day suggested that we develop a system in the whole of the UK, partly because postal sorting was becoming mechanised. Norwich was selected as the town where this experiment would be carried out, and all addresses in Norwich were given a code of NOR, representing Norwich, followed by a two- or three-figure numeral. This was shown to be very efficient indeed. So, a second town was chosen, Croydon, and they were given the letters CRO, for Croydon. From this we developed a system that today we have a specific pattern of postcodes, where every post town is given one or two letters followed by one or two digits. That is for outgoing sorting. For example, Luton might have LU and then LU1 and LU2 and so on. Then there is the inward part of the postcode, which consists of a digit and two letters. That has now been established for quite a while for every address in the British Isles. When I say every address, not necessarily your individual house, it might be a string of ten or twelve houses in one street, on one side of the road, before it changes to the next ten or twelve, or if you are a business that has a vast quantity of mail every day, you might have your own individual postcode.

Now postcodes can be used for insurance purposes. Insurance companies will determine, for example, that your premium on your car insurance, because you live in postcode XYZ, is going to be much higher as the crime rate for stealing vehicles is very high in this postcode area. We hear of people speaking of 'a postcode lottery', if you live in the 'wrong' postcode, you may not be entitled to certain drugs by your local health authority and so on. In another postcode, you may be entitled to them. It is an artificial barrier, very often. Some people favour it, while some people say, 'Oh, I have been disadvantaged'. House prices, for example, can be linked to postcodes, rightly or wrongly. So, nothing to do with the postal system, but they have been used in this way.

MMcQ: While the postal system for the delivery of material or physical letters may die out in the future, or might look very different in the future, the importance of the postcode grows more and more significant.

DW: That is a very interesting question. If there is a postcode, but there is no post attached to it, would the country be divided by some other arbitrary identifier? Possibly, I don't know, but as you can understand, postcodes came about for other reasons, as a means of increasing the efficiency of sorting and delivering mail.

FILMING DECONSTRUCTION/
DECONSTRUCTING FILM

Jonathan Lahey Dronsfield

I.

A scene in Safaa Fathy's film *D'ailleurs, Derrida*, at once both simple and 'normal', indeed perhaps over-determined in its signification, in which Jacques Derrida is shown posting a letter or post card into a post box, is voiced-over by Derrida saying that writing is a betrayal for which "he cannot but [he walks straight towards the camera] ask for forgiveness . . .". We cut to footage of a close-up of Derrida much younger, turning to face the camera, faking a laugh, before theatrically resuming the turn of the head, the voice-over continues, ". . . for the perjury which consists in writing, in signing". This shot follows on immediately from a sequence of Derrida writing by hand at his desk at home, voicing his worry that by writing he erases the singularity of the reader or the addressee, that even the most singularly addressed remark does this, that as soon as one writes to someone secretly 'there, I love you, this word is meant for you alone' the uniqueness of the intended reader is lost, denied, wounded. Another cut, this time to Derrida leafing through a manuscript, between the pages of which are letters, addressed envelopes. Those in the know will notice that it happens to be *La Contra-allée*, written with Catherine Malabou, a book on what it is to journey and journey with. Derrida continues, "I no longer address such and such a person, I address anyone", and finally we cut to a sequence of Derrida posting what he posts into a yellow letterbox. These short scenes, totalling one and a half minutes, on the mark and structure of writing, referenced to the sending of a post card, we might say stage the problematic of Derrida's book *The Post Card*.

In his *abécédaire* to the film Derrida says that these scenes illustrate his writings on *adestinerrance*. The film needed a postman of truth, and the Actor is this postman (the capital letter is Derrida's, a capitalisation on the distinction between Actor and Author). And I am too, he says, a counter-postman. As one or other of those 'I's that I am in the film will tell you. The Actor knows me, and the card that we are talking about. What is written on this card by the Actor, or by me, and to whom? But nothing is more inappropriate than the word 'illustration', he says—for reasons that we will discuss later in this essay—because this image becomes the gesture of the Author signing the film, by which Derrida means the director Safaa Fathy. The addressees of the film and what the film addresses to them are indeterminable, yet its sender is not. She is all too determinable; she is the director. Moreover, the film is inextricably a self-portrait of Fathy.[1] She signs the film because she edits it. Derrida the Actor can betray the film in what he says in the film, and betray his addressee in what he the Actor says in the film, but the director, the Author, remains determinable.[2] Yet no words were ever suggested to him by the director, Derrida says. Derrida characterises himself in the film as an Actor, an Actor divorced from himself as an 'I', an actor made up of many 'I's, other 'I's, 'I's as others, others who displace him, a divorce to which the film stays faithful in allowing him these multiple 'I's. Thus the Actor plays many parts in this film, parts which started 'in' him well before the film, parts the 'symptoms' of which he acts. But Derrida would not have been able to play these parts were it not for the discontinuous, wandering, ruptured and essentially adestinal *way* of the film, achieved in how it was cut and edited. And because Derrida did not know in advance where the film was going or to whom it was addressed, he could not see the film and was essentially blind to the parts he played. Thus did those parts become possibilities. But the 'symptoms' Derrida refers to will themselves be 'signed' by the filmmaker's *own* symptoms. Therefore between the two, the truth of the film, if there is any, will involve the betrayal of what is acted, and no one's, symptoms will be freely or fully explored.[3] But this dispossession and displacement of self is surely a necessary condition of filmmaking, whether or not that film is 'on' a philosopher who philosophises those very matters. A film on Derrida, or on a text by him, ought not to reflect Derrida.

II.

One translation of the title of *Tourner les mots* is 'roll the words'. The essential task, it seems to me, when making a film of a philosophical text, is how to 'roll the words', how to shoot the words of the text cinematographically, how to inscribe into the screen the words from the book, but not as a book. Whether they be uttered by the philosopher acting 'himself' (*D'ailleurs, Derrida*), or voiced by an invisible narrator (*Derrida*), or intertitled (*The Ister*), or filmed 'on the page' itself (*Disturbance*)—and we will come back to all these works—the task remains the same: how to inscribe words of philosophy? How to graft the written word onto video? How to shoot the words without allowing them a discursive authority over the film? How to make of the words of philosophy something filmic or aesthetic, without reducing the film to an illustration, and without utilising mimetic substitution or presupposing its veracity? How to make the film philosophical without reducing philosophical texts or ideas to captions or legends of the image? In short, how to achieve the aesthetic without negating or sacrificing the philosophic—and *vice versa*? Not to fall back on the presuppositions of representation, and at the same time not to be simply 'against representation'. The great era of non-representational thought, of which Derrida's works are among the most exemplary, was not 'anti-representational', or not simply or straightforwardly that; it put representation into question; it questioned representation as the destiny of thought.[4] What is 'beyond representation' is not outside of representation; it is *in* representation. The point is to think representation not as some indivisible and unified 'sending', as he takes Heidegger to do—and this is why representation is unrepresentable: 'the essence of representation is not a representation' he says (after Heidegger's 'the essence of technology is nothing technological'), 'it is not representable, there is no representation of representation'[5]—but to think it in its dissemination, its divisibility, its multiple sending, its *différance*,[6] and to think it in terms of what is other to it, to think the otherness of representation not as something we can put before ourselves as something outside representation, a conception in which the frame still plays the governing principle, but to think the otherness of representation, as 'inventions of the other' in representation.[7]

Representation presupposes that the world is prior-constituted as visible, and that it is the visibility of the world that representation can render present, make present again in the form of a picture framed and put in front of the subject by the subject. And with representation, the subject, says Heidegger, places himself there, as the scene of representation, as if he himself is on stage.[8] Derrida will develop the 're-' of representation, its making present *again*, in his notion of spectrality, the organising principle of much of what he says about cinema. Ghosts do not come; they come *back*. As Derrida remarks in Ken McMullen's film *Ghost Dance*, cinema is 'the art of allowing ghosts to come back'. 'Come back' [*reviens*] is at the origin or end of every 'come'.[9] If we are talking about the representation of a philosophical text, then we might say that a representation would render present again, in the form of a visible picture, what it says. But what a philosophical text says is as much a matter of the unsaid as it is of the said. Both Heidegger and Derrida take this as their point of departure. Derrida is paraphrasing Heidegger when at the beginning of the film *D'ailleurs, Derrida* he states that 'whatever I may say here and now in this short time . . . it will be selective, finite and, consequently, as much marked by exclusion, by silence, by the *unsaid* [*non-dit*], as by what I say' [my emphasis].[10] However, Derrida equates the unsaid in this film with the invisible.[11] Why should the unsaid be co-extensive with the invisible? Are not ghosts the material of the unsaid? The problem is how, in film, or aesthetically, to draw out the unsaid of a text of philosophy without falling back on the metaphysical presuppositions of representation. If we are talking about Derrida's *Post Card*, then the answer is: deconstructively, which is no 'answer' at all. But it will be only by countersigning the *Post Card* in such a way that it brings into question its, film's, 'own', presuppositions regarding how it represents or renders visible that of which it speaks that the film will stay 'faithful' to the text, even if in doing so it draws out what the text does not say in such a way that it begins to deconstruct it. This would be an act of love on the film's part.

'In *The Post Card*', Derrida says in 'Negotiations', 'the signatory of the dispatches says somewhere, "In the end, I deconstruct" (and I will quote from memory) "the things I love."'[12] Leaving aside the odd elision here between 'the signatory' and the 'I' quoting, referred to in the interview by Derrida himself and referred to as himself, as far as I can tell, Derrida does not in the *Post Card* say, 'I deconstruct the things I love'.[13] But perhaps, given that he is 'quoting' from 'memory', he is quoting from those parts of the correspondence which did not arrive or have been burned or lost or otherwise erased and which are 'indicated' or, better still, represented by the spaces, those wide white spaces which punctuate the text. It would be an act of love were the film to deconstruct the book because deconstruction is a way of making the thing itself possible, it would be to make something that the book *The Post Card* makes possible. To film the *Post Card* deconstructively, to deconstruct the book with film, is to make it possible both as a film and as the possibility that the book itself is. In the interview to which we have just referred, Derrida says this: 'One could also say that deconstruction "involves the structures" or the constructa, the things constructed that make life or existence possible. Deconstruction makes the constructed character appear as such, which is not artificial in opposition to the natural (precisely this opposition needs to be deconstructed) but constructed or structured in view of making possible—of making possible . . . what?'[14] Of making possible an on-screen, or rather in-screen, character in such a way we see what constructs him. And that character will itself be a construct, and it would be important not to cover over that constructedness but to affirm it. Deconstruction is as much an affirmation as it is a threat. And this would be the risk the film would take, and the risk would inform its rhythm and its tonalities.

We might agree with Alain Badiou when he says of Paul Thomas Anderson's film *Magnolia* that its multiplicity is bound up with 'deliberate tonal indecision', that it shows that a world from which love is withdrawn is a world from which 'true life is absent', and that its 'determining factor' is 'the relationship between idea and construction'. But we must disagree when he goes on to oppose construction to deconstruction: 'if you want to bring about, in the world as it is today, something that takes a stand on a possible meaning of generic humanity, even if you're using traditional materials, the path has to be that of *construction*, not deconstruction.'[15] The opposition between construction and deconstruction is a false one. Derrida's works are constructions, and they are affirmations. And they are inspired by the editing possibilities of the moving image. The technologies of cut and paste, re-composition, quotation, bring writing and cinema closer and closer together. 'Deconstruction or not, a writer has always been an editor [*monteur*: film editor]. Today more than ever'.[16] Indeed, the signature is itself a product of the technologised 'thinking-body'; in its relation to the technology of its writing and composition and editing the 'thinking body' 'invents its own machine', a machine which is stronger than it, but nonetheless its, and it is this excess, its excess to itself, that would legitimise and empower, as if it were its own invention, its signature.[17] In many places Derrida affirms the importance of tone and rhythm for the composition of his writing. Words and written images continuously join and disjoin in his work, constructing sensory possibilities of the written word, words as bodies in movement made audible, affirmative constructs of the visible and the sayable as possibilities of world; but always mindful of a certain necessary non-translatability between word and image, and between idioms of them, and the stakes involved in joining and disjoining them. Badiou locates deconstruction on the side of the avant-garde rather than kitsch (another false opposition), and whereas avant-gardism established itself in the visual arts, cinema has remained more on the side of kitsch: 'Cinema is a harsher critic than is generally believed. The deconstructionist figure has had a lot of trouble becoming established in it and in the final analysis has hardly become established in it at all.'[18] Putting aside our strong disagreement that deconstruction has been sensed in visual arts to anything like the degree it has in literature, the point of interest is that deconstruction has not been felt in cinema. Compare this to what Derrida himself says about his love of film when an adolescent in Algeria: that 'first and foremost they said "America"', that American films were simultaneously exotic and close, pure entertainment. This has stayed with him, he says, to the extent that cinema is linked to a love of the image rather than to philosophy, that it stays closer to emotion than to knowledge.[19] There will always be a certain suspicion about Derrida's work, that it privileges the discursive and literary—the written word—over the visual; after all, Derrida himself admits that 'it may be that a certain general theoretical formalization of the deconstructive possibility has more affinity with discourse' than with the non-discursive, non-verbal, spatial, or visual— a remark he prefaces with the explanatory force of *autobiography*: 'for reasons related to my own history, I feel more at ease with philosophical and literary texts'.[20]

III.

At a public Q&A following the screening of *Derrida: The Movie* at the Locarno Film Festival in August 2002 the two directors, Amy Kofman and Kirby Dick, are asked what, if any, say Derrida had had in the editing process in terms of what footage to leave out and what to include. Kofman gave as an example of something that she had wanted to show, but which was vetoed by Derrida, a scene in which he was filmed signing the contract for the film. According to Kofman, this was because Derrida did not want the film to be seen as 'his', authored by him. In the event, the scene did not even make the 'Deleted Scenes' 'extra' for the DVD. Both directors offer a take on this episode, and they differ in important respects. In Kofman's words, 'the deal we had with Jacques was that before the film could ever be released publicly, he would have the right to view it and exercise any type of final cut. That is, anything he wanted removed would be removed or the film would not go out. No questions asked.' After viewing a rough cut of the film Derrida called Kofman and 'requested' (Derrida's word according to Kofman) that the directors 'remove a scene which showed Jacques and me discussing the terms of our filmmaking contract'. Kofman agreed with Derrida that to have included the contract scene could indicate that Derrida 'had had more collaborative input on the film than he did'.[21] Dick describes the contractual situation thus: 'In 1995, before shooting began, Derrida had added a handwritten clause to the contractual release of his image that gave him the right to view the film before it was exhibited, and to excise any scene or footage he wished.' For Dick, this entailed the directors 'ceding editorial control', which perhaps explains why 'few documentary filmmakers ever agree to give a subject this kind of power'.[22] Derrida too offers his own take on the excised scene. Asked whether he had had any control over the editorial process, or had asked to take anything out of the film, Derrida answered, 'Not that I remember. Of course, there was a contract. Written or not written—there was a contract between us. It stated that I would give the authorization (for the film's release) only after I had seen the completed film; which meant that I wouldn't participate at all in the editing. Not at all. . . . I never asked for anything except one thing, I remember. I never asked for anything, any change, anything to be removed. I did not intervene at all except—if I remember correctly—once.' That one change, according to Derrida, was to the image of Marguerite, his wife, 'all the time in the kitchen'. When prompted to verify that this was his only intervention Kofman reminds him that there was in fact a scene he asked to be removed. That scene, according to Kofman, was of Derrida eating yogurt.[23] Precisely because he has no input, Derrida is given output. If he is not given output he will be put out to such an extent that he will refuse to allow the film's release—or rather, the release of his image. Derrida would be the first to say that to put a scene out is no less an editorial move and decision than to put one in. It is an acknowledgement of this to input into the contract a clause which allows him to put scenes out of the film.

In view of Derrida's refusal to allow the 'signing the contract' scene to be included, we would do well to raise the question how might its inclusion have affected Derrida's contention, made in the film itself and everywhere he talks about it, that the film is as much, if not more, autobiographical about the filmmakers than it is biographical about him,[24] whereas the real biography is to be found in the philosophy.[25] The question is worth asking because it affords an approach to the question of whether, and if so how, film can be deconstructive. It points to a certain paradox at the heart of films 'on' philosophers and filmic renderings of philosophical texts. There is biography in a philosopher's text; there is autobiography in a filmmaker's film 'on' the philosopher. Derrida countersigns the film *Derrida* in agreeing to its release, even if it is on condition that his signing is not seen, and that its not being seen is for Derrida not to be seen to counter-sign the film. But this does not mean that his signature is nowhere to be seen. Derrida is seen to be refusing to discuss certain things about his life, for instance his relationship with his wife. Derrida is at that moment editing what he will or will not divulge about himself. It is an editorial decision, even if it is not his decision to include that scene in the film. But the editing begins before the camera starts rolling. This is what is given by the clause in Derrida's own handwriting in the contract that Derrida signs. On the other hand, the existence of a scene in which Derrida is shown signing the contract for the film testifies to the fact that the film was begun before any contract was signed, even if this scene had been staged for the camera. Whatever the 'image' of Derrida is, a right over it is established in advance. Derrida's right over his own image is countersigned by the filmmakers removing his signature from it. Were the image of the contract scene to be included in the image over which the contract establishes rights, then it might be said that such rights are established by the film itself; or in other words, as much by the filmmakers as by Derrida; or, if we go along with Derrida's insistence that he does not at all sign the film, by the filmmakers *rather than* by Derrida. One might speculate what it may have been about his experience of the film *Derrida* that led him, in the year of its release, to say about contracts that he does not believe in them. He makes this remark in a discussion about the other film 'on' him, *D'ailleurs Derrida*, and implies more explicitly that there was no contract, but instead an 'accord' between him and the director Fathy, in the sense of a musical accord and an alliance, in which a mutual dissymmetry pertained such that Fathy initiated whatever there is in the film, created the place for the film, and held the secret to the film.[26]

Pointing out of the film *Derrida* to its directors, Derrida says, 'it will be your signature, and your autobiography in a certain way'. Pointing to 'behind the camera', to the cameraman (Dick) and interviewer (Kofman) 'in front of the screen', out of the screen into the space that separates us from what the screen shows and brings us close to it, a gesture with the finger which cuts the on-screen space, dividing it up into an 'on' and an 'off', into a 'behind' and a 'front' Derrida makes of this scene a post card. Not only does he mimic the gesture of *Plato* pointing over *Socrates'* shoulder to the space that separates and joins *Socrates* to the page he writes or is poised to write on or is being dictated to write on the post card in question,[27] but he puts into question what is front what back, what comes first, picture or text.[28] And to whom is he sending this post card, the viewer or the directors? To what does the contract scene belong, Derrida's biography, Derrida's autobiography, or the filmmakers' autobiography? Who is speaking when Derrida requests that the scene in which he is shown signing the contract for the film be taken out of the film, or when Derrida does not mention that scene when talking publicly about what he asked to be taken out of the film? The contract scene exists at precisely those moments when Derrida insists on maintaining that he did not sign the film. We might say that the utterances are autobiographical. What interests Derrida about autobiography is that 'there is always someone else': 'The most private autobiography is explained with great transferencial figures which are *themselves*, and also themselves *plus* someone else'.[29] The *Post Card* is, by Derrida's own admission, autobiographical.[30] It 'takes the risk' of making part of his life what is written there.[31] Gregory Ulmer is right to say that the 'Envois' section of *The Post Card* is 'in the process of becoming a (film or video) script', and that, as if a screenplay, it gives 'directions concerning the video portion of the broadcast'.[32] Part of the task of filming that screenplay would be to work out, to invent or construct, who the transferencial figures of its autobiography might be. The autobiographical 'I' does not exist until such figures are constructed.[33] The 'abyssal question of the signature': only when the *autos* of its self-relation is disturbed, through the encounter with 'autobiographicity' located elsewhere, the 'ghosts' at the origin of any 'to come', would the 'I' of *The Post Card* be drawn forth.[34] I would argue that one, or more than one, of the transferencial figures of Derrida the autobiographer is Derrida the actor in the two films on him.

A film 'of' Derrida's *Post Card* could not be deconstructive 'in itself' unless it were to counter-sign that book by betraying it, doing a certain violence to it, having it say something other than what it wants to say or thinks it is saying, by bringing back the ghosts, and the transferencial figures of other films on Derrida are no less ghosts in this regard, and no matter that the films themselves post-date *The Post Card*. Ought not the Derrida signing the film contract be asked to come back? Yet by betraying *The Post Card* in this way the film would be remaining faithful to the book, by assisting the book's betrayal of itself in its sending, by saying what remains unsaid there, *right there* in the book, what remains to be said by the book. It would need to do something that a recent filmic adaptation of a philosophical text was unable to do. The film *The Ister* remains unfaithful to Heidegger's lectures on Hölderlin's 'hymn' *Der Ister* precisely because it does not betray them in terms of what Heidegger himself has to say about film, his presuppositions regarding what film is—film as the abolition of remoteness, the film frame as photographic objectification, the film camera as a weapon, and perhaps most importantly of all, his disparagement of the movie theatre as 'American' (to which we would also have to add what Heidegger says about 'Americanism' and its 'giganticism' in the *Ister* lectures). Without this, the film is merely a companionable 'accompaniment' to Heidegger's text—as is stated at the beginning of the film. The film *D'ailleurs, Derrida* is not deconstructive 'in itself', it is deconstructive to the extent that it can be counter-signed as such, in which the counter-signature would show or reveal—or even invent—how the film puts into question distinctions between author and actor, self and acted self. This is what Derrida does with the book *Tourner les mots*. At the same time, that book opens up the possibility of deconstructing the film—showing how it is always already in deconstruction—because of what Derrida says there about his and Fathy's signatures in relation to the film.

IV.

Everywhere in Derrida's *Post Card* one reads played out the negation of the unique addressee at the hands of the 'anyone' of its address.[35] There are in fact texts which we might say are representations of this structure, indeed ones in which we see it performed by the sending of a post card between lovers, a post card which happens to be intercepted en route by the state police: Milan Kundera's novel *The Joke*, published in 1967 just months before the Prague Spring, and Jaromil Jireš' film adaptation of the book, sent during the Prague Spring, when it was shot and produced, but which arrived only after the 'Spring' had been crushed, released after the Warsaw Pact had invaded Czechoslovakia. There is a telling difference between the book and its film adaptation. Unable to accept that Marketa, his lover, away on a Communist Party training course, should be happy while he misses her so much, Ludvik buys a post card and, 'to hurt, shock, and confuse her', writes 'Optimism is the opium of the people! A healthy atmosphere stinks of stupidity! Long live Trotsky! Ludvik'.[36] Ludvik is hauled in front of the 'District Party Secretariat'. It soon becomes clear that his post card has been intercepted. To 'refresh his memory' they recite it back to him. His own words sound so terrifying they frighten him; they carry a 'destructive force' he is 'powerless to counter'. Nonetheless he protests that the card had been a joke. In the novel, Marketa did not hand in the card of her own accord, but willingly gave it over when asked to; she agreed with the state that what Ludvik had written was subversive, saying 'the Party has a right to know exactly who you are and what you think'. And with this she countersigns what is irreducible about the post card: that it is open. Marketa gave the card to the state police not because they 'knew all about it', but because she is at one with the state, and it is obvious from what he writes on the card that Ludvik is not. The card betrays what is 'inside' Ludvik. She appeals to the same 'invincible logic' his interrogators had employed: "They said I had written my sentences on an open post card, there for everyone to see, that my words had an objective significance that could not be explained away by the state of my emotions."[37] It is the openness of the card which reveals not just the obvious truth of what is written on it, but the truth of its obviousness. The truth of its obviousness is that it is true because it is obvious. It is in this sense in which the card is open.

But what is at stake in the relay of this openness is staged more per-formatively in the film 'adaptation' of Kundera's book by Jireš.[38] What the film does which the novel does not is have Marketa see the card through the eyes of those who intercept it. In the film version, when Marketa receives the post card, when it reaches its addressee, she cannot believe that it has not already been read by the state police, and that she is receiving it only because the police are testing her; so she voluntarily takes the card to the police. In other words, she sees that once the card had been intercepted it had no chance of reaching *her*. Or if it does arrive at her, it arrives not at a lover, a unique addressee, but to someone who is essentially anyone—Derrida's beloved reads on a post card he sends her: 'Once intercepted—a second suffices—the message no longer has any chance of reaching any determinable person, in any (*determinable*) place whatever. This has to be accepted, and *j'accepte*.'[39]—Marketa sees that the post card had not reached her through the sending of its signa-tory, on the contrary, it had reached the police, and it is the police who are now sending her this post card in order to find out whether she will admit to having received it, to ascertain whether she will admit to who the card says she is. The card can only have been destined to her now, having been sent by the police, because what is written there is obvious. If she keeps the post card to herself and makes of its openness her secret then *she* will have signed it. So she voluntarily takes the post card to the police. And in doing so she countersigns the truth of its obviousness.[40]

Ludvik is sentenced to six years 're-education', in the army, in mili-tary prison, in the mines. But not before he too begins to 'see' the three sentences on the post card '*through the eyes*' of his interrogators.[41] 'I my-self began to feel outraged by my words', says Ludvik, 'and to fear that something serious did in fact lurk behind their comedy.' This, he says, is at once what is 'most upsetting and revealing'. It is upsetting because revealing, for what is revealed in its not arriving is the very principle by which his post card might have arrived. This, to use Derrida's words, is an 'an unbearable certainty', unbearable because of its certainty, so certain that the author himself cannot not accept: his post card cannot not be read by anyone, and in its openness to being read by *anyone* it cannot be destined to *one* at *any* given place. Derrida writes to his beloved 'The message no longer has any chance of reaching any determinable person, in any (*determinable*) place whatever. This has to be accepted, and *j'accepte*. But I recognize that such a certainty is unbearable, for anyone'.[42] Ludvik and Marketa accept, and what they accept is that the post card can bear no one addressee, no determinable addressee, unless that one be anyone, that they are in one party, and that there is and can only be one party, and that every 'anyone' must belong to that party. Absolute publicness and certain openness can serve only totalitarianism. It is not, in the film, that Marketa betrays Ludvik's post card; it is that the post card betrays Ludvik. But Ludvik comes to accept that the post card can always betray him, can always arrive at another to whom it is not addressed, and mean something there, something other, something he can neither decide nor legislate in advance, defenceless in front of the obviousness of its openness.

Jireš' film 'adaptation' of Kundera's novel deconstructs totalitarianism not just through the sending of a post card, but in how it shows the postal principle to be deconstructive of the presuppositions of sending and destining our writings with certainty, and of the uniqueness of their most determinate addressee. In *The Post Card* Derrida wants to 'demonstrate' to his beloved that a letter 'can always—and therefore must—never arrive at its destination'. More than that, to demonstrate that this is 'not negative' but 'the condition (the tragic condition . . .) that something does arrive'.[43] But it is the arrival of the post card on which he says this that refutes the demonstration. Not just because it arrives, which would be a performative contradiction, but because in arriving it draws the refutation from its addressee, his beloved, and it's her (if it is a 'her') response which obliges Derrida to agree, knowing as he does that if it arrives it negates her specificity as the unique addressee. On the one hand, then, 'one of the paradoxes of destination, is that if you wanted *to demonstrate*, for someone, that something never arrives at its destination, it's all over. The demonstration, once it had reached its end, would have proved what it was not supposed to demonstrate. But this is why, dear friend, I always say "a letter *can* always *not* arrive at its destination, etc."'[44] But on the other, even if it arrived it would not arrive, for in its very openness lies the erasure of the specificity of the addressee: 'Understand me, when I write, right here, on these innumerable post cards, I annihilate not only what I am saying but also the unique addressee that I constitute, and therefore every possible addressee, and every destination. I kill you.'[45] This is what is monstrous about the postal principle, what is unbearable about it. Deconstruction does not demonstrate anything, if it did, the 'demonstration' would itself already be undergoing deconstruction. Rather, it monstrates, it lets what demonstrates monstrate, it pushes demonstration to monstrate, it deconstructs the 'de-' from monstration by monstrating it. This is precisely what the *The Post Card* does. And what any film of *The Post Card* must do, to *The Post Card*. It must let monstrate whatever the *Post Card* demonstrates. It must 'bear within itself a force and a structure, a straying of the destination, such that it *must* also not arrive in any way'.[46] This would be the film's chance—of arriving. The only chance is monstrousness,[47] an innocent monstrousness,[48] in monstrousness lies fidelity.[49]

V.

Derrida wanders across the seven monitors of Gary Hill's *Disturbance (Among the Jars)*, reading from the Gospel of Thomas, one of the Gnostic texts found buried in a jar (together with a Coptic 'translation' of part of Plato's *Republic*[50]) near Nag Hammadi in Egypt in 1945, composed around the end of the first century beginning of the second AD. No directions, no script, simply asked to walk and to read out loud 'a fragmented sentence that he was weaving through'.[51] It looks as if Derrida is walking through the space of multiple monitors—but rhythmed haltingly, syncopatedly. But this 'walking through' is achieved by having Derrida pace back and forth across a single frame only, which in postproduction is 'reversed' each time; so the book, which Derrida holds in one hand only, appears to change hands from one screen to the next.

Asking what went on in that piece, not knowing whether he was coming or going, Derrida wonders whether the newness of video consists in its being not a medium of art, reducible to a specific support, but a 'new experience' of the already existing arts, a way of *reading* them. Compare this to what Derrida says is new about cinema in an interview on the 'spatial arts' from the same year as 'Videor': that it is 'the possibility of another way of playing with the hierarchies', between discourse and non-discourse, for example. This play leads to a greater degree of difference *within* cinema than it does between cinema and photography. There are many different arts 'within the same technological apparatus', to the extent that there is no unity to cinema, and hence a certain cinematic style might be closer to literature than to another cinematic style.[52]

Derrida points out that Hill works extensively with heterogeneous discourses and texts—'secret names and dead tongues'—and certainly *Disturbance* scrolls text in many ways into its screens. Indeed, Hill's work can be seen as the visible instating of word into image. Video appears to be more discursive than the other arts, more textualised, says Derrida. But if we cannot be certain of what is new about video, and if its textual production is reading, then the already existing discourses we have for articulating its newness can only be inadequate, or we might say in an essential sense redundant. It is necessary to invent something about the discourses we have. The newness of video is 'to come'. Yet at the heart of this 'to come' there is repetition. If video is new it is because its writing is a reading again of all the other arts, and not just visual arts but literature too, 'another mode of reading the writings one finds in books'. If the newness of video involves the reading again, and thus the writing out, of all other media, all the other arts, then not just the newness of video, what is truly new about it, is still to come, but all other arts too, all of them are also 'to come', we have yet to see what they can be in their being read again by video. This is the familiar double chance of Derrida's 'to come', the chance of a writing as if for the first time, and the threat of writing mechanically repeated. The 'to come' of video is comprised both of the promise of a radical newness, and of the risk of a return of the worst: 'the most mechanical repetition of genres or stereotypes, for example narrative, novelistic, theatrical, cinematographic, or televisual'.[53] That it be a modality of reading helps explain why cinema, its new digital face, has turned to philosophical texts for its material, and raises the question in what way a videoed 'adaptation' of a philosophical text can in its reading remain faithful to that text without repeating the 'old' codes.

If video is a way of reading anew, a way of reading we have yet to see, then its coming is of a body. Such is what Jean-Luc Nancy proposes. The images which come on to a movie or TV screen are not 'images of', they are the *'coming to presence . . .* coming *from* nowhere behind the screen, *being* the spacing of this screen, existing as its separation'.[54] *Video* is not 'I see', it is the 'generic name for the *techne* of coming into presence'. Video does not give us something to see, it is what happens on our eyes, it is the spacing of our seeing, its screen the plasticity our bodies. Ours is a video-body. The passage in *Corpus* in which Nancy sets this out has a walk-on part, a corpulent part, in the book Derrida devotes to Nancy, *On Touching*—in the manner of Hitchcock striding passerby-like as if by chance through the films that he himself is directing. Derrida does not discuss Nancy's video-body and remains undisturbed by it; it is left as a passage elsewhere.[55] The digital 'image' incorporates the voice. Never in film has the voice been absolutely separated from the image, because the image is itself a body, and film always a question of screening the play of separation and non-separation between image and voice, even silent film. The task is to film words, to produce cinematised words, to construct the video-word. This goes as much for a film which disjoins the voice from the speaking body (Godard), or unearths it from the ground of dead bodies (Straub), or remarries it to the body's desire (Fassbinder), or disembodies it from the characters' hearing (Cassavetes), or displaces its truth to the fictionalised utterances of an off-screen narrator (Marker)—as much as it does for the most formulaic Hollywood remake. 'Image' in Derrida's contract stipulating the conditions of his releasing his image incorporates reference to his voice. In the film *Derrida* Derrida's 'own' speaking voice is not disjoined from his face, his talking head. To this extent the film *Derrida* utilises a standard conventional mode of documentary filmmaking, an 'old code'. Derrida might want to say that this is not his doing, but his asking for the removal of the contract scene puts such stance into question. Derrida deconstructs *Derrida* through the counter-signature of the texts by him read during the film, and by what he 'himself' says in the film about the filmmaking process. But he can only do so by unifying the voice and face, by presupposing the proximity of voice to face, through the standard conventional documentary code of the 'talking head', a 'discursive head', and by protecting the authorial authority of that 'discursive head' with a contract establishing in advance a determinate link between that authority and the 'release' of *his* 'image'. It is a procedure which out-puts him from the film, removes his signature from the film, relocating it back into his texts. But it is precisely this move that opens his position, his stance on his signature, how he stands behind the autobiographical fiction that is his signature, to deconstruction.

Derrida was one of a number of readers and poets to participate in the Gary Hill piece. He says of the experience that it was if he were a passerby using his body his voice his passing steps (the only thing he could calculate, he says, was the rhythm of his steps) 'as no art, no other art, one would say, would have done'.[56] In other words, only the rhythm of his participation was present unto him. 'Glory is the rhythm, or the plasticity, of this presence–local, necessarily local.'[57] So Nancy.[58] It is

Sophie in the gallery.

the rhythm, precisely, to which Derrida attends in Nancy; and we will remark here that it is rhythm which is 'beyond opposition' in *The Post Card, différance* and rhythm.[59] And it is rhythm by which Derrida makes the opposition between one side of the post card and the other work, and work to give it a body. Rhythm is *fort:da*, and *fort:da* the scene of writing, the scene of writing is the post card, and the post card's *envoi* is *fort:da*: '*fort:da* is the post, absolute telematics'.[60] There is nothing of *The Post Card* which does not dance or fall to this rhythm: 'what is there, rigorously, in our letters that does not derive from the *fort:da*, from the vocabulary of going-coming, of the step, of the way or the away, of the near and the far, of all the frameworks in *tele-*, of the adestination, of the address and the maladdress'.[61] And it is through rhythm, the rhythm of the cut, that one may remain faithful in any adaptation of *The Post Card*, the filmic rhythm of image to text, seeing to saying, the body between one side of the video screen and the other, one side of the video screen that gives seeing and the other, the voice and its dispossession, pace the faithfulness speed the betrayal, disject the public figure, anject the ghost, divide the philosophy by the autobiography, disjoin the head from sovereignty, intensify the other on the face of the *autos*.

NOTES

Work for this paper was begun for the Forum for European Philosophy satellite panel, 'Filming Deconstruction', at the forty-eighth annual conference of the Society for Phenomenology and Existential Philosophy (SPEP), George Mason University, Washington D.C., in October 2009. The other members of the panel were Martin McQuillan and Catherine Malabou.

1. Derrida, 'Trace et archive', 8–9.
2. Derrida, 'Lettres sur un aveugle', 88–89.
3. Derrida, 'Lettres sur un aveugle', 97.
4. We may be at, as is argued by Martin Heidegger, Derrida, and Jean-Luc Nancy among others, the closure of representation; but, following Heidegger, Derrida took as part of his task to show how representation is sent by Greek thought, despite the fact that Greek thought has no adequate or equivalent word or concept that could be said to translate 'representation' or the Latin *repraesentatio*. Heidegger, 'Die Zeit des Weltbildes', 91f.

5. Jacques Derrida, 'Envoi', in *The Post Card: From Socrates to Freud and Beyond* (Chicago: University of Chicago Press, 1987), 111.

6. Derrida, 'Envoi', 127.

7. Derrida, 'Envoi', 123.

8. Heidegger, 'Die Zeit des Weltbildes', 91.

9. Derrida, 'Artifactualities', 12.

10. "Die 'Lehre' eines Denkers ist das in seinem Sagen *Ungesagte*, dem der Mensch ausgesetzt wird, auf daß er dafür sich verschwende." Heidegger, 'Platons Lehre von der Wahrheit', 203 (my emphasis).

11. "Ce qui se voit dans le film a moins d'importance sans doute que le nondit, l'invisible". 'Le cinéma et ses fantômes', 83.

12. Derrida, 'Negotiations', 16.

13. And let's not forget that Derrida never fails to insist that as the speaker in an interview he is never his 'true' 'I', that is his 'writing' self, because he is obliged to improvise and to answer the imposed imperative to 'speak!', that in an interview he speaks with the least calculation and says things in a form in which he 'does not usually say them', as indeed he does in this interview. Derrida, 'Negotiations', 20.

14. Derrida, 'Negotiations', 16.

15. Badiou, 'Say yes to love, or else be lonely', 190–92.

16. Derrida, 'Le cinéma et ses fantômes', 82.

17. Derrida, *Tourner les mots*, 106–7.

18. Badiou, 'Say yes to love, or else be lonely', 192.

19. Derrida, 'Le cinéma et ses fantômes', 75–77.

20. Peter Brunette and David Wills, 'The Spatial Arts: An Interview with Jacques Derrida' in *Deconstruction and the Visual Arts: Art, Media, Architecture*, ed. Peter Brunette and David Wills (Cambridge: Cambridge University Press, 1994), 14.

21. Kofman, 'Making "Derrida"—an impression', in Dick and Kofman, 25. It is worth noting that beneath Kofman's text, as if 'illustrating' something about what she is stating (but what comes first in this instance, what is shown or the signature that exercises and excises what is shown? what is the ground what the grounded? is the image an illustration or the legend? is the legend the image or the writing it represents? does the image resist the contract or does its presence marry the two? does the image finally master the signature, or does the signature have the last word in not having to authorise an image which in end shows itself to be defenceless and indefensible? or if the image does finally master the word is it only on condition of the death of the author?), there are three photographs arranged linearly as if in a sequence. The first two show Kofman and Derrida in each other's company, first from

Derrida's side, then from Kofman's, each reading what could be a contract; the third is a close-up of Derrida writing by hand (or Derrida's hand writing, or a hand we are led to believe is Derrida's writing) on, and/or indeed signing, a sheet of paper, the top half of which is typed, the lower half of which consists of half a dozen lines of handwriting and/or signature(s).

22. Kirby Dick, 'Resting on the Edge of an Impossible Confidence', in *Derrida: Screenplay and Essays on the Film*, by Kirby Dick and Amy Ziering Kofman (New York: Routledge, 2007), 39–40.

23. Jacques Derrida, 'Derrida on Derrida: Q and A with Jacques Derrida', in Dick and Kofman, *Derrida*, 114.

24. "I had to accept the experience of knowing that this film would . . . in fact, be signed by the filmmakers . . . the film would be their work and I had no real initiative in it, no initiative. So I knew from the beginning that I would be exposed to their own autobiographical signature; that this would be their autobiography." Derrida, in Dick and Kofman, *Derrida*, 113.

25. Right at the beginning of the film *Derrida* we see Derrida speaking, in English, at a 'biography conference', the first words of philosophy by Derrida in the film. He insists that the rigorous study of a single paragraph by a philosopher will yield more about the biography of that philosopher than the one 'official' biography published by a reputable press.

26. Derrida, 'Trace et archive', 9. It is worth noting that nowhere during this discussion about *D'ailleurs, Derrida* does Derrida mention the film *Derrida* by name, despite the fact that the latter film came out that year; but there is a reference to 'other films' about him. It comes when speaking about how, in its reservation, *D'ailleurs, Derrida* authorises him, allows him without his feeling obliged to, to renounce whatever there is most proper, ownmost, in what he says there. And it does this through its cutting, how it cuts him. And this would not be the case with every film about him (11). The emphasis, though, remains on the said. Even if he does not recognise himself in his voice, he can stand behind what he says in the film (31). But he cannot stand behind the film; again, only its 'author', the director, can do that (5).

27. The post card is of a drawing by Matthew Paris, *Plato and Socrates*, the frontispiece of the thirteenth-century 'fortune telling' book *Prognostica Socratis basilei*, MS. Ashmole 304, fol. 31v, Bodleian Library, Oxford.

28. Derrida, 'Envois', 13.

29. Jacques Derrida and François Ewald, 'A Certain "Madness" Must Watch Over Thinking', *Educational Theory* 45, no. 3 (September 1995): 284.

30. Kristine McKenna, 'The Three Ages of Jacques Derrida: An Interview with the Father of Deconstructionism', *LA Weekly*, November 6, 2002; Derrida and Ewald, 'A Certain "Madness"', 284.

31. 'I have the impression that everything comes to resemble itself, and me first of all, in a post card, the post card—that I am'. Derrida, 'Envois', 35.

32. Ulmer, 56.

33. Derrida and Ewald, 'A Certain "Madness"', 279.

34. Jacques Derrida, *A Taste for the Secret* (Cambridge: Polity, 2001), 41–42.

35. 'Understand me, when I write, right here, on these innumerable post cards, I annihilate not only what I am saying but also the unique addressee that I constitute, and therefore every possible addressee, and every destination. I kill you.' Derrida, 'Envois', 33.

36. Milan Kundera, *The Joke* (New York: HarperCollins, 1992), 34.

37. Kundera, *The Joke*, 38.

38. Jaromil Jireš (dir.), *Žert [The Joke]*, *Czechoslovakia*, Filmové studio Barrandov, 1968.

39. Derrida, 'Envois', 51.

40. We might ask why we are never told by the book or by the film what is on the other side of the post card, what image is 'behind' the words. But we would be missing the point; the book and the film are that image. Certainly the film understands itself as such. This is partly what we are being invited to accept by the specific way the film has Marketa see the post card through the eyes of her interrogators. And if we say also that both the film and the book are images of the 'other side' of the 'Iron Curtain', we must add the other side of that other side.

41. Kundera, *The Joke*, 45 (my emphasis).

42. Derrida, 'Envois', 51.

43. Derrida, 'Envois', 121.

44. Derrida, 'Envois', 123.

45. Derrida, 'Envois', 33.

46. Derrida, 'Envois', 123.

47. Derrida, 'Envois', 127.

48. Derrida, 'Envois', 175 and 177.

49. Derrida, 'Envois', 175 and 243.

50. Plato, *The Republic*, 588A–589B; where we are asked to *picture* man as—*internally*—a many-headed beast.

51. Hill, 'Liminal space', 16.

52. Brunette and Wills, 'The Spatial Arts', 14.

53. Derrida, 'Videor', 178. Derrida gives a literary example of this 'mechanical repetition' in the interview 'The Ghost Dance', 64–65. Compare the reasons Derrida gives for rejecting work submitted by two of his students in the form of video cassettes: whilst the videos addressed the problematic of the subject adequately enough, in their 'passage to the image' they lost something of the

'demonstrative power' of the discourse, such that they arrived 'in the place' of discourse. Jacques Derrida and Bernard Stiegler, *Echographies of Television* (Cambridge: Polity, 2002), 142–43. Compare too the reasons Derrida decided against including in the corpus of his own thesis to be defended those writings which experiment typographically. (*La carte postale* was published the same year that Derrida defended his thesis, 1980.) What makes those texts unable to defended, leaving them defenceless, is not the 'demonstrative positions' to which they hold, but the performativity of the writing acts those positions produce, acts which are inseparable from what they demonstrate. Derrida, 'Punctuations', 49. I discuss these examples in 'Writing as Practice', in James Elkins (ed.), *Artists with PhDs*, 2nd edition (Washington, DC: New Academia, 2014).

54. Jean-Luc Nancy, *Corpus* (Bronx, NY: Fordham University Press, 2008), 63.

55. Jacques Derrida, *On Touching—Jean-Luc Nancy* (Stanford, CA: Stanford University Press), 222. We might add that there is but one mention of video in the *Post Card*: to *Videotex*, of which Minitel is the best-known example: "Read this. It's falling into place . . . if it appears, it will be at the moment when the so-called 'telematic revolution' . . . will make it spoken of." Derrida, 'Envois', 206. When asked about Minitel, Derrida characterises it as a 'sexual network' and therefore a problem for political organisation. 'The Ghost Dance', 64.

56. Derrida, 'Videor', 178.

57. Nancy, *Corpus*, 65.

58. 'Being, as the rhythm of bodies—bodies, as the rhythm of being. The thought-in-body is rhythmic, spacing, pulsing, giving the *time* of the dance, the *step* of the world.' Nancy, *Corpus*, 115.

59. 'Beyond opposition, *différance* and rhythm. Beyond a beyond whose line would have to divide, that is to oppose entities, beyond the beyond of opposition, beyond opposition, rhythm.' Derrida, *The Post Card*, 408.

60. Derrida, 'Envois', 44.

61. Derrida, 'Envois', 222.

BIBLIOGRAPHY

Badiou, Alain. 'Say yes to love, or else be lonely, an interview about Paul Thomas Anderson's film *Magnolia*' [2002]. *Cinema*, translated by Susan Spitzer, 176–92. Cambridge: Polity Press, 2010.

Derrida, Jacques. *La Carte Postale: de Socrate à Freud et au-delà.* Paris: Flammarion, 1980.

———. 'Punctuations: the time of a thesis' [1980]. In *Philosophy in France Today*, edited by Alan Montefiore, translated by Kathleen McLaughlin, 34–50. Cambridge: Cambridge University Press, 1983.

——. 'Envois' [1980]. In *Psyche: Inventions of the Other, Volume 1*, translated by Mary Ann Caws and Peter Caws, 94–128. Stanford: Stanford University Press, 2007.

——. *The Post Card: From Socrates to Freud and Beyond*. Translated by Alan Bass. Chicago: University of Chicago Press, 1987.

——. 'The Ghost Dance'. Interview with Andrew Payne and Mark Lewis, translated by Jean-Luc Svoboda. *Public* 1 (1987): 60–73.

——. 'The spatial arts', an interview with Peter Brunette and David Wills [1990]. In *Deconstruction and the Visual Arts: Art, Media, Architecture*, edited by Peter Brunette and David Wills, translated by Laurie Volpe, 9–32. Cambridge: Cambridge University Press, 1994.

——. 'Negotiations', interview with Deborah Esch and Tom Keenan [1987]. In *Negotiations: Interventions and Interviews, 1971–2001*, translated by Elizabeth Rottenberg, 11–40. Stanford: Stanford University Press, 2002.

——. 'Telepathy', trans. Nicholas Royle, *Oxford Literary Review* 10 (1988), 3–42.

——. 'Videor'. In *Passages de l'image*, edited by Raymond Bellour, Catherine David and Christine van Assche, translated by Peggy Kamuf, 174–79. Barcelona: Fundació Caixa de Pensions, 1990.

——. 'A certain "madness" must watch over thinking', interview with François Ewald [1991]. *Educational Theory* 45, no. 3 (September 1995): 273–91.

——. 'A taste for the secret' [1995]. In *A Taste for the Secret*, by Jacques Derrida and Maurizio Ferraris, translated by Giacomo Donis, 1–92. Cambridge: Polity Press, 2001.

——. 'Artifactualities' [1993]. In *Echographies of Television: Filmed Interviews*, by Jacques Derrida and Bernard Stiegler, translated by Jennifer Bajorek, 1–27. Cambridge: Polity Press, 2002.

——. 'Lettres sur un aveugle: Punctum caecum'. In *Tourner les mots: Au bord d'un film*, by Jacques Derrida and Safaa Fathy, 71–126. Paris: Éditions Galilée/Arte Éditions, 2000.

——. 'Le cinéma et ses fantômes', entretien avec Antoine de Baecque et Thierry Jousse. *Cahiers du cinéma* 556 (avril 2001): 74–185.

——. 'Trace et archive, image et art'. Bry-sur-Marne: Institut national de l'audiovisuel, 2002.

——. 'Countersignature' (2000). Translated by Mairéad Hanrahan. *Paragraph* 27, no. 2 (July 2004): 7–42.

——. 'The three ages of Jacques Derrida', interview with Kristine McKenna. *LA Weekly* (November 6, 2002). A fuller, more detailed, and in some places slightly different version of the conversation is to be found in Dick and Kofman, 118–26.

——. *Copy, Archive, Signature: A Conversation on Photography*. Translated by Jeff Fort. Stanford: Stanford University Press, 2010.

Derrida, Jacques, and Amy Ziering Kofman. Q&A at the Film Forum, NYC, 23 October 2002. In *Derrida: Screenplay and Essays on the Film*, by Kirby Dick and Amy Ziering Kofman, 110–17. Manchester: Manchester University Press, 2005.

Derrida, Jacques, and Bernard Stiegler, 'Echographies of Television' [1993]. In *Echographies of Television: Filmed Interviews*, by Jacques Derrida and Bernard Stiegler, translated by Jennifer Bajorek, 29–143. Cambridge: Polity Press, 2002.

Dick, Kirby. 'Resting on the edge of an impossible confidence'. In *Derrida: Screenplay and Essays on the Film*, by Dick and Kofman, 36–49. Manchester: Manchester University Press, 2005.

Dick, Kirby, and Amy Ziering Kofman. *Derrida: Screenplay and Essays on the Film*. Manchester: Manchester University Press, 2005.

Heidegger, Martin. 'Die Zeit des Weltbildes' [1938]. In *Gesamtausgabe*, Band 5: *Holzwege*, 75–113. Frankfurt am Main: Vittorio Klostermann, 1977.

———. 'Platons Lehre von der Wahrheit' [1940]. In *Gesamtausgabe,* Band 9: *Wegmarken*, 203–38. Frankfurt am Main: Vittorio Klostermann, 1976.

———. *Hölderlins Hymne* 'Der Ister' [1942]. *Gesamtausgabe*, Band 53. Frankfurt am Main: Vittorio Klostermann, 1984.

Hill, Gary. 'Liminal performance: in conversation with George Quasha and Charles Stein'. *PAJ: A Journal of Performance and Art* 20, no. 1 (January 1998): 1–25.

Kofman, Amy. 'Making "Derrida"—an impression'. In *Derrida: Screenplay and Essays on the Film*, by Kirby Dick and Amy Ziering Kofman, 22–35. Manchester: Manchester University Press, 2005.

Kundera, Milan. *The Joke* [1967]. Translated by the author. London: Faber and Faber, 1992.

Malabou, Catherine, and Jacques Derrida. *Counterpath: Traveling with Jacques Derrida* [1999]. Translated by David Wills. Stanford: Stanford University Press, 2004.

Marie-Françoise Plissart avec une lecture de Jacques Derrida. *Droit de regards*. Paris: Editions de Minuit, 1985.

Ulmer, Gregory. 'The post-age', review of Jacques Derrida. *La Carte Postale: de Socrate à Freud et au-delà, Diacritics* 11, no. 3 (Autumn 1981): 39–56.

FILMOGRAPHY

Anderson, Paul Thomas (dir.). *Magnolia*. Ghoulardi Film Company/New Line Cinema, USA, 1999.

Barison, David, and Daniel Ross (dirs.). *The Ister*. Black Box Sound and Image, Australia, 2004.

Dick, Kirby, and Amy Ziering Kofman (dirs.). *Derrida*. Jane Doe Films Inc., USA, 2002.

Fathy, Safaa (dir.). *D'ailleurs, Derrida*. Gloria Films / La Sept Arte, France, 1999.

Hill, Gary (dir.). *Disturbance (Among the Jars)*. Installation video, seven monitors, 22'55", Collection Centre Georges Pompidou, Paris, 1988.

Jireš, Jaromil (dir.), *Žert [The Joke]*. Filmové studio Barrandov, *Czechoslovakia,* 1968.

McMullen, Ken (dir.). *Ghost Dance*. Channel 4 Television, UK, 1983.

INDEX

ABOUT THE CONTRIBUTORS

Joanna Callaghan is a filmmaker and director of Heraclitus Pictures. She is a Senior Lecturer in Filmmaking at the University of Sussex. Before entering academia she worked in the film, television and radio industry in the UK and France.

Martin McQuillan is Professor of Literary Theory and Cultural Analysis at the London Graduate School and Pro Vice Chancellor of Research at Kingston University. He is the author of *Deconstruction after 9/11* (2009), *Roland Barthes, or, the Profession of Cultural Studies* (2011) and *Deconstruction without Derrida* (2013).

Theo Marks is Professor of Modern Literature at University of Wessex. He is the author of *Love in the Time of Deconstruction* (2002) and *Dead Letters: A History of the Post from Plato to Derrida* (forthcoming).

Geoffrey Bennington is Asa G. Candler Professor of Modern French Thought at Emory University. His recent books include *Not Half No End: Militantly Melancholic Essays in Memory of Jacques Derrida* (2010) and *Géographie et autres lectures* (2011).

Ellen S. Burt is Professor of French at University of California, Irvine. Her publications include *Poetry's Appeal: Nineteenth-Century French Lyric and the Political Space* (2000) and *Regard for the Other: Autothanatography in Rousseau, De Quincey, Baudelaire, and Wilde* (2009).

Catherine Malabou is Professor of Philosophy at Kingston University. Her recent publications include *The Ontology of the Accident: an Essay on*

Destructive Plasticity (2012) and *The New Wounded: From Neurosis to Brain Damage* (2012).

J. Hillis Miller is Distinguished Research Professor of English and Comparative Literature at University of California, Irvine. His recent publications include *Theory and the Disappearing Future: On de Man, on Benjamin* (2012) with Tom Cohen and Claire Colebrooke, and *Reading for Our Time: Adam Bede and Middlemarch Revisited* (2012).

Samuel Weber is Avalon Foundation Professor of Humanities at Northwestern University. From 2012–2014 he was Distinguished Anniversary Chair in Medialogy at Kingston University. His recent publications include *Benjamin's—abilities* (2010) and *Inquiétantes singularités* (2013).

David Wilson is a postal historian and philatelist. His specialist interest is in the use of the half penny stamp of Great Britain. He recently published his first book on the Postal History of Euton and District.

Jonathan Lahey Dronsfield is Director of the Research Project Space, Wilkinson Gallery, London. Previously, he held posts at the University of Reading and the University of Southampton.